AGRICOLA

AGRICOLA

ARCHITECT OF ROMAN BRITAIN

SIMON TURNEY

AMBERLEY

First published 2022

Amberley Publishing
The Hill, Stroud
Gloucestershire, GL5 4EP

www.amberley-books.com

Copyright © Simon Turney, 2022

The right of Simon Turney to be identified as
the Author of this work has been asserted in
accordance with the Copyright, Designs and
Patents Act 1988.

ISBN 978 1 4456 9674 4 (hardback)
ISBN 978 1 4456 9675 1 (ebook)

British Library Cataloguing in Publication Data.
A catalogue record for this book is available
from the British Library.

1 2 3 4 5 6 7 8 9 10

Typesetting by SJmagic DESIGN SERVICES, India.
Printed in the UK.

CONTENTS

Julius Frontinus succeeded Cerialis both in authority and in reputation: But the general, who finally established the dominion of the Romans in this island, was Julius Agricola, who governed it in the reigns of Vespasian, Titus, and Domitian, and distinguished himself in that scene of action.

David Hume, *History of England,* 1778

INTRODUCTION

Almost uniquely among non-ruling Romans, we have a full biography of Gnaeus Julius Agricola courtesy of his son-in-law, the famous writer Tacitus. Tacitus is one of the widest read and most investigated of all Roman writers, and his Agricola is probably the most evaluated and divisive of all classical texts. It is all things to all men in the world of Roman history. It is at one and the same time a history, a biography, a eulogy, a political statement, a declaration of the values of Rome and, of course, a damn good read to boot. And since it is all these things and more, it can be somewhat difficult to unwind those threads and attempt to view it as any one thing, and scholars have argued over its veracity and its value for centuries.

The purpose of this book is not to rehash the many attempts to investigate Tacitus per se, nor is it a reflection of the current trend to use Tacitus to re-examine the Roman conquest of the north of Britain. Both of these things are part of my research, but the main purpose of this book is to attempt to divine the most probable course of events in Agricola's life and, using that, to biographise him, focusing on the man himself more than the conquest for which he is famous. In addition to Tacitus as our primary source, I shall use contemporary accounts and archaeology to corroborate (or occasionally fail to do so) the information to be found in the Agricola, using the text as objectively as possible.

Agricola has come down to us through the centuries as one of the most noble of Romans, and as the man almost single-handedly responsible for the conquest of northern Britain. On a personal level, his is one of the first Roman names of which I became aware in my youth. My grandfather, whenever we passed over the bridge on the A1 near Catterick, would note that we had just crossed 'Agricola's bridge', and would joke that Agricola was the 'first cousin of Cocacola.' Such is the level to which Agricola has permeated the national consciousness. A visit to Bath's Roman bath complex confirms it. Around the walkway above the main pool are Victorian carvings of the various Roman characters who have been influential in our island, in chronological order. Most are emperors, a few: governors. But a simple examination of their names will reveal in just what august company we keep Agricola:

Julius Caesar
Claudius
Vespasian
Ostorius Scapula
Suetonius Paulinus
Agricola
Hadrian
Constantine

An impressive list in which Agricola finds himself, then, since many of those names are ones synonymous with Roman Britain, and some of the most famous in history: the man who built the wall, the man Asterix beat with the aid of a magic potion, the builder of the Colosseum, Robert Graves's stuttering fool, and the man who legalised Christianity. Yet of those names, Vespasian fought but one campaign here, Claudius visited for a matter of weeks with all his pomp and pachyderms, Caesar dropped in twice for a summer jaunt, Hadrian came briefly as part of his empire-wide tour, and Constantine fought a single campaign in the north with his father before running back south and taking the legions with him. The three governors among those emperors (Scapula, Paulinus and Agricola) obviously spent more time on the island than the emperors and were more intimately involved with Britannia, and we shall learn more of them in due course, but of that entire list, if we are to believe Tacitus at least, only Agricola spent the majority of his career on the island. He served

Agricola, Tacitus and the Caledonian leader Calgacus in the painted frieze by William Brassey Hole inf the Great Hall of the National Portrait Gallery of Scotland, 1897. (Author's collection)

in Britain as a military officer, then a legion commander, and finally as governor. Compared to the rest, with a maximum of a five-year tenure (Scapula), Agricola served in total some fifteen years or so on the island. In that light it is possible to see Agricola as more important to Roman Britain than *any* of those other illustrious names, no matter how many walls they built or indomitable Gauls they fought.

We will examine Tacitus's biography in detail in due course and attempt to build the most likely possible picture of the man it portrays, but to continue with this introduction, let us examine who Tacitus is, and see where Agricola draws a powerful parallel, especially in his work.

Gaius (or possibly Publius – Roman writers helpfully rarely note a character's first name in their work) Cornelius Tacitus was born *c.* AD 56, some sixteen years after Agricola and early in the reign of the complicated emperor Nero. His origins are obscure, but there are persuasive arguments that he was from what is now the area of northern Italy and southern France. This is a somewhat central point to the entire history of he and his father-in-law, and it is perhaps unfortunate that we have as yet no confirmed geographical origin for our biographer. *Sic vita east* (such is life, as the comedian Terrentius would have us know.)

His father is likely, based on his unusual name, to be the Cornelius Tacitus who was procurator of Germania, mentioned by Pliny the elder, which would make the father a member of the Equestrian order (Rome's upper middle class). Born into the equestrians, then, our Tacitus acquired Senatorial status under the Flavians.

Based upon his own writings and a funerary inscription discovered on the Via Nomentana in Rome believed to be that of Tacitus ((the legend 'CITO' – *taCITO* – is visible, along with corroborating positions), we can tentatively rebuild the man's political career, following the common line of the Cursus Honorum (the path of a Roman's career). Starting with a minor magistracy in perhaps 76, he would have served as a military tribune for a number of years thereafter, stomping around the provinces and running errands for a legionary commander. We have no record of this and cannot therefore be certain of this period of his life, but there is a case to be made here that is very pertinent to our work. His military tribunate would have begun around AD 77/78, which was also coincidentally when he married Agricola's daughter, and the time when Agricola was appointed as governor of Britannia. Since there is a solid tradition in imperial Rome of men serving their military tribunate under a patron or a father or father-in-law (nepotism being a prime factor in Roman politics), it is highly likely that Tacitus served his first military stint with Agricola in Britain. This is critical to the question of his account's veracity. It has long been argued how much of Tacitus's work is comprised of second-hand information, hearsay, or indeed simply fiction. If, however, we are to say that Tacitus was actually in Britain with Agricola early in his governorship, then that adds a great deal of credibility to his account. It is better, after all, to say 'I came, I saw, I conquered' than 'I heard about it, I wrote it down, I made money from it.'

After his tribunate, Tacitus seems to have been in Rome once more by the end of AD 79 and can therefore only have served two or three years with his father-in-law, but that is certainly enough for him to gain a good grounding as a foundation for his account. Two or three years out of seven is not a bad foundation of research, after all.

A quaestor *c.* AD 81, Tacitus likely served as an Aedile – a sort of faceless mid-level bureaucrat – in 82 or 83, and by 88, with the favour of Domitian, held the Praetorship at the expected age of thirty, as well as being one of the prestigious quindecimviri. By 90, Tacitus and his wife depart from Rome, and do not return until some four years later, following the death of Agricola. It is probable that he spent that time in one of the border provinces serving as the commander of a legion. Returning from such a post he likely secured a governorship from Domitian soon after and was in Rome in time to witness that emperor's fall and the end of the Flavian dynasty. His ties to Domitian, and the favour he enjoyed, clearly did not ruin his reputation, for in 97, under Nerva, he secured the consulate. Given his switchback allegiances in a time of imperial strife, the image of Tacitus we can glean is one of a survivor. Condemning the despised Nero he gained much from Domitian, only to condemn that emperor in turn when he fell from grace and Nerva and Trajan came to power. From here until the end of his life in around AD 120, Tacitus had reached the top rung of the Roman political ladder.

It is in the year after that consulship that he published his first literary works, the Agricola and the *Germania*, with which we are, of course, most concerned. He would go on to write his more famous Annals and Histories and become one of the most notable literary figures in the ancient world, but by AD 98, we have seen of his life that which is most pertinent to our work.

Tacitus had been a toddler when Boudicca revolted with her Iceni in Britain, but must have been aware of the disaster even as a child. At four or five years of age I remember the Queen's silver jubilee, as well as fixing my bike with my next door neighbour, and therefore I imagine a massive native revolt that sent shockwaves through the empire would have come to my attention – so it must have done with our biographer. Tacitus lived through the events of which he writes, even if he heard them only as news reported in Rome. He was tied to Agricola by marriage to his daughter, and likely served in the military with him. He would have been in Rome for a number of years with his father-in-law as an old man and we can accept from phrases used in his work that Agricola and Tacitus corresponded and conversed during that time, for the writer gives us anecdotes from his father-in-law. Finally, he returns to Rome to give a funeral oration for Agricola. When the 'reviled' Domitian dies in 96, Tacitus manages to escape any consequences

Nineteenth-century statue of Tacitus on the Austrian Parliament Building in Vienna. (Public domain, Pe-Jo)

of his ties, but his writing in the Agricola, penned within two years of Domitian's death, heaps criticism upon that of Domitian's death, heaps criticism upon that emperor and lauds the new reign (possibly Nerva, but more likely the first days of Trajan).

In recently writing a fictionalised biography of the emperor Commodus I had call to question the modern reader's perspective. Commodus has historically been hailed as a megalomaniac, with some of the reasons being his relabelling of the months of the year after his own twelve names, and his intention to rebrand the city of Rome 'Colonia Commodiana' after himself. With some musing on these signs of megalomania, it occurred to me how such things can easily be interpreted in different ways. After all, two months of the year had already been renamed for Rome's great and good, and are Julius Caesar and Augustus vilified for the months of July and August? Of course not. Better yet, the benchmark emperor Constantine is still lauded as one of the best incumbents in four centuries of Rome's rulers. He is even sainted. And what did he do? Take the great city of Byzantium, make it New Rome and *name it after himself*: Constantinople. So why do we consider Commodus a megalomaniac for similar decisions?

I bring this up because these days I find myself constantly re-evaluating what history tells me, and that applies with Tacitus no less than Commodus. The general consensus on Tacitus's biography is that it is likely to be heavily biased due to his familial connection and should therefore be treated with a huge pinch of salt. Tacitus is the only 'inside' source we have on Agricola, though, and if we dismiss his account as too biased to be trusted, then we suffer an almost total lack of information. In essence, if we write off the veracity of Tacitus, then we remove any real hope of learning of Agricola. In this case rather than fly in the face of conventional accepted wisdom as I did with my account of Commodus, I am more concerned with why we should not so easily write off our main literary source.

I ask why, because there is the *possibility* of bias, we are not to trust the information held within the Agricola. The great 'inside' source on Julius Caesar is his *De Bello Gallico*, or 'Gallic Wars', an account of the eight years of his conquest and consolidation of Gaul, written by the man himself. Yet while when one speaks to a student of Tacitus they will mostly decry his biases and then grudgingly admit that without an alternative source we are forced to at least consider his words, a student of Caesar will usually laud the detail, insight and prose of Caesar's autobiography and then grudgingly accept that there might be a touch of bias about it. Yet they are much the same proposition for the historian.

Having mentioned Caesar, then, we might perhaps briefly consider a comparison not between his writings and those of Tacitus, but between his life and that of Agricola. Parallels are easy to draw, with Caesar as an active and renowned politician and general during the troubling and dangerous times of the late Republic. The same might be said of Agricola during the reign of Domitian. Moreover, Julius Caesar is unusual in that his tenure as the proconsular governor of Gaul was already stretched at five years *before* it was extended by a further five. A ten-year governorship is unprecedented and, I believe, unmatched. One character who comes close to that record, though, is Gnaeus Julius Agricola, who achieved eight years as governor in Britain.

Throughout the late republic and early empire, few governors actively sought conquest, being content to achieve imperial favour while amassing small personal fortunes. We will experience the corruption and avariciousness of governors more than once in our tale. Caesar, though, is given control of Cisalpine Gaul (that part of Gallic territory that occupies the northern part of Italy), and immediately sets out on a mission to conquer and incorporate the rest of the Gallic world. Agricola is given Britannia, which at the time reaches only to perhaps the future site of Hadrian's Wall, and immediately sets out to incorporate the remaining territory. Caesar has a daughter only, without a dynasty, and his legacy will pass to a great-nephew (Octavian/Augustus). Agricola has only a daughter, and via her his legacy has come to us through his son-in-law.

Parallels abound between Tacitus's Agricola and Caesar's De Bello Gallico. Woolliscroft and Hoffman[1] suggest that Tacitus has adapted the latter for his own first opus, and it is easy to see why. They note seductively that both immediately campaign late in the season, both rescue men from a night attack, both are thwarted in attempts to annex islands, and both fight a grand set-piece battle at the end. They go on to cite individual sections of text that seem to have been borrowed or adapted from other works. Yet when we compare the two accounts, the Agricola contains a great deal of directly biographical information that we cannot find in Caesar. The reuse of phrasing, allusion, and reference was ancient even in Roman times, yet we do not knock Plato for directly reusing Alcaus's 'wine and truth' more than a century after the latter, let alone Theocritus paraphrasing it another century on. Try to discern who first used the phrase 'History is written by the victors,' and you might get the idea. There is simply no way to satisfactorily confirm or deny whether Tacitus is too derivative to be of direct value, but these parallels should be borne in mind throughout as we attempt to evaluate the life of Agricola largely from his son-in-law's account.

There are myriad difficulties in attempting to prove Tacitus right or wrong by cross-referencing with contemporary accounts and archaeology. Just as we have to bear in mind Tacitus's own biases and the undoubted additional purpose of the Agricola as a political statement, we must apply the same caution to other accounts. Every ancient writer (just as any modern one) is inherently biased in some way, and it is therefore their lesser, almost incidental, anecdotes, mentioned on the periphery of greater things, which bear the higher likelihood of truth.

In my youth I was taught that arts were subjects that were subjective, while sciences had definite answers that were empirically provable. That was before I discovered archaeology. Archaeology might be the only science whose results are largely arguable and mutable. A science in which being able to say 'we can be reasonably confident that' is as good as it gets.

In terms of archaeology, the least arguable and most certain dating evidence upon which we can rely comes from either dendrochronology or *specifically dated* inscriptions. In the case of Roman forts and camps that have been constructed solely of timber and earth (which is generally the case in our investigation), dendrochronological work on unearthed timbers gives us a good date. They can usually be placed as trees felled in a single season, and since the timbers used for forts were not carried around on carts but felled at the time of construction, we can comfortably date those forts to the same year as the felled timber.

Inscriptions, on the other hand, are often undatable and vague. In the perfect world a farmer would have unearthed a stone slab somewhere in the Moray region that says, 'G I AGRICOLA WOZ ERE AT MONS GRAUPIUS DCCCXXXVI AD URBE CONDITA' and we would verify everything we hoped for in one fell swoop. The reality is that inscriptions rarely have any way to date, and most manage such indecipherable and weird fragments as '...O...EGI...X'. Imagine trying to decipher a message when two thirds of the letters are missing, and you don't know who wrote it, where, when, or why, and you hit the main stumbling block of epigraphy. In fairness there are exceptions. An inscription inscription found at St Albans, for example, references the emperor Titus and the governor as Agricola and can therefore be dated to somewhere between AD 79 and 81.

Coin evidence is of some value too, though with considerably less certainty. We can estimate the first and last dates of a site from the discovery of earliest and latest coins, but since coins would usually stay in circulation for a huge period, the leeway we give those dates has to be equally huge. Certain examples are of more value, though. A coin that is still in recently minted condition, for example, found in the foundations of a wall, can give us a reasonably certain period of construction, but such cases are relatively rare. Patricia Southern and Andrew Tibbs both note particularly pertinent and successful cases of coin evidence dating, which we will discover much later in the text.

Similarly, pottery is poor dating evidence, for an article carried by soldiers might be datable to a period of years in terms of its production, but since such items would probably be used for many years, only being discarded when broken and being carried from site to site, they can only help us estimate periods of occupation at best. I still have a mug I used at university twenty-some years ago because I like it and it has miraculously survived my ham-fisted washing up over the decades to bear tea stains an archaeologist could only dream of.

The only evidence for Agricola in Britain that does not come from Tacitus consists of three things: the aforementioned St Albans inscription, a lead pipe found at Chester bearing his name, and a writing tablet from Carlisle. A fourth inscription (RIB793) found at the fort of Hardknott in Cumbria is dubious. Discovered in 1855 and now lost, the inscription read GRIC[O]LA COII. However, since the only other datable evidence found at Hardknott is post-Hadrianic, it seems likely that this is not our Agricola, but Sextus Calpurnius Agricola, who governed Britain in the early 160s.

Somewhat like this book, the first three sections of Tacitus's Agricola set the scene for us. He begins by suggesting that long-ago biographers were free to produce such works without fear or censorship, and that those works were regarded as impartial. Lord, but I wish that were true now! Indeed, he even suggests that autobiographies were written without conceit. He goes on to hint that he had needed to seek permission for such a work, suggesting that perhaps the Agricola was planned or even started during the oppressive reign of Domitian. That emperor he then damns, telling us that a man could not even converse without being the subject of espionage, that freedom of thought was purged, and that men who wrote biographies and eulogies were prosecuted, their works publicly burned in the forum. Domitian is very clearly painted as a führer figure in the Agricola.

Finally, before speaking of his father-in-law he lauds the new regime of Nerva and Trajan (likely having written the Agricola during the last days of the former and the first days of the latter). He hints that he intends to write a history of the oppressive fifteen years of Domitian's reign, and hopes that until that time, his dutiful tribute to his father-in-law will be commended.

Given that we know Tacitus to have enjoyed the favour of the very same Domitian he now repeatedly damns, having been promoted and granted commissions by him, it is very tempting to see this opening of his first ever written work as an attempt to ingratiate himself with the new regime and to effectively distance himself from the old. That being said, while there are places in the Agricola where the author could be accused of using his work to vilify the former emperor, since much of the work focuses on Britannia with only passing commentary on what happens in Rome, we can be comfortable that such instances can easily be identified in the text and worked around.

While Tacitus's accuracy and impartiality have been endlessly questioned, there have been discoveries that suggest a certain level of accuracy. In October AD 19 the great general Germanicus, father of Caligula and brother of Claudius, died in Syria in suspicious circumstances. His passing was blamed by both himself and his wife upon the governor Piso, suggesting poisoning at the behest of the emperor Tiberius, as Tacitus tells us: 'The cruel virulence of the disease was intensified by the patient's belief that Gnaeus Calpurnius Piso had given him poison.' He goes on in the same chapter to tell us of Piso's house with cinematic style that 'it is a fact that explorations in the floor and walls brought to light the remains of human bodies, spells, curses, leaden tablets engraved with the name Germanicus, charred and blood-smeared ashes, and others of the implements of witchcraft by which it is believed the living soul can be devoted to the powers of the grave'.[2]

This sounds almost like horror novel fiction, yet Germanicus's possible poisoning by Piso[3] can be seen to be corroborated in a Senatorial decree recorded on bronze tablets (the Tabula Siarensis) discovered in Spain in 1982, and this reminds us not to lightly brush aside his words without due consideration. For a full discussion of these bronze tablets and their comparison with Tacitus, I would direct you to 'Tacitus, Germanicus, Piso, and the Tabula Siarensis' by Julián González in vol. 120 of the *American Journal of Philology*.

We must remember, after all, that Tacitus was writing within living memory of these events, and his potential audience would include people who had experienced them first-hand. While it seems unlikely that Suetonius Paulinus would be one, as he would have been in his eighties then, it is feasible that Petilius Cerialis would live to read it aged in his sixties, let alone young officers who had served as tribunes in Agricola's campaigns, who would only be middle-aged by the time the Agricola was published. In essence there will have been plenty of people to read Tacitus's work who knew Agricola personally and had lived through what the writer described. Thus, while his veracity can be questioned constantly, one might wonder why, if it was erroneous, history does not record anyone arguing with its content.

With all of this in mind, then, my goal cannot be to prove Tacitus either right or wrong. What I have done is to examine and evaluate each aspect of Agricola's life from the text and attempt to build a suggested and plausible biography that fits entirely with the archaeological evidence, with contemporary accounts and what we know of the military, social and political framework of the era, and as far as possible agrees with Tacitus's own work. In doing so, we will build the most reasonable account of his life available based upon the evidence we have.

I

AB ORIGINE

The origins of Agricola's family, his parentage, birth and childhood, and some background on the time and the region.

Critical to our understanding of a person, before we even consider their physicality and their personality, is an appreciation of whence they came. Tacitus understood this, giving us an introductory passage in his Agricola that addresses the issue in a succinct form. For the modern historian it would have been more useful if Tacitus had been a little *less* succinct and told us more, but we can only work with what we are given. Fortunately, in addition to Tacitus's own writings, we are able to look at other contemporary accounts, odd mentions that coincide, and even epigraphy, which all help expand upon that short paragraph crammed with data.

Firstly, let us examine the geographical background, just as our first biographer did. Tacitus tells us 'Cnaeus Julius Agricola was born at the ancient and famous colony of Forum Julii.'[1] In actual fact, in the original Latin, we find the wording 'Gnaeus Iulius Agricola, vetere et inlustri Foroiuliensium colonia ortus.' An important point here is the potential variation in translation of Latin texts. The word *ortus* can be translated a number of ways. Mattingly and Handford translate it as 'was born in', but Birley prefers 'came from'. While the distinction between the two is subtle, it allows for great variation in meaning. As we shall see, it seems almost certain that Agricola was actually born in Rome, though since his formative years were spent at Forum Julii and it is likely his family were from the area, Birley's choice of 'came from' therefore makes a great deal more sense.

What Tacitus tells us, then, is that Agricola came from Forum Julii. There are several ancient towns that bore this name (the name being 'Market of Julius'), but one in particular fits the bill far more than any other and has long been accepted as the man's home. This town is now known as Frejus, and it lies on the southern coast of France between Marseilles and Nice. Agricola, then, was born rather pleasantly on the Cote d'Azur.

A little background on Frejus will prove invaluable in understanding Agricola's connections (see map 1 for the general geography.) In the mid-first century BC northern Italy was considered to be Gaulish, though still part of the Roman republic. Its provincial name was Cisalpine Gaul, its border ending just to the east of Nice, and in 58 BC Gaius Julius Caesar was appointed as its governor. Governorship of a province was a lucrative position for an ambitious man, and many governors would use their time in office to increase the contents of their own purse. Occasionally truly ambitious men would use their province, as long as it was one that came with legions, to conquer new lands, for conquest brought both riches *and* fame. Engineering an excuse for a war, Caesar pursued the Helvetii tribe from what is now Switzerland into France, initiating an eight-year campaign of conquest that would end with *Trans*-alpine Gaul becoming a province (and Asterix forging a thirty-eight-book campaign of resistance!) The city of Marseilles (ancient Massalia/Massilia) had been an independent Greek colony, but following a siege in the civil war of 49 BC when they backed the wrong horse – never bet against Caesar – Massilia (Latin) was annexed and the entire region became Roman.

Following the siege, close to Massilia and just outside the border of Cisalpine Gaul, Caesar established the town of Forum Julii, likely on the site of an older native settlement, and settled his veterans there. His association with the town, and not just in name, resonated down to Agricola's time a century later, as it still does today. Le Cesar restaurant is near the port for when you visit.

A generation after its founding, the emperor Augustus settled his own veterans from the Eighth Legion there and raised the town to

Ruins of the 12,000-capacity amphitheatre in Frejus. (Public domain, Patricia. fidi.)

the status of Colonia, granting its population Roman citizenship and other rights. Forum Julii grew rapidly and by the time of Agricola was a true Roman city, complete with theatres and public buildings and all the trappings of urban Roman life. For reference, its theatre and aqueduct, among other ruins, remain in excellent condition for the visitor.

Agricola's family must have lived through and experienced that growth as they rose within Roman society. The earliest members we know of are mentioned by Tacitus. Both Agricola's grandfathers were high-ranking imperial procurators. At this time, procurators were drawn from the Equestrian order, and their duties were to take care of financial and judicial matters in a province, serving under a governor or directly under the emperor. It was an important and prestigious position for those so honoured. Both Agricola's mother and father, then, were born into the equestrian class.

The 'tria nomina' form of male Roman names			
Praenomen	Nomen	Cognomen	Agnomen
The personal or first name, of which there are a limited number, and which are often common within families (Gaius, Lucius, Titus, etc.)	The clan or family name of the person, indicating their line of descent (Julius, Cornelius, Flavius, etc.)	A nickname, often based upon a physical characteristic, sometimes passed down through the family (Caesar, Sulla, Vespasianus, etc.)	Increasingly through time, nobles acquired more than three names, often including victory titles (Germanicus, Parthicus, etc.)

Agricola's father was Julius Graecinus (Tacitus, as usual, records only two names – nomen and cognomen – of the tria nomina), and these two names are remarkably informative. Given the connection with Forum Julii, the gens name of Julius suggests that the family received its citizenship perhaps not from Augustus along with the rest of the population, but earlier, from Caesar, probably at the end of the Gallic Wars and around the time of the city's founding (while Asterix is just warming up). This would fit with a rise of the family to the equestrian class within half a century or so. The cognomen 'Graecinus' is interesting, too. Though a cognomen was commonly used to identify branches of a family and could be inherited, the fact that Graecinus's son did not in fact inherit this name suggests that the practice is not uniform, and that perhaps in some circles the cognomen was still applied as it had once been – as a descriptive (such as Celer 'The Quick', Nasica 'Big Nose', and so on.) Graecinus, then, is derived from Graecus ('Greek') and while it may have been inherited from his own father, it did not pass down to his son, Agricola. Given the high probability of a Gallic origin and a connection to Caesar, we might be tempted to look in the direction of Massalia, a thriving formerly Greek colony just a stone's throw from Forum Julii.

Can we corroborate Tacitus's account of Agricola's father? Well yes, as it happens, we can. He tells us in that same opening paragraph 'His father, Julius Graecinus, a member of the Senatorian order, and distinguished for his pursuit of eloquence and philosophy, earned for himself by these very merits the displeasure of Caius

Caesar. He was ordered to impeach Marcus Silanus, and because he refused was put to death.' What we can discern from this was that while Graecinus was born into the equestrian class, he rose to the senatorial order at some point during the reign of Tiberius. Let us then examine non-Tacitan evidence and see what we can glean.

In 1940 a tombstone was unearthed on the Esquiline hill in Rome. The inscription reads:

LIVLIO.LF.ANI
GRAECINO
TR PL PR
MIVLIVS.L.F.ANI
GRAECINVS
QUAESTOR.F[2]

Which can be translated as:

Lucius Iulius, son of Lucius, of the Aniensis voting tribe
Graecinus
Tribune of the Plebs, Praetor
Marcus Iulius, son of Lucius, of the Aniensis voting tribe
Graecinus
Quaestor made this

As a piece of evidence this is immensely valuable. If we are willing to accept that one of these Julius Graecinuses is the same man who is named as Agricola's father, and it seems highly likely since the name is far from common, then we now know his praenomen is either Lucius or Marcus, the other being a brother.

We can also corroborate what Tacitus says about his senatorial rank, for he would need to be such to achieve the position of Praetor or Quaestor. We can confirm a link to the city of Frejus, for that city falls within the territory of the Aniensis voting tribe, and we can even say that Agricola's paternal grandfather was called Lucius. What's more, we know that either Agricola's father interred his uncle, or the other way around, apparently in Rome. Of the two brothers, Lucius would be the older, as it was common practice for a father to pass his praenomen down to the first male child.

One important theory is supported by this inscription. Since the tombstone was found in Rome and both brothers had to have been in the city when one died, and since both were climbing the Cursus Honorum, then Agricola was very likely born in Rome. This being the case, I am inclined to agree with Birley's translation of 'ortus' as a more vague 'came from' rather than a definitive 'born in'.

Do we know anything else about this man who had risen to the heights of the social ladder from a family of humble origins, whose name means Greek and who has ancestral ties to Caesar, who was a praetor or quaestor and lived (and possibly died) in Rome? As it happens, other Roman writers tell us more about Graecinus than Tacitus does, and miraculously such works have survived the ages.

Seneca not only tells us something about Graecinus's character, but also partially corroborates the information from Tacitus that he was put to death by Gaius (Caligula). 'If there is need of an example of a noble spirit, let us take the case of Julius Graecinus, a rare soul, whom Gaius Caesar killed simply because he was a better man than a tyrant found it profitable for anyone to be.'[3] He goes on to laud Graecinus for refusing contributions towards expensive public games from people he considers of poor reputation.

Columella tells us 'And his [Julius Atticus] pupil, as it were, Julius Graecinus, has taken care that two volumes of similar instructions on vineyards, composed in a more elegant and learned style, should be handed down to posterity.'[4] So we know also that Graecinus was a writer and a keen student of viticulture.

Even the great Pliny notes 'Graecinus states that there have been cases of vines living 600 years.'[5] Given these notes on his interests, it seems highly likely that either Graecinus, or his wife after his death, gave Agricola his cognomen, for *Agricola* unsurprisingly refers to agriculture.

There is a question about Graecinus that arises from Tacitus's brief account. The biographer notes 'He was ordered to impeach Marcus Silanus, and because he refused was put to death' (by Caligula). The relationship between this Silanus and the infamous emperor I explored in my novel *Caligula*. Since we know from a later mention that Agricola was born in June of AD 40, and we know that the *famous* Marcus Silanus who was Caligula's father-in-law was killed in AD December 37, there is a period of two and a half years between the reason for Graecinus's execution and its carrying out. It is, of course, possible that the cause of Caligula's displeasure did not lead immediately to Graecinus's death, and then the two-and-a-half-year gap is less jarring, but there is a more seductive possibility. Perhaps we need to look further afield. There was another Marcus Silanus contemporary with both Caligula and Graecinus, one M. Junius Silanus Torquatus, and he seems all the more obvious when we discover that Tacitus has mentioned him elsewhere in a similar vein: 'But in course of time Caligula, prompted by his restless temper and by his fear of Marcus Silanus, who then held Africa, took away the legion from the proconsul, and handed it over to a legate whom he sent for that purpose.'[6] While it seems likely that Silanus fell foul of Caligula and it may well be he that Graecinus refused to prosecute, it seems that he managed to survive that difficult reign, for we are told that a Torquatus Silanus in the reign of Nero, 'finding his condemnation imminent, severed the arteries in his arms'.[7] So endeth our chosen Silanus. *Arma virumque.*

Whatever the truth of the Silanus incident, Julius Graecinus, keen Viticulturalist and vir egregius (illustrious man),[8] died towards the end of Caligula's reign, likely before his son was born.

What of Agricola's mother, then? The daughter of a respected equestrian procurator and wife of the celebrated Graecinus, who was left alone to bring up her son? Tacitus tells us 'His mother was Julia Procilla, a lady of singular virtue. Brought up by her side with fond affection, he passed his boyhood and youth in the cultivation of every worthy attainment.'

Julia's name brings us back to the connections we noted initially. Her first name once more suggests an ancestral link to Caesar, but it is her second name that holds real fascination. Procilla, or its male variant Procillus, is of a somewhat confused origin. It may be a corruption of Procilius, which is commonly attached to one of Rome's oldest patrician families, or it may be a Latinisation of Troucillus, with which Procillus seems to be interchangeable even in the writings of Caesar, and which is most definitely a name of Helvian Gaulish origin. Procillus appears on numerous inscriptions in Gaul (such as 'qui … moratus est in dispensatione Boion[i]ae Procillae et Aureli Fulvi'[9]), and in the first year of his Gallic Wars,

Julius Caesar selects as an important emissary a Helvian named Gaius Valerius Procillus (or Troucillus). Thus, we find Caesarian and Gallic connections on both sides of Agricola's parentage. That he 'came from' Frejus now seems unarguable.

As another regional link, I offer a second line from Columella: 'He [Graecinus] relates that he often used to hear his father say that a certain Paridius Veterensis, his neighbour, had two daughters, and also a farm planted with vineyards.'[10] This Paridius seems to have had family estates near Albimintilium, some 40 miles or so east along the coast from Forum Julii, and where in AD 69 Julia Procilla resides.

Tacitus goes on to illustrate how Julia Procilla brought Agricola up with notable personal care. The mid-first century AD is an era when the wealthy and the important relied heavily upon wet-nurses, slaves and tutors for the welfare of their children. It is uncommon (though not unheard of) for a woman of status to so personally involve herself in her child's growth and life. There are parallels, for certain, such as this excerpt from an epitaph to Gratia Alexandria from Rome: 'an outstanding exemplar of modesty. She even brought up her children with the milk of her own breasts'.[11] Tellingly, this fragment shows us how unusual that closeness was at the time, an old custom that was no longer in common practice. Indeed, it is an example of the *mos maiorum* (the vital Roman sense of ancestral custom) at work.

Tacitus tells us in his other work 'Thus it was, as tradition says, that the mothers of the Gracchi, of Caesar, of Augustus, Cornelia, Aurelia, Atia, directed their children's education and reared the greatest of sons. The strictness of the discipline tended to form in each case a pure and virtuous nature which no vices could warp.'[12] This seems to be echoed in his description of Julia Procilla, placing the family firmly alongside those other illustrious names.

It is likely that Tacitus uses Agricola's parents' adherence to the old ways to enhance the family's Romanitas. Rome may now have been a superpower, but every Roman knew that they descended from men who had farmed the land, and had only taken up the sword when the need arose. A thousand years after the founding of Rome, when asked to resume power after his retirement, the emperor Diocletian replied: 'If you could see at Salonae the cabbages raised by our hands, you surely would never judge that a temptation.' In bringing out these traits Tacitus makes Agricola's family a line to be proud of despite relatively humble origins. There is also a sense in this early chapter that the Gauls from which the family undoubtedly descend should be seen as noble and traditional even prior to their Romanisation. A practical provincial family.

Since we can reasonably assume that Agricola was born in Rome, but we know from ensuing text that he spent his formative years in provincial Gaul, we can perhaps put a tentative sequence to events so far. Agricola's father is a respected advocate in Rome but refuses to prosecute a man on the emperor's orders. Caligula, being ever quick-tempered, has Graecinus executed, while Julia is pregnant. Agricola is born in Rome, but without Graecinus around she takes him far from the emperor's direct influence and to family estates at Frejus.

So far so good. We have a solid idea of Agricola's ancestry and where he came from. We are then told of his youth and his adolescence in similarly brief summation, and I shall treat this with similar brevity, largely through more corroborative example. Tacitus states: 'He was guarded from the enticements of the profligate not only by his own good and straight-forward character, but also by having, when quite a child, for the scene and guide of his studies, Massilia (Massalia), a place where refinement and provincial frugality were blended and happily combined. I remember that he used to tell us how in his early youth he would have imbibed a keener love of philosophy than became a Roman and a senator, had not his mother's good sense checked his excited and ardent spirit. It was the case of a lofty and aspiring soul craving with more eagerness than caution the beauty and splendour of great and glorious renown. But it was soon mellowed by reason and experience, and he retained from his learning that most difficult of lessons – moderation.'[13]

From the age of seven, then, when a Roman boy passed from infancy to adolescence and required further schooling, Agricola was sent to Massalia for his formative education. We do not have to look far to find accounts of that great old city to understand why this choice was made.

Strabo, writing only a generation before Agricola, tells us 'Their present state of life makes this clear; for all the men of culture turn

Statue of the Massalian explorer Pytheas on the palais de la Bourse in Marseilles, one of the luminaries of the ancient city of learning. (Public domain, Rvalette)

to the art of speaking and the study of philosophy; so that the city, although a short time ago it was given over as merely a training-school for the barbarians [...] at the present time has attracted also the most notable of the Romans, if eager for knowledge, to go to school there instead of making their foreign sojourn at Athens.'[14]

Valerius Maximus tells us 'They are quite remarkable for their austere way of life, their adherence to old ways, and their love for the Roman people,'[15] and Cicero even describes 'a city, the strict discipline and wisdom of which I do not know whether I might not say was superior, not only to that of Greece, but to that of any nation whatever'.[16]

Clearly, then, it would be natural for the son of a well-to-do family in the region of Forum Julii to be educated in Massalia. His mother continues to play a part, dampening his urge to explore the very Greek love of philosophy far more than was acceptable for a Roman student. A century later, following the influence of the Hellenophile emperor Hadrian and the 'Philosopher King' Marcus Aurelius, such learning becomes favourable, but in Agricola's era the focus remains on the *mos maiorum*, on maintaining traditional Roman values of practicality, hard work and austerity. I know, not the image of Romans we have been handed down from tales of Caligula and Nero, of lark's tongues and golden barges, but even in the time of those lavish emperors, the heart of Rome remained a very practical and plain one. To some extent, then, the Greeks with their philosophy, languidity and love of the naked human form represented the polar opposite of the mos maiorum. No wonder Agricola was prevented from becoming too philosophical.

While Cato might not be typical of Roman attitudes at the time he does exemplify the ascetic and severe character of old Rome, and that character is very clear in Plutarch's description of him: 'he was wholly averse to philosophy, and made mock of all Greek culture and training, out of patriotic zeal. He says, for instance, that Socrates was a mighty prattler, who attempted, as best he could, to be his country's tyrant, by abolishing its customs, and by enticing his fellow citizens into opinions contrary to the laws.'[17]

Of course, not all Romans shared this anti-philosophic zeal. Quintillian takes a contrary position: 'no one will achieve sufficient skill even in speaking, unless he makes a thorough study of all the workings of nature and forms his character on the precepts of philosophy and the dictates of reason'.[18] Cicero perhaps makes the best statement of all with 'I sometimes fear that what we term philosophy is distasteful to certain worthy gentlemen, and that they wonder that I devote so much time and attention to it.'[19]

Roman education, then, is something of a balance between the acceptance of philosophy as an integral part of learning and life, and a fear that too much philosophy risks going against the mos maiorum and being essentially 'too Greek to be good for you'.

Thus is a picture painted for us of Agricola the youth. A man who, like his vaunted father, has an interest in science, who is at once open-minded and progressive, wishing to learn and press deeper in subjects of intellectual value, and yet who achieves moderation and control in life partially through his own character, partly from the austere nature of the Massalian populace, and partially from the continued influence of his mother.

At eighteen years of age Agricola, born in Rome but raised and educated in Frejus and Marseilles, finally enters the political world and begins to climb the cursus honorum, starting with the traditional role for the senatorial class: the tribunate.

2

THE BRITISH SITUATION

Given the connection between Agricola and Britain, it is important that we understand the progress of the Romanisation of Britain in the two decades leading up to his arrival. Interest in the island had been building since Caesar first landed on the Kentish coast in 55 BC in what is still often referred to as a planned invasion, but was in truth much more of a publicity stunt. Following Caesar, the island was largely left alone for almost a century, though contact was maintained and some of the tribes treated favourably with Rome.

The empire first staked its claim to Britain when Agricola was but three years old. Invaded in AD 43 by the forces of the emperor Claudius, the attack had been led by General Aulus Plautius and had consisted of four legions and accompanying auxiliaries. Those four legions we must take note of, for they will reappear in this text throughout and are tied to Agricola's life. They were II Augusta, IX Hispania, XIV Gemina and XX Valeria Victrix. Among Plautius's officers came a number of famous Roman names. The future emperor Vespasian commanded the Second, the evidence of his campaign still evident in missiles found at Maiden Castle in Dorset, and his brother Sabinus is noted as being present too, perhaps leading a legion. Gnaeus Hosidius Geta, victorious general of the Mauretanian Wars, was also involved, perhaps in command of the Ninth. Plautius, incidentally and wholly coincidentally, had a wife whose cognomen was Graecina, just like Agricola's father.

Remains of the triumphal arch celebrating the conquest of Britain, located at Richborough. (Author's collection)

Claudius himself even came over for a few days once there was little chance of him facing any real danger, and he brought elephants with him – must have been a bizarre sight for the conquered locals watching this pampered lord and his parade of pachyderms. Within months the south-east was secured, the south-west being gradually subsumed, and the capital of the resisting forces at Colchester had been captured and garrisoned by Rome. Colchester remained of import even after the dreadful events of AD 60 to which we will come, and the man from whom it was taken, the British chieftain Caratacus, will reappear shortly, having fled the victorious legions to rally further resistance against the Roman invaders. Britain was, to some extent, conquered.

Plautius, then, became the first governor of the new province, and during his tenure (from 43 to 47) Roman forces pushed north and west from Kent, gaining control over land as far as Lincolnshire and the Severn Valley either directly or through tribes ruled by client kings, securing the south-west under Vespasian's

Second Legion. By 47, Britannia as a province was recognisable and increasingly stable, or so it would appear.

It is Plautius's successor upon whom we must concentrate, for his tale will become extremely pertinent in our biography. Publius Ostorius Scapula, a former consul, took command of the burgeoning province in 47. If we are to follow the sequence of events in Tacitus's *Annals* (and we have less reason to cast doubt upon the writer's later histories than on his *Agricola*) the departure of Plautius had sent out troublesome ripples. Those tribes as yet outside Roman influence had taken advantage of the change, believing that a successor would not be prepared to campaign late in the season with an army to whom he was new. It seems they underestimated Scapula, who immediately set to work with the forces available, despite the lateness of the season, pushing the tribes back and making them regret their impetuousness.

With winter looming Scapula, having recovered control, decided that the only way to prevent future risings would be to disarm the entire populace within Roman-controlled territory, behind the line of the Severn and Trent rivers. This rather radical decision did not go down well with many of those to be disarmed, including allied tribes like the infamous Iceni, who were the first to rebel. Goading their neighbours into war, the Iceni prepared to meet the Roman force to assert their self-government. Scapula marched to their chosen field of battle leading a force comprised solely of auxiliaries, which is worthy of note for later. With only auxiliaries and dismounted cavalry and no heavy legionary force, Scapula overcame the Iceni and crushed the revolt, still early in his tenure as governor. Rebellion across the region collapsed with the decisive defeat of the Iceni and despite the seeming rashness of his disarmament plan, with speed and decisiveness Scapula achieved precisely what he'd set out to do. His excellent military reputation must have spread far and wide in the late 40s.

The following year, Scapula campaigned in North Wales against the Deceangli with notable success, and several military sites in their original incarnations may date to this campaign, including Chester. Scapula was temporarily drawn back to northern England to put down a revolt within the northern tribe of the Brigantes who were nominally allied to Rome, but this was not a long-winded campaign and seems to have been achieved quickly and without issue, allowing him to move on once more. It is also possible that Verulamium, the modern St Albans, was founded by Scapula this year, once the military push was over. This lull was not to last.

Enter upon our scene that (in)famous Caratacus, great enemy of Rome. The Catevellauni chief had been one of the excuses for the Roman invasion in the first place, ruling from his capital in Colchester and expanding his lands at the expense of pro-Roman interests on the island. When the invasion had come it had been Caratacus who led the defence of Kent and the battle of the Medway against the armies of Aulus Plautius. Beaten and with his tribe subdued and his capital taken by Rome, Caratacus had vanished in the mid-40s, defeated but uncaptured.

Half a decade later the Silures of south Wales rose against Rome, pushed to action by Scapula's military construction on the periphery of their lands, and against the odds the man who emerged to lead them was Caratacus, reappearing from the shadows to head the war against Rome once more. Scapula responded in force to this thorn in Rome's side, initiating a new campaign in south and central Wales. The war continued over several seasons and it was only in 52 when the two forces met in a full engagement and Scapula carried the day, once more proving his military prowess. Attempts have long been made to place the location of this battle at sites such as British Camp in the Malvern Hills, or the appropriately named Caer Caradoc, though the late great Barri Jones preferred Blodwel Rock hill fort, based largely upon synchronicity with Tacitus's account. Wherever the battle was fought, the result was conclusive. Blood, mud and victory for Rome.

Never one to accept defeat, Caratacus, once more with his forces smashed and his power base broken, fled in search of aid from new tribes. Unfortunately for him, fleeing north away from the sphere of Roman influence he found himself at the court of the Brigantes, allied to Rome and so recently chastised by them, whose queen Cartimandua immediately handed him back to the Romans. Caratacus was taken to Rome and imprisoned for a time, eventually, according to Tacitus, being released and living out his

The hillfort of Caer Caradoc. (Author's collection)

life in that great city to which he had been so opposed. It seems incongruous that the man who had led two major armies against Rome and been dragged from the island in chains should in the end live a comfortable life as a Roman in the capital.

The defeat of the Silures and the capture of Caratacus seemingly did little to end the matter, though. According to Tacitus, the tribe was driven to further action by comments of Scapula's in which he stated the value of exterminating the Silurian name completely – presumably Scapula's version of Cato's famous '*Carthago delenda est*' statement. In the face of ongoing tribal conflict, Scapula was forced to construct garrison forts to control the Silures, who raided and attacked the cohorts involved and their foraging parties.

The situation had not been satisfactorily resolved by the time that Scapula died suddenly while in office in 52, but in addition to his defeat of the Iceni with just auxiliaries and his intent to wipe out a tribe entirely, there is one last very important aspect of his tenure that we must bear in mind. Scapula had campaigned throughout the entire Welsh border during his five years, first against the Deceangli in the north, and then the Silures in the south, pushing that war into the territory of the Ordovices in the middle. That Scapula was building not mere temporary camps for the winter but garrison forts is significant. The dating of sites is troublesome, but with best approximation it is possible to identify a series of sites that have been suggested as Scapulan installations (see map 2 and the table below).

Chester (*Deva*)	Alleged pre-Flavian box rampart and ditch located beneath fortress's 'elliptical building' combined with Neronian urn finds suggest existence of a fort that pre-dates the Deva fortress. *Roman north west England* p.10 (Shotter, 1996) and *Roman Chester* by David Mason (History Press, 2012)
Hope	Recent work (2019) places a turf ramparted fort/ camp on a hill above Hope. Local legend places a Roman bathhouse and buried Roman timbers at the site of twentieth-century quarrying between Hope and Caergwrle. (Info: Park in the Past, Caergwrle); also Barri Jones postulated an early fort at Farndon nearby.
Rhyn Park	Two overlapping sites, with pottery finds dated to mid-first century and a brooch considered of Neronian date suggesting that the earlier, smaller fort may be Scapulan, overlaid by a later vexillation fortress. (https://www.pastscape.org.uk/hob.aspx?hob_id=66831)
Abertanat	No dating of fort and two nearby camps has yet been possible, but box rampart suggests possible pre-Flavian or early Flavian date and more permanence than a temporary camp.
Brompton	No finds have appeared to date the fort, but its proximity to the early Flavian installation at Forden Gaer (4 miles) suggests a prior use. Forden Gaer has produced evidence of occupation from the late first century, including a Mortarium of 50–85 (Blockley, 1990, *Excavations in the vicinity of Forden Gaer Roman Fort, Powys*, 1987, Montgomeryshire Collections 78, 17–46). Brompton could therefore date from Scapula's push.

Stretford Bridge	A fort and series of marching camps remain undated.
Jay Lane	The earliest of a series of forts around Leintwardine, Jay Lane has produced solely pre-Flavian finds of Claudian and Neronian date and has been dated between AD 47 and 61. (Woolhope Naturalists' Field Club Transactions, 1968, p230-237, 55)
Hindwell Farm	Claudio-Neronian finds point to a pre-Flavian date, and several local marching camps indicate possible campaign use. (See pp 17-23 of Radnorshire Society Transactions1979 for find dating)
Clifford	Believed to pre-date the nearby fortress of Clyro, which has been dated to *c*. AD 60 (Nash-Williams, *Roman Frontier in Wales*, University of Wales 1969). Positioning with flood risk and distance from Roman road supports proposition.
Longtown Castle	Recent excavations have unearthed first-century pottery in a later reused site with turf ramparts; the suspected period is supported by radiocarbon dating. (http://longtowncastles.com/index.php/summary-of-excavations/)
Abergavenny *(Gobannium)*	Fort dated through pottery, coin and other finds in military refuse tip to a period between late Claudian and early Flavian. (Webster, *Rome Against Caratacus*, p75, Book Club Associates, 1981)
Usk *(Burrium)*	Recent 'Phase I' finds include a Claudian coin suggested as belonging to a construction camp for the fortress of AD 54, but may instead pre-date the Neronian site (Excavations at 10 Old Market Street, Usk, Britannia 20, 1989). Boon postulated a Scapulan site here based on other earlier finds. (G. C. Boon, *Remarks on Roman Usk* in Monmouthshire Antiquary 1.2, 1962)
Caerleon *(Isca)*	Possible earlier site beneath fortress of *c*. AD 70 based on a Samian find dated AD 35–55, whose origin is now lost, but which may have come from either Usk or Caerleon. (Webster, *Rome Against Caratacus* p75, Book Club Associates, 1981) Also, a rectangular enclosure at Coel y Caerau across the river could have a Roman date, which might suggest a fortlet site pre-dating the legionary fortress.

What this gives us appears at first glance to be a frontier, a military control zone along similar lines to the later Stanegate system. But as Webster mentions,[1] there might be more to it than that. After all, in this era the notion of a permanent border anywhere in the empire is still an alien idea, and such installations are always intended as merely a temporary measure until the next push. The positioning of these forts does not simply create a border with the Welsh tribes (since it often cuts through their territory, dividing it), but it does something rather more specific.

If one notes the terrain in relation to the installations, it can be seen that this postulated Scapulan system effectively seals all the major valleys and inroads to the territory of the tribes, on the very edge of the hills and mountains. It is possible, as Webster suggests, that these forts were so planned to deny the Silures and the Ordovices access to the rich farmland of the Severn Valley and the Cheshire plain. Perhaps in his inability to end the Silurian threat through field action, Scapula intended to break them through starvation and desperation? Did he still intend to remove their very name from history? Such a line of valley-controlling forts will reappear later, then referred to as the 'Glen-blocker forts', and so this theory is of great significance.

It is possible that Scapula's reputation reached the ears of the populace not only in Rome but also in Gaul, as he was awarded triumphal honours for his defeat of Caratacus. Agricola would have been twelve years old at the time of the general's death, learning at Massilia and almost old enough to take the adult toga. I find it very unlikely that word of the governor's success did not reach Agricola's ears. Britain, then, has thus far seen two very strong militaristic governors in the persons of Plautius and Scapula.

Didius Gallus now arrived from Rome to serve the next five-year term, from 52 to 57. Gallus had served as the commissioner of Rome's aqueducts in AD 38,[2] and Quintillian tells us 'Afer [...] replied to Didius Gallus, who, after making the utmost efforts to secure a provincial government, complained on receiving the appointment that he had been forced into accepting, "Well, then, do something for your country's sake."'[3] Gallus was seemingly not pleased at this troubled borderland. At this early juncture we can see something of a difference between the soldier-generals thus far sent to Britain and this next governor. Tacitus tells us 'Didius Gallus consolidated the conquests of his predecessors, and advanced a very few positions into parts more remote, to gain the credit of having enlarged the sphere of government,'[4] which is as damning as any account of a general's career.

Fortunately, two decades later Tacitus picks up Gallus's life once again in his Annals and reveals more. He tells us that a legion under Manlius Valens had suffered a defeat against the Silures. Presumably, based purely on geography, this was the Twentieth, who garrisoned Kingsholm near Gloucester, since the II were at Dorchester, the IX at Leicester, and the XIV at Mancetter, all far from Wales. There had also now been a horrible break-up between Venutius and Cartimandua, the king and queen of the ever-problematic Brigantes, possibly arising from her handing a resisting British king over to Rome. Venutius took an anti-Roman stance and Cartimandua sent to the governor for help. One can only imagine how the former aqueduct commissioner, who had begged for a comfortable and lucrative province but had been landed with war-torn Britannia, reacted to all this trouble. Tacitus tells us that he essentially relied upon his generals, who supported Cartimandua and aided her against her former husband. This is, sadly, almost all we know of Gallus. Given his apparent personality and abilities, his appointment may have been a political/nepotistic decision. If we are to be kind, an alternative possibility is that the apparent inactivity of the governor could be explained by the sudden change of rule as Claudius dies and Nero takes the throne. Nero, we are told, considers abandoning the province altogether and so expensive campaigns might have been put on hold against the possibility of withdrawal from the island.

Where Britannia had seen almost a decade of powerful military governors, at a time when the bordering tribes were being restive and troublesome Gallus apparently did little more than put out some advance posts from his predecessor's frontiers. While we cannot corroborate or deny this, Tacitus has no reason to lie on this subject, given how he had held forth on the value of Gallus's predecessors. It may be, however, that he is deliberately downplaying Gallus in order to cast his successors in the best possible light, since this is something we'll see Tacitus do in spades later on, so we might want to give Gallus the benefit of the doubt.

Gallus was replaced in 57 by Quintus Veranius, former consul and general of sufficient fame that Onasander dedicated a book on strategy to him. Nero, having now decided against withdrawal from the province, had perhaps seen the value of assigning more military-minded and proactive governors once again. Veranius arrived on the island, noted the ongoing situation with the Silures, and immediately launched into a campaign against them. Unfortunately, Veranius also died within the year, the cause of death unmentioned in sources. What Tacitus tells us of his appointment and death are confirmed by Veranius's epitaph from Rome (CIL vi.41075): 'legate of [...] the province of Britain, in which he died'. One begins to wonder why any noble Roman wanted to govern Britain now that two of the four men in the job had died in office on the island. It must have looked like a poisoned chalice at best.

After an initial strong start, then, with the powerful figures of Plautius and Scapula, from 52 onwards the burgeoning province had suffered a death in office, an ineffectual commander, and a strong leader who had lasted just a few months, all the time seething with disaffection and revolt. Two of the most powerful tribes on the island, the Iceni and the Brigantes, had been in revolt, while all the tribes of Wales continued to attack the military on the border. Rome must have looked at the island of Britannia and decided that something needed to be done. Britannia needed sorting out. It needed a strong commander, a veteran general who could bring the island back to heel.

Enter upon the scene Suetonius Paulinus.

3

AD SIGNUM

When a Roman male of substance reached eighteen years of age, he began to climb the social ladder. This involved a series of posts in the political and military spheres that sent a man from youth to the apex of Roman political life, if he played things right. This cursus honorum ('path of honour') had age limits defined in the days of the republic by the Lex Villia Annalis.

Posts of the Cursus Honorum with defined age requirements	
Vigintivir (required only for equestrians)	18
Military tribune (the senatorial class would achieve this directly at 18)	20
Quaestor	25
Aedile or Tribune of the plebs (non-mandatory for senatorial class)	27
Praetor	30
Governor of a lesser province (Propraetor* or Proconsul**) or commander of a legion	
Consul (age limit often varies at the whim of imperial choice)	32
Governor of a major province (Propraetor or Proconsul) or Urban Prefect	

* A propraetor had to have served his praetorship and would have his tenure extended into this position.

** Proconsuls theoretically had to have previously served as a consul, though in this era provincial governors are sometimes found referred to as proconsul even before their consulship.

Tacitus was of the equestrian class initially and therefore, as we noted earlier, he sought a minor administrative position at eighteen and moved on to take on a military tribunate at twenty. His father-in-law Agricola, however, had been born into senatorial ranks, and therefore he secured his first tribunate directly at eighteen. Admittedly, Agricola was only eighteen in June of that year, and so we must assume that the appointment of military tribunes was not at this point set on a specific date. Livy (Histories 42.31.5) gives us at least one clear example of the appointment of tribunes being amended for convenience during the days of the republic: 'leave the consuls and praetors free to appoint them.'

Each legion (of which at this time there were twenty-five) had six tribunes. Positioned directly beneath the legatus who commanded the unit and above the centurions who ran the day-to-day military activity, these six men served a number of purposes. Five of them were junior tribunes (tribuni angusticlavia) drawn from the equestrian class, who were young, inexperienced, and using the military as a springboard for a political career in Rome. They may have served as runners, administrators and in all sorts of non-critical positions. The sixth tribune was the senior one (the tribunus laticlavius). He was of senatorial blood, and as such he would be too important and well-connected to saddle with menial tasks.

In the period of the early empire the appointment of senior tribunes seems to have involved patronage and nepotism more than social order or plain ability. Pliny wrote to the senator Falco, saying 'I have been in such haste to ask you to bestow a military tribuneship on my friend.'[1] Birley has Falco commanding a legion in Dacia from 101 to 102, and he is attested as consul in 108. In the intervening six years, Birley places him as governor of first Lycia et Pamphylia, and then Judea,[2] presumably both for three-year terms. This would put him in command of Judea and its two legions when Pliny wrote his letter, and this is indicative of how such military appointments came about. Again, Pliny, clearly not a man reluctant to push his luck, wrote to to the senator Cornelius Priscus 'I have decided to choose you of all people as the one from whom to ask a favour which I am very anxious to have granted me. You are in command of a magnificent army, which gives you abundant material for conferring favours, and, moreover, has provided you with ample time during which you have advanced the interests of your own friends. Now give my friends a turn, please.'³

Similarly, when Vespasian was assigned to put down the Jewish revolt in 66, it can hardly be coincidence that one of the three legions involved was led by his son Titus. It seems that the general or governor had considerable say in requesting his officers, as suggested by the aforementioned Pliny letter. Also, though it dates from the late Republic, Julius Caesar's account of his Gallic Wars is replete with instances of him assigning men again and again to individual commands.

Thus, when in AD 58, at the age of eighteen, Agricola secures the position of senior tribune in one of the legions of Britannia, it is easy to see it as having been secured through connections. What connections might Agricola have had, given that he was but eighteen, had lived in Forum Julii and Massilia throughout his youth, and his father had died before he was born?

Simply, Rome ran on a network of social and political connections, clients and patrons, favours owed and long-standing loyalties. Without his father around, it is entirely possible that his mother helped secure him his tribunate, for well-positioned women were not as powerless as one might think. Perhapso Agricola had grown up knowing of his father's connections, even though he had never met Graecinus.

Remembering Pliny's letter to Falco, one can imagine a similar situation arising in 58. The man assigned to govern Britannia in that year was Suetonius Paulinus, a tried-and-tested military man as we have already noted, a man with a successful history of campaigning in mountainous terrain, no less. Paulinus was born *c.* AD 10, around the same time as Agricola's father. Paulinus had been a praetor in AD 40 (the year Agricola was born, the family were in Rome, and almost certainly the time of Graecinus's death). If Graecinus *is* the man mentioned on our tombstone from the Esquiline, then he had been a praetor at the latest point in his career, quite possibly alongside Paulinus in AD 40. Even if they did not serve together they will undoubtedly have been at Caligula's court in Rome at the same time. A potential connection rears its head. Silanus, the man who Graecinus refused to prosecute, would have been another member of that court. Interestingly, Vespasian was also a praetor in 40, which puts the future emperor also in that same circle.

If one were to further expand upon the court in AD 40 – the web of important figures who must have known one another – we can already say that Graecinus very likely knew Paulinus and Vespasian. Vespasian was involved in the invasion of Britain three years later, alongside Aulus Plautius and Hosidius Geta, and in the short gap between Vespasian's praetorship and the invasion, Hosidius Geta had been serving in a famed campaign in Mauretania with Suetonius Paulinus. The complexity and web-like nature of Roman patronage is becoming clear, but what we are left with is a series of connections between influential military characters forming within the first half decade after Agricola's birth. It is possible that through his father, Agricola enjoyed connections to not only Vespasian, but to Geta, Aulus Plautius and to the all-important Suetonius Paulinus.

By the time Agricola reached adulthood and sought a military posting, Paulinus was a celebrated war hero and a respected general and politician, a man who might very well have been close to Agricola's father once upon a time. In other words, the perfect patron. It is therefore easy to see how Agricola himself, or perhaps his uncle or his mother, or both, secured him a position with one of Paulinus's legions in war-torn and career-making Britain.

Whatever the case, when Suetonius Paulinus departed for Britain in 58, Agricola went with him as the second in command of one of Britain's four legions, which makes him, of course, one of the nine most senior military officers on the island, including Paulinus himself.

At the time of their arrival the north of the province was relatively stable under the control of the client kingdom of the Brigantes, who for once were not actively kicking seven shades of stercus out of each other, though the simmering hatred between their king and queen continued to make future trouble a very real possibility. Thus the concentration of the military lay upon the restive Welsh frontier. The Ninth legion was at this time garrisoning Lincoln and commanded by Petilius Cerialis, the only legion based in the settled south and east of the island. The Second Augusta was at Exeter and may possibly have been under-strength, with vexillations deployed away from the fortress. The Fourteenth was now based at Wroxeter in Shropshire, on the River Severn and very close to the Welsh trouble zone, as was the Twentieth at Usk, similarly bristling on the Welsh border.

This deployment is important for we know that, like the proactive soldier he was, Paulinus immediately launched into campaigning against the Welsh tribes, for which the heart of his force consisted of those two legions based at the frontier, the Fourteenth and the Twentieth. It is possible to see one of these, or even the Ninth, as the unit to which Agricola was assigned, though the most likely is the Second in Exeter. Two years later, when the stercus hit the fan, the Second was called for from Exeter and declined to move, the refusal coming from the legion's camp prefect, its third in command. Had the legate or the senior tribune been present it would have been they who issued such an order, and therefore it is reasonable to suggest that Agricola had been assigned to the Second, but since that legion was positioned in a region of little danger, the two most senior officers were were seconded to the governor's staff for the campaign in Wales, leaving the camp prefect in command. This neatly explains and supports Tacitus's description of his father-in-law's assignment to Britain:

'He served his military apprenticeship in Britain to the satisfaction of Suetonius Paulinus, a painstaking and judicious officer, who, to test his merits, selected him to share his tent. Without the recklessness with which young men often make the profession of arms a mere pastime, and without indolence, he never availed himself of his tribune's rank or his inexperience to procure enjoyment or to escape from duty. He sought to make himself acquainted with the province and known to the army; he would learn from the skilful, and keep pace with the bravest, would attempt nothing for display, would avoid nothing from fear, and would be at once careful and vigilant.'[4]

The opening line refers to his assignment and tells us that Agricola was selected to serve on Paulinus's staff. This might seem odd, given his youth, rank and position, but it is not as unlikely as it might seem. Remember that even at eighteen and new to the military, Agricola was one of the nine most senior officers on the island. Throughout the army's history we can see evidence in support of such appointments. In the republican era, so Suolahti tells us, of the six tribunes in a legion, two would command at any one time on a rota, and suggests that the other four, while unoccupied, would serve on the general's staff.[5] Over the years of his wars in the late republic, Caesar regularly assigns men from his staff, his 'lieutenants', to command legions or vexillations. This republican system of using tribunes and senior officers as a pool of staff officers clearly worked, and so there is no reason to assume that the practice died out simply with the formalisation of the military under Augustus. Very likely tribunes and legates were still taken from their units to serve directly with the general. Adrian Goldsworthy admits 'The only thing that does seem clear is that there was no standard complement for a general's staff,' and goes on to add that 'its effectiveness depended upon the commander's own abilities and the qualities of the officers that he had chosen'.[6]

What Tacitus goes on to tell us, in a headache-inducing river of praise, is how while assigned to Paulinus's staff Agricola does not choose to idle away his time in a sinecure of a position as most such appointees did, but that he took an active interest in the military, his role in it, and the province in which he was now serving. Simply, that he learned.

If one gently sweeps the torrent of compliments beneath the carpet and sees just the bare bones of it, then the picture of a serious young military man emerges, and it is not an unlikely or unrealistic one. Assigned to serve with a bona fide war hero who seems to have taken the young tribune under his wing, Agricola's attention and professionalism seems a likely and appropriate response.

We are told little of Agricola's first two years in Britain, for in Tacitus's text, as well as in his Annals, the tale properly picks up in AD 60/61 with Paulinus poised to invade Mona, the island of Anglesey. What can we say of those missing years, then? Well the best clue comes later in the Agricola, in chapter 14, where Tacitus tells us 'Suetonius Paulinus enjoyed success for two years; he subdued several tribes and strengthened our military posts.'

We read in the Annals that Paulinus was 'in military skill and in popular report [...] a formidable competitor to Corbulo, and anxious to equal the laurels of the recovery of Armenia by crushing a national enemy'.[7] Paulinus, then, while already a successful and acclaimed general himself, is hungry to match the greatest name of his day: Gnaeus Domitius Corbulo. Paulinus arrives in Britain with the writ to settle the trouble in Wales, which has continued to rage and fester. With peace across the majority of settled England and the allied Brigantes controlling the north, naturally Paulinus would turn straight to Wales.

The Silures had been defeated by Scapula, but not conquered, and had continued to cause trouble ever since. Gallus had made advances against them, perhaps, but they remained a resistant tribe. The Ordovices had been involved in the actions during Scapula's tenure, but are not mentioned again until AD 70. Only the Deceangli in the north seem to have been truly overcome. It seems most likely that from 58 to 60 Paulinus took the Fourteenth and Twentieth legions into Wales, firstly subduing the Silures, likely securing the Demetae in modern Pembrokeshire, then moving north to overcome the Ordovices.

Pre-Roman settlement of the Ordovices at Din Lligwy on Anglesey. (Author's collection)

Despite the fragmentary literary evidence for these two years, there may be archaeological evidence to support this theory in the form of temporary camps. The problem we have with this possibility is the vague character of said temporary camps. Their very nature means that they were devoid of permanent structures, which denies us most useful archaeological evidence, and they were only ever occupied for very brief periods, which eliminates the rest of our potential proof. What we are largely left with is a turf rampart, a few rubbish pits and things thrown away or lost. From that scant evidence it is extremely difficult to date such a site.

Added to this is the fact that the purpose and nature of a temporary camp is extremely difficult to determine with any confidence. Sites that appear on the ground as vague ramparts and nothing else cannot tell us in a straightforward manner whether they were used as practice camps for training soldiers in fortification techniques, training camps for artillery practice and the like, siege camps, marching camps to protect a unit on the move during campaign, or even camps built to temporarily garrison a location for strategic purposes. There *are* clues to be had, however. Placement in a line roughly a day's march apart suggests campaign marching camps, positioning next to native hill forts might mean siege camps, and clusters close by a fort might identify practice camps. But with the best will in the world all we can say for certain is that they were simply 'temporary camps of some sort'. For an in-depth discussion on this subject, see Alan Leslie's 1995 thesis 'Roman Temporary Camps in Britain', chapter 4.

Barring practice/training sites, though, what we can say about the camps in Wales is that they were extant in only a limited period. The first campaigns in Wales took place under Scapula in 47, and the last under Agricola in 78, and thus any temporary campaign sites were almost certainly active only during that thirty-one-year window. Given that we know Scapula to have built forts to pen the tribes in, and we now can reasonably assume we have identified the rough line, the various temporary camps beyond that line must belong to one of his successors, and a prime suspect must be the two years of Welsh campaigning under Suetonius Paulinus. After him only Frontinus and Agricola would campaign in Wales, the former against the Silures in the south and the latter against the Ordovices in the north.

Those later campaigns further complicate the identification of sites involved in these two years of war, but a quick look at the distribution of temporary camps in Wales (map 3), in which I have made no attempt to separate out their purpose for my previously stated reasons, shows concentrations of activity. It is reasonable to say that some of these sites (and the many that have yet to be identified, since temporary camps are located every year) suggest that Tacitus was not far off the mark when he told us that Paulinus enjoyed success and subdued tribes. Agricola, then, almost certainly spent his first two years in the army at the side of Paulinus across the entirety of Wales on a campaign of conquest and subjugation.

The reason I have devoted so much time to this is because there is something important lurking between the lines here. Agricola, at an impressionable age and while learning the military ropes from a war hero, perhaps acquires his own role model at this time. Just as we are blatantly told that Suetonius Paulinus holds himself up against the measure of Corbulo, it is possible that here Agricola begins to stand in the shadow of the former governor Ostorius Scapula and attempts to outgrow it.

Agricola's first two years of campaigning are spent amid the reminders of Scapula's feted campaigns, for which he was given triumphal honours. Scapula did not have a chance to fall from grace, dying in office and leaving a powerful legacy of Romanitas. Agricola must have approved of the man, and there are odd clues to be found in support of this. Scapula's notion of wiping out a tribe will recur later, that time on the lips of Agricola. The very idea of forts positioned to block the enemy's routes to good farmland will become very important towards the end of Agricola's career. And the fact that Scapula had used auxiliaries alone to defeat the Iceni will re-emerge. This, then, is the time when Agricola takes in Scapula's achievements first-hand, standing amid their reminders, and is perhaps the first true formative time of his adult personality.

So from 58 to 60 Paulinus, with Agricola on his staff, settles the tribes that have been troublesome for years. This perhaps explains why Mona (now the island of Anglesey) becomes so important at the culmination of this period. It is commonly assumed that the campaign against Mona was politically motivated due to it being the heart of druidic culture in Britain. That was perhaps *part* of Paulinus's purpose, but it is reasonable to assume that enemy survivors of his campaigns had taken refuge there – in the annals Tacitus even refers to Mona as 'a haven for refugees'.[8] Moreover, as we shall see from another unexpected angle, there is good reason to suspect that Paulinus had never intended to make such a focus of Mona, but that the invasion came about purely as a consequence of pushing the resistance ever more northwards.

The Romans had a fortified and garrisoned line from Chester to the Bristol Channel courtesy of Scapula's foundations. As the legions secure first the south, the south-west, the centre and the west of Wales, and then push into the north of Ordovices territory, then those warriors resistant to Roman domination must have been systematically squeezed further and further into the north, finally being forced across the strait and onto Mona. Perhaps with this being a druidic stronghold and protected by water they felt it to be, as Tacitus noted, a safe haven.

They were wrong. After all, Britain itself was an island, and the English Channel had not stopped the legions. Paulinus seemingly now had all of Wales under control and the remaining troublemakers on one island. We have no evidence of the site of Paulinus's invasion of Mona, sadly, and even the temporary camps are very rare in the area. Traditionally, locals claim the site of Llanfair-is-gaer as the crossing point, and despite the fact that there is no record of a Roman fortification there, the name does translate as 'the church of Saint Mary beneath the fort', and it is on a slight bluff with perfect terrain for both embarkation and landing across the water close by. It is not difficult to stand at Llanfair-is-gaer and picture the scene.

We are told of the war on Mona not in the Agricola, but in Tacitus's Annals: 'in view of the shallow and variable channel, [Paulinus] constructed a flotilla of boats with flat bottoms. By this method the infantry crossed; the cavalry, who followed, did so by fording or, in deeper water, by swimming at the side of their horses.'[9]

The construction of flat-bottomed boats is perfectly logical and believable. We can see this action as a smaller-scale early version of the Normandy landings, and there is no reason to doubt Tacitus's words here. He may have been only four years old at this point, but by the time he was writing about it he would have heard first-hand accounts of these campaigns from Agricola, and likely from others who had been involved.

The way the cavalry cross to Mona is revealing. That they swim alongside their horses gives us a definite clue as to the identity of these units, and it is their first appearance of several during Agricola's time. We first come across them in Caesar's writings. In an attempt to cross a narrow river and engage the forces of the Pharaoh of Egypt, 'scattered groups of German cavalry, looking for places to ford the river, swam across it at some points where the banks were lower.'[10] These Germans were almost certainly of the Batavi and the Tungri, tribes from the Rhine, whom Caesar had adopted as his cavalry during the Gallic Wars. Caesar's use of Germanic cavalry is well documented and began a centuries-long tradition of such units employed as elite squads by Roman generals and emperors.

These Germans reappear time and again in Roman history, with Cassius Dio telling us of their actions during the invasion of Britain, where Aulus Plautius at the battle of the Medway River 'sent across a detachment of Germans, who were accustomed to swim easily in full armour across the most turbulent streams'.[11] Dio also tells us of an incident witnessed by the emperor Hadrian: 'So excellently, indeed, had his soldiery been trained that the cavalry of the Batavians, as they were called, swam the Ister with their arms,'[12] an incident confirmed by the inscription CIL III 3676. Even as late as the fourth century, there are records of the Cornuti (an imperial mounted bodyguard of Germanic origin) 'swimming on their shields, which they put under them like canoes'.[13]

Here it is important to note the role (or lack thereof) of the Roman navy in this campaign. We hear from Tacitus of the importance Agricola places on his naval capabilities in later days, and Rome learned hard lessons as to the importance of the navy from the Carthaginians centuries ago. So why at this juncture is Paulinus building makeshift rafts for his men?

Roman imperial trireme on a relief in Baia archaeological Museum. (Author's collection)

There is a simple and illuminating answer to this. Mason suggests that the fleet assigned to Britain, the Classis Britannica, operated around the west and north coasts of Wales during this campaign. Indeed, Nash Williams[14] suggests that even as far back as the Claudian era a fleet might have been based in the Bristol Channel, perhaps at Sea Mills. I am less convinced by the notion of the fleet's presence during the campaigns of 58-60. Firstly, the fact that Paulinus is forced to improvise suggests a lack of naval support. Where campaigns in the north of England or in southern and eastern Scotland might benefit from naval support, with navigable rivers making much of the interior reachable as far as the Pennines, Wales is a different proposition entirely. Any campaigning in the heartlands of Wales would be out of reach of the navy, who would be restricted to coastal landing or the Severn, barring a few short inlets and unable to penetrate far into the land. While Nash-Williams suggests the use of the Usk and the Tywi in dealing with the Silures, neither is navigable above the tidal area by more than canoes and flat-bottomed boats. The Carmarthen Rivers Trust sums it all up: 'Most tidal waters are navigable as are the lower (English) reaches of the river Wye, but there are no other navigable inland waters in Wales.'[15] Rome would have learned from early exploration, and most definitely from the campaigns of Paulinus's predecessors, that the navy would be of very little use in support of an upland Welsh campaign. As such it is no surprise that the navy are not in attendance when Paulinus attacks Mona. Most likely they remained on the Kentish coast, awaiting a time when they would be of use. Within the next twenty years, Caerleon will exist with its impressive harbour capability, and so will Chester in its grand form, and coastal stations such as Cefn Gaer will arise in the ensuing years, but at this stage there is simply no sign of Rome making provision for the navy in Wales.

This also raises a secondary question of import: if Paulinus set out to conquer Mona as Tacitus tells us, then why did he clearly not arrange naval support, and why was he left building makeshift rafts? This is not the level of planning one would expect from such a man. The clear inference from this is that Paulinus never set out to make a grand political statement with the extinction of the druids and the invasion of the Celtic heartland. Instead, what he had done, and what any good general would have done, was to conquer Wales in stages, grinding down resistance and pushing the last pockets into a corner, where, sadly, he suddenly discovered he needed boats and had none. This makes a great deal more historical and logical sense.

So with legions on rafts and German cavalry swimming the channel, Paulinus crossed to Mona and engaged the enemy. Once more it is not hard to picture an Iron Age version of the opening scenes of *Saving Private Ryan*, with arrows and spears and slingshots whipping into the waves as men approach the beach in water pink with the blood of fallen legionaries. In one of Tacitus's most famous passages, we are told of the action that ensued.

'On the beach stood the adverse array, a serried mass of arms and men, with women flitting between the ranks. In the style of

Furies, in robes of deathly black and with dishevelled hair, they brandished their torches; while a circle of Druids, lifting their hands to heaven and showering imprecations, struck the troops with such an awe at the extraordinary spectacle that, as though their limbs were paralysed, they exposed their bodies to wounds without an attempt at movement. Then, reassured by their general, and inciting each other never to flinch before a band of females and fanatics, they charged behind the standards, cut down all who met them, and enveloped the enemy in his own flames.'[16]

We need not explore too deeply the battle itself, which may have taken place at Llanidan, based upon three local names: 'Hill of Graves', 'Field of the Long Battle', and the most excellently named 'Field of Bitter Lamentation'. We may never be able to confirm the truth or falsehood of Tacitus's account, but there is no real reason to lie in his portrayal of Paulinus in the Annals, and the format of *Roman troops unnerved by a feral enemy and then roused to victory by the heroic words of their commander* is hardly new.

We cannot guess at the nature of the black-clad females mentioned, though women had a much more varied public and important role in Celtic society than in Rome, and so it is not impossible by any means that this is true. The druids being at the heart of the issue and whipping up a frenzy among the defenders is wholly in keeping with their role as priests, scholars and leaders of the tribes. Caesar describes the druids of Gaul in much the same way. After all, we are not talking about Asterix's friend Getafix here but warrior priests, political masters and fervent freedom fighters. It is the last line of Tacitus's description that intrigues the most:

'The next step was to install a garrison among the conquered population, and to demolish the groves consecrated to their savage cults: for they considered it a duty to consult their deities by means of human entrails.'[17]

It might strike a modern reader as odd to learn that human sacrifice was one of the trigger points of unacceptable barbarism in Roman society, having been banned by Senatorial decree in 97 BC. After all, we are talking about a culture of blood, whose capital punishments were gruesome, who had no qualms about making butchery a public entertainment and sacrificed animals just to check whether it was time to feed the kids, but Rome was a strictly ordered society, and moral lines drawn were uncrossable. Human sacrifice was one of them. Rome had frowned upon the practice among Carthaginians, perhaps in early Geto-Dacian culture, and wherever else they found it. While we should naturally accept Roman accounts of druidic practice with a pinch of salt, the number and detail of such writings suggests a certain veracity; for example: 'There stood a grove [...] matted boughs entwined prisoned the air within. No sylvan nymphs here found a home, nor Pan, but savage rites and barbarous worship, altars horrible on massive stones upreared; sacred with blood of men was every tree.'[18] This poetic line is a reference not to Mona, but to the Gallic groves in the time of Caesar, but the parallels are clear. Archaeological evidence also supports the existence of druidic sacrifice. Lindow Man may represent such evidence in the form of the infamous 'three-fold death', and shackles found in the lake of Llyn Cerrig Bach may even point to sacrifice taking place on Anglesey.

It would seem that Roman revulsion at druidic practice, when combined with the need to destroy the druidic power that remained a rallying point for resistance to Rome, led Paulinus to the decision not simply to conquer and settle the island, but also to make a point of wiping out all evidence of the druids and their culture, going as far as destroying their *nemetons*, or sacred groves.

The importance of this decision cannot be overstated. Rome had an inclusive stance to non-Roman gods and religions, and Romans were by nature a superstitious people. Any decision that might anger a god was not taken lightly. Indeed, in the whole gamut of Roman history, there are only two instances of the Roman military actively going to war with a religion. One is the case of Judea, where the sacred temple of Jerusalem was levelled and replaced with a Roman one. The other is Paulinus on Mona. No wonder his troops were nervous before the battle. They faced not only rabid Celts, but the possibility of angering powerful gods on their own soil. Still, thanks to Paulinus, the druidic culture disappears in AD 60.

We are told that it was Paulinus's intention to garrison the island, which indicates that he considered the region settled and ripe for inclusion into the province, which by extension also suggests that the rest of Wales was now under control. Though it has long been assumed that no garrison was left on Anglesey, the discovery of a fortlet at Cemlyn Bay, the possible ditches at Aberffraw, and the unconfirmed camp at Caer Helen, all point to the possibility that Paulinus did not entirely abandon his plans for the island. Still. his great victory in Wales was somewhat overshadowed by what happened next: 'While he was thus occupied, the sudden revolt of the province was announced to Suetonius.'[19]

It is not my intention in this work to explore in detail the events that followed. The revolt of Boudicca and the Iceni has been covered in many works and explored in full, and is at best peripheral to this book. For a full account, I refer the reader to Webster's 'BOUDICA: The British Revolt Against Rome AD 60' (Batsford, 1993). Here we need not examine the veracity of Tacitus, for the details he gives are in the annals and not connected to Agricola, and the basic facts of the revolt are supported by the accounts of Cassius Dio and Suetonius, albeit that both are later writers and likely used Tacitus as their source. The simple fact is that archaeology supports the accounts of the disaster.

Before we briefly note the activity of the following months, two important points must be raised. The first is the attempt of Petilius Cerialis to put down the revolt in its early stages. Cerialis was commanding the Ninth at Lincoln, and it is possible that his legion was split with a second base at Leicester. Indeed, it is quite possible that further vexillations of his legion were elsewhere in temporary garrisons. Whatever the case, Cerialis takes a force of infantry and cavalry and rushes to the rescue of Colchester, only to blunder into a trap which sees his infantry butchered and Cerialis escaping with only his cavalry. We will encounter later both the Ninth and their commander, who Tacitus describes as 'better fitted by nature to despise a foe than to guard against him [...] declaring that he would not delay a moment when he had a chance to engage the enemy'. A fierce and impetuous man.[20]

The second point of note, while Paulinus turns to face this unexpected threat, is the action of one Poenius Postumus, camp prefect of the Second Legion in Exeter. Paulinus called for the Second to march, presumably immediately as he abandoned his activity in Mona. As noted earlier, the legatus and senior tribune must have been absent, for it was the third in command who refused the order. Tacitus treats the man unkindly, though in truth it could not reasonably have been cowardice that was the cause, for a camp prefect is a veteran who has risen to the position through merit, rather than a political appointment. More likely, Postumus was called to march by the governor, but only a small part of the Second remained in garrison, the rest farmed out across the south-west and near the Welsh border, as well as protecting Britain's lead mines in the Mendips, critical to the Roman war machine. With the news of what had happened in Colchester, it is even possible that other tribes were becoming restive and that Postumus did not fancy the chances of the Second making it across the country without being annihilated in detail. The Teutoburg disaster in AD 9 had seen three legions destroyed in column as they travelled across the German forests in an attempt to put down a fictional rebellion in a settled province. That epic disaster was still a relatively recent memory, and no man wanted to be the next General Varus.

Agricola's last year in Britain as a tribune, then, would have seen him once more riding alongside Paulinus as the general made with his cavalry for London across an unsettled province. Arriving in the city, Paulinus decided that London could not be saved with troops so far away and so few men in the area. He decided that to save the province as a whole he would need to sacrifice the city. This he did, riding back north-west to meet his army, who were marching in his wake.

As Paulinus rejoined his legions, Boudicca ravaged London and St Albans. Then, perhaps arrogant and full of hubris, confident after their sacking of three cities and their defeat of the Ninth, the Boudiccan rebels turned north to meet the advancing Romans. The story of the rebellion ends there, where Paulinus defeated the British soundly and recovered the province, further enhancing his military reputation.

It is worth remembering that although Tacitus was not present at any of these events about which he writes, not only would he have had ample opportunity to learn of them from his father-in-law, it is also plausible that he obtained the accounts of other officers involved. It is entirely possible that Suetonius Paulinus lived long enough to give an account to the historian, and the same is true of

Petilius Cerialis, though there is a suggestion that Tacitus's writing displays a dislike of the latter.

Two further matters deserve attention in the aftermath of the revolt, before Paulinus gives up his governorship and Agricola moves on to the next stage of his career. Firstly, the Ninth were left seriously under-strength at the end of the season, and to rebuild the force manpower was sent from the continent. Tacitus tells us 'Its strength was increased by the Caesar, who sent over from Germany two thousand legionaries.'[21] The identity of this 'Caesar' is not given. It seems unlikely to be Nero, the emperor of the time, but a clue might be found in Suetonius's life of Titus: 'He served as military tribune both in Germany and in Britain.'[22] Tacitus lived through the Flavian era and had been tied to the family, and it seems almost certain that it is the future emperor Titus to whom he is referring as sending troops. Titus was born only half a year before Agricola and they would have served as tribunes at the same time. This makes it very likely that it was Titus who was serving in Germany and who brought the reinforcements to Britain. Here, then, is a second occasion in which Agricola can be tied to the Flavians. He and Titus very likely first met as tribunes in Britain, while their fathers had been praetors together in Rome.

The second point of note is the change in governor. The procurator who had caused the revolt in the first place had fled the island, and was now replaced by a man called Gaius Julius Alpinus Classicianus. Tacitus tells us that this new procurator and Paulinus were 'not on good terms', and Classicianus began to send reports to Rome to the effect that no peace could be expected on the island until the warlike Paulinus was replaced. He would get his wish, for Publius Petronius Turpilianus was assigned by AD 62. Thus ends a run of strong and militaristic governors of Britain, which is significant with regard to what happens in the ensuing years.

For now it is AD 62, Agricola is twenty-two years of age, and has spent four years of an apprenticeship in war alongside Paulinus, familiarising himself with the island of Britain, especially Wales and the settled east. He has seen the legacy of the impressive Ostorius Scapula, and has now fought the Silures, the Ordovices and the Iceni, just as Scapula had. Agricola is recalled from Britain to advance his career elsewhere.

4

CURSUS HONORUM

His term of service in the Tribunate over, Agricola returned to Rome. Uniformly, across the breadth of scholarly works on Agricola, scant attention is paid to this period, often little more than the paragraph Tacitus allots. However, I see this period as worthy of note, not only for the fact that it covers almost a decade of the man's life and the lion's share of his political career, but also for the lessons he learned during that time, which would come to bear later in his career.

Tacitus tells us '[he] allied himself with Domitia Decidiana, a lady of illustrious birth. The marriage was one which gave a man ambitious of advancement distinction and support. They lived in singular harmony, through their mutual affection and preference of each other to self. However, the good wife deserves the greater praise, just as the bad incurs a heavier censure.'

What can we say, then, of the woman that Tacitus lauds so? Her father appears to have been one Domitius Decidius named on inscription ILS 966 as having been *Quaestor Aerarii* (supervisor of the treasury) under Claudius in AD 44, and later a praetor. Syme[1] and Birley[2] both speculate a Gaulish or Narbonensian origin for Domitius, which would make him, and therefore his daughter, Agricola's countrymen, though there is no reason to assume a tie or connection between the families prior to this.

It was normal at this time for a man of Agricola's age (early twenties) to marry a girl of perhaps thirteen or fourteen, and given that Domitius Decidius must have been born around AD 19, and likely had children in his late twenties, then that would quite reasonably put his daughter at a marriageable age in AD 63. Domitia was therefore almost certainly this man's daughter.

Birley also suggests a relation in one Decidius Domitianus, a procurator of Lusitania during the reign of Augustus. If this is true, then that would make this another example of a Gallic provincial family who achieved equestrian status early and was raised to senatorial ranks in the principate. We can therefore see something of a parallel between the family of Agricola and that of his wife.

With perhaps a year of civic life and marital bliss for Agricola in Rome, Tacitus then tells us: 'Appointed Quaestor, the ballot gave him Asia for his province, Salvius Titianus for his proconsul. Neither the one nor the other corrupted him, though the province was rich and an easy prey to the wrongdoer, while the proconsul, a man inclined to every species of greed, was ready by all manner of indulgence to purchase a mutual concealment of guilt. A daughter was there added to his family to be his stay and comfort, for shortly after he lost the son that had before been born to him.'

We have a minor date issue with this period of Agricola's career, though upon investigation there is a solution. Since in *Agricola* 44 Tacitus tells us directly that the man was born on 13 June AD 40, in 63, which is the year commonly assumed for his posting to Asia, Agricola would be twenty-three years old. The minimum age for such a posting was twenty-five and so under normal circumstances, this seems unlikely. So what accounts for the two missing years?

Our answer might come in the form of the Augustan Lex Papia Poppaea, which promoted an increase in the number of children in Senatorial families. At the time, the patrician blood of Rome seems to have been waning, and this law was one part of Augustus's push to turn the empire back into a moral society and one in which patrician power remains strong.

Adam describes one effect of the law as giving a man 'priority in bearing offices',[3] and in more detail Field tells us that 'An ingenious system of rewards and penalties was formulated, inheritance of bequests and precedence of entry into public office were made dependent upon marriage and the number of children.'[4] Pay attention now, for we are about to play the shell game with children, and their existence at any time makes many differences in Agricola's career path.

Though Agricola would have to be twenty-five to achieve his quaestorship, if he had a child at this point his required age could be reduced to twenty-four. We are told by Tacitus that Agricola had a daughter while in Asia and that he already had a son who died soon after. We can assume, therefore, that the boy had been born by the time of Agricola's appointment (within his marriage's first year) and that the son's existence brought Agricola's age requirement down by a year. This accounts for one of our two years' discrepancy. The second year can be similarly accounted for by the same law, all because of one line in Tacitus. Once again, the translation of the Latin is here critical. In the Church & Brodribb edition, we are told that while in Asia 'A daughter was there added to his family to be his stay and comfort,' while the Birley translation gives us 'While he was there he was blessed with a daughter, which was both a consolidation of his position and a consolation.' When we take Birley's translation, the meaning shifts from the daughter being a consolation for the loss of a son to being both that *and* a legitimization of his position. This suggests that he had secured the quaestorship an extra year early on the grounds that he was about to have a second child, and that her arrival confirmed him in the position while he was already there.

We are told in no uncertain terms by Tacitus that Salvius Titianus was 'a man inclined to every species of greed', and though we have no corroborating evidence of Titianus's misdeeds and it is possible that this is a Tacitan invention, such a character is quite feasible in the post. Salvius Otho Titianus is the older brother of the short-lived emperor Otho, who we will encounter shortly, and the only other time he is attested is his service in the civil war, where he acquitted himself with aplomb. However, corruption among provincial governors was not only known, it was rife. In the days of the late republic one man, Gaius Verres, abused his position with such corruption that in 70 BC he was brought to trial by the famous Cicero, who addressed the court with powerful words: 'For we have brought before your tribunal not only a thief, but a wholesale robber; not only an adulterer, but a ravisher of chastity; not only a sacrilegious man, but an open enemy to all sacred things and all religion; not only an assassin, but a most barbarous murderer of both citizens and allies; so that I think him the only criminal in the memory of man so atrocious, that it is even for his own good to be condemned.'⁵

Tacitus tells us not only that Agricola resisted the temptation of corruption in rich, easy Asia, but that he also resisted advances from Salvius Titianus to join him in his criminal activity for a union of 'mutual concealment of guilt'.

Cicero, writing to his brother Quintus, notes of the man's own tenure as governor of Asia four years previously 'the inhabitants are not being ruined by your progresses, drained by your charges, agitated by your approach? That there is the liveliest joy, public and private, wheresoever you come, the city regarding you as a protector and not a tyrant, the private house as a guest and not a plunderer?'⁶ That Cicero feels the need to laud his brother for *not* being corrupt suggests just how common said corruption was, and indeed, though Agricola might resist the temptation himself, there is no indication that he made any attempt to bring Salvius to justice, allowing the man and his crimes unpunished. An earlier, Republican, example in the same province is noted by Mitchell: 'In case a community was unable to pay taxes, they borrowed from Roman lenders but at exorbitant rates. This more often than not resulted in default on said loans and consequently led Roman lenders to seize the borrower's land, their last remaining asset of value. In this way and by outright purchase, Romans dispersed throughout Asia province.'⁷ Clearly, the corrupt management of a province was nothing new under the emperors.

If we accept Tacitus's account, Agricola was assigned in the role of financial overseer of Asia under a corrupt governor. Given that his earlier posting as a tribune had revealed in Boudicca's revolt the potential consequences of provincial mismanagement, Agricola's experience in Asia can only have driven home the damage such corruption could do. For a man climbing the cursus honorum and destined for a governorship himself, this is an important step in his ongoing political education.

In 63/64 Agricola chose a good time to be absent from Rome, a time when Nero's dangerous autocracy was waxing, and it seems he would not have had to worry for his family back in

Rome, either, for they were with him abroad. We are told in the Annals 'Caecina Severus moved that no magistrate, who had been allotted a province, should be accompanied by his wife. ...Weakness and a lack of endurance were not the only failings of the sex: give them scope, and they turned hard, intriguing, ambitious.'[8] This senatorial argument is rebutted, including the line 'How often had the deified Augustus travelled to west and east with Livia for his companion.' Ulpian states 'while it is indeed better that a proconsul go out to his province without his wife, he can also do so with her.'[9] So wives accompanying their husbands on provincial assignments was a matter of debate, and Tacitus states that Domitia accompanied her husband to Asia, for their daughter is born in Asia during this tenure. Agricola and his familia, then, had been absent from the capital during the apogee of imperial viciousness.

Having served in Asia, by the latter part of AD 64 Agricola was back in Rome where his time 'he passed in retirement and inaction, for he knew those times of Nero when indolence stood for wisdom'.[10] Simply, who could blame Agricola for staying out of the limelight? Tacitus tells us that 'the evils of the state were growing daily more serious',[11] and that 'Regulus survived [because] he was shielded by his quietude of life.'[12]

A simple check-in of events in Rome during the years 64–66 will bring to light many reasons a man might want to keep out of the emperor's sights. In the July of 64 Rome suffered its 'great fire', and Nero's persecution of Christians began, leaving human candles as a reminder of who the emperor blamed for the conflagration. His increasing autocracy led to a massive conspiracy to murder the emperor led by a senator named Piso (not the same Piso who had probably poisoned Germanicus as mentioned earlier), which resulted in a round of proscriptions, suspicion and execution unlike anything seen in half a century. Nero continued his decline, kicking his pregnant wife to death, killing his former tutor Seneca and his sister-in-law Claudia Antonia. Navigating the eddies and currents of imperial favour at court must have been like white water rafting in a shoebox. In short, Rome was becoming a place in which no one wanted to stand out.

The great fire of Rome by Hubert Robert, 1785. (Public Domain)

Having managed to avoid the worst of the Neronian troubles with a year in Asia, Agricola continued to spend time away from the emperor's notice upon his return. Wise man. If we were to speculate as to his activities and whereabouts during this period of retirement, it is very tempting to see him as self-exiling, like so many Roman nobles, to his family's country estate. We are not told of his activity in Rome then, despite this being the time of chaos left by the great fire and the uncovering of the Pisonian conspiracy, and the gap in information suggests that Agricola was elsewhere during these great events. If Agricola happened to be in those family lands around the Ligurian border, then there is another odd moment of synchronicity. In Annals 16.14-15, Tacitus tells us that Ostorius Scapula, the son of the man who built those fortifications Agricola had walked among in Wales, was living on the Ligurian frontier at this time when Nero sent men to force him into taking his own life. The notion that Agricola might have spent several months as a neighbour of Scapula's son appeals to me, and is far from unrealistic.

His short period of anonymity over, it is commonly agreed that Agricola was in Rome as Tribune of the Plebs in AD 66. It is tempting to see in this appointment Agricola's need to continue his career while maintaining a quite reasonable desire to keep himself safe from the ever-increasing dangers of the imperial court. While securing this important post on the ladder, there is no record of Agricola doing anything public with the role. His colleague Arulenus Rusticus offered to use his veto to save the beleaguered Thrasea (Publius Clodius Thrasea Paetus) from imperial legal attacks, himself risking reprisals, yet there is no mention of Agricola standing up for justice in the corrupt world of Nero's Rome. This suggests that he achieved a fine balance between the required public service and healthy obscurity – not an easy thing to do.

The plebeian tribunate was a single-year appointment, and so Agricola once more spent another year in private life before moving on to his next position. We have, with the praetorship, a seemingly unsolvable date issue in Tacitus's account. We know when Agricola was born, and we know he was praetor when Galba was on the throne, so that makes him praetor in 68, and he was just twenty-seven in January when praetors were selected.

These dates are unarguable, and so we are left with a problem, since even with two children Agricola would still be a year too young for the post. There are two possibilities to consider here that might explain the missing year.

Firstly, that there is some unaccounted-for factor that granted him an even earlier shot at the post. It sounds thin, but there are possibilities. The system was by necessity flexible. Even back in the republic, when the age-restricting provisions of the 180 BC Lex Villia Annalis were still new, Scipio Africanus was elected to the consulship when five years too young because, due to public demand, the senate introduced a bill exempting him from the restrictions. The powerful Cinna in the late republic had served four consulships back to back, while the law demanded a ten-year gap between consulships. It is not hard to imagine against such a history that Agricola secured a post half a year early. And to follow a similar tack, I posed to a serious group of Roman historians and enthusiasts the question of how a man might further reduce the age requirements of the cursus honorum beyond the acquisition of children. The first answer I received, given as a joke, was simply: 'money'. I laughed, but I also wrote this down, because the old adage that 'money talks' was as apt in ancient Rome as it is now. A joke it might be, but it is worth bearing in mind. Crassus almost secured an empire through his acquisition of huge wealth, after all, even if he ended his days in the Parthian desert with (purportedly) a mouthful of molten gold.

Secondly, we might consider the possibility that Agricola did not achieve the praetorship in January 68 as is generally assumed, something that Birley seems to support, given that he states that Agricola would be twenty-eight at the time of his praetorship in 68 under Galba. Though the praetors were traditionally elected in the new year, we only know for certain that Agricola was praetor when Galba gave him a second commission in AD 68. A browse of Suetonius's life of Galba reveals something interesting. 'It was thought too that he intended to limit the offices open to senators and knights to a period of two years [...] had all the grants of Nero revoked [...] there was nothing that he did not allow his friends and freedmen to sell at a price or bestow as a favour, taxes and freedom from taxation.'[13] What this might tell us is that when Galba came to the throne, he immediately reorganised offices and the men who served in them to his advantage. And, of course, Suetonius reminds us here that money really does talk. But it is worth noting that if Galba dismissed praetors and wished to replace them, he came to power on 8 June 68, and Agricola would be twenty-eight and eligible for the praetorship as of his birthday just five days later.

Whether this is a case of merit overriding legal niceties, of Galban reorganisation, or simply of money talking we cannot know. The alternative, of course, is to label Tacitus's words a lie. One has to wonder, though, if Tacitus was to fictionalise any part of his account, why he would bother with such a small and trivial thing. The praetorship is of such insignificance in the grand account that it is hard to see Tacitus fabricating the details. The answer then, is almost certainly something miscellaneous and uninteresting, along the above lines.

Of this post, Tacitus tells us 'His praetorship was passed in the same consistent quietude, for the usual judicial functions did not fall to his lot. The games and the pageantry of his office he ordered according to the mean between strictness and profusion, avoiding extravagance, but not missing distinction.' The praetorship was a high-profile position but varied in nature, with more than a dozen praetors elected annually with roles in the military, gubernatorial, infrastructural, legal and financial spheres.

Given the prominent position of the praetors, it is interesting to note how Agricola once more stays out of the limelight despite being in a very prominent public post. There were, however, praetors whose role was to oversee a specific region of Rome, and it is possible that Agricola secured one of those positions, which would secure the rung on the political ladder while allowing him to remain on the periphery of Nero's court. It is darkly humorous to imagine Agricola securing a position administering a region of Rome that was now little more than charred ruins. He did clearly hold games, though, and we are told that they were not too lavish, yet not too sparse. In other words, just enough to keep everyone happy and yet not draw the attention of the empire's increasingly dangerous ruler.

Depending upon precisely when Agricola became praetor, if he *had* been in the position since the new year it may be that this somewhat peripheral role is why, when Nero falls and Galba makes his bid for the throne, we are not told of any involvement of Agricola's in the beginning of a civil war that must have swept like a tidal wave across the politicians in Rome. Our story picks up again during the short reign of Galba. We have, sadly, no information about what Agricola did or thought during those last days of the Julio-Claudian dynasty, but we do at least have a clue as to where his loyalties lay.

In the latter half of 68, with Galba ascendant, Agricola is in his praetorship yet he is given a second role by this new emperor, suggesting that Galba valued him, which in turn leads us to suspect that Agricola threw his support behind this new emperor's bid for the throne.

Tacitus tells us 'He was afterwards appointed by Galba to draw up an account of the temple offerings, and his searching scrutiny relieved the conscience of the state from the burden of all sacrileges but those committed by Nero.'[14] The accusation levelled at the end there is supported by Suetonius, who tells us of Nero that 'At last he stripped many temples of their gifts and melted down the images of gold and silver, including those of the Penates, which however Galba soon afterwards restored.'[15] This adds a certain veracity to Tacitus, and there is an earlier parallel to this seemingly unique appointment, too. Livy tells us in Republican days of 'two sets of triumviri; one to search for the property belonging to the temples, and to register the offerings'.[16] An official defined role in the Roman administration that would also fit the bill is the post of *Curator Aedium Sacrarum*. Although this post was theoretically open only to ex-consuls, A. E. Gordon notes the case of C. Julius Galerius Asper who, according to the inscriptions CIL XIV 2505, 2507, 2508, 2509, and 2510, had secured the post at the start, rather than the end, of his career. Once again, we are pointed towards the flexibility of the system. If there were simply insufficient ex-consuls to fill the roles at the time, then Galerius Asper might have been drafted in against legal precedent to fill an open position. Perhaps, then, it is this post to which Galba assigns Agricola in 68.

Once again, here Tacitus presents us with the image of a man incorruptible and decent. A man who is assigned to root out wrongdoing and sacrilege in the temples of Rome. While some might argue that Tacitus is 'bigging up' his father-in-law, we must continue to bear in mind that there will have been people around to read this book who remembered that time and Agricola's part in things. In fact, this is more true of that particular year than most others, since the infamy of the year of the four emperors must have lived on in the memory of all concerned for the rest of their lives. Thus, can we accuse Tacitus of being creative with the truth when so many readers might be able to gainsay him?

Agricola was now in Galba's camp. How grateful he must have been to have laid down his praetorship at the end of AD 68, given his apparent siding with Galba, when at the start of the new year the German legions rebelled and proclaimed Vitellius emperor, and within weeks Galba was dead and Otho raised to the purple in Rome. We are not told what Agricola was doing in the first part of that dreadful year, and it is reasonable to assume he was once more stepping back into the shadows. Following the praetorship, a mandatory two-year period of non-service was required before any possible consulship, and Agricola would have found himself very conveniently out of the political limelight once more, while Rome seethed with rebellions and usurpers.

We learn of his next activity in the Spring of 69. In one of the most savage passages of the *Agricola*, Tacitus tells us 'The following year inflicted a terrible blow on his affections and his fortunes. Otho's fleet, while cruising idly about, cruelly ravaged Intemelii, a district of Liguria; his mother, who was living here on her own estate, was murdered. The estate itself and a large part of her patrimony were plundered. This was indeed the occasion of the crime.'[17]

With Nero and Galba now dead and Otho and Vitellius both claiming the throne, the former in Rome and the latter in Germany, civil war begins to rage across the Alps and the northern borders of Italy. Only Tacitus tells us of the military activity here, though he does so in both the *Agricola* and the *Histories*. In the passage above from the *Agricola* we see the Othonian navy, who had been dispatched to secure the coastal

NERO	GALBA	OTHO	VITELLIUS	VESPASIAN
OCT 54 – JUN 68	JUN 68 – JAN 69	JAN 69 – APR 69	APR 69 – DEC 69	DEC 69 – JUN 79

The year of the four emperors in statuary. (Author's collection)

regions between between Rome and the Vitellian forces, ravaging the country estates there, and during one dreadful raid killing Agricola's mother and ransacking the family's estate.

The Histories concentrates more on the land war, giving us the names of three Othonian generals, all of whom fail for varied reasons. As an interesting aside, one of Otho's generals (and not one of those three) was the very same veteran Suetonius Paulinus under whom Agricola had trained in war. A battle is fought in which the Othonians are victorious, but are starved of plunder in the aftermath, which sends them on a rampage through the city of Albimintilium (modern Ventimiglia). We are told of the heroic actions of one woman in saving her son, but this is not Agricola's mother. Therefore, though these two passages tell of events in the same region at the same time, there is no direct corroboration.

Once again, here we are beset by coincidences. The new emperor in Rome, Otho, whose forces are ravaging Agricola's homeland, and whose navy has killed his mother, is the younger brother of the 'corrupt' Salvius Otho Titianus who had governed Asia while Agricola had served beneath him. Agricola must have been in a quandary as to who he might consider giving his support at the time. As a former appointee of Galba, he had to be unsure of what reception he would get from Vitellius, and Otho's name would undoubtedly sour his opinions, even before the man's soldiers had killed Julia Procilla and plundered the estate.

A second interesting coincidence comes in the form of the forces sent against Otho's men by Vitellius. A combined mass of infantry and cavalry is dispatched to garrison Gallia Narbonensis, and Forum Julii, Agricola's hometown, is specifically named as garrisoned against Otho. Additionally, a unit included in that force was of Treveri cavalry – the Treveri being a Belgic/Germanic tribe from the Moselle valley. Yet more Germanic horsemen like those with whom Agricola had crossed to Mona years earlier were probably now garrisoned in his hometown.

Agricola's response to the horror and outrage of his mother's murder is only very briefly noted in Tacitus, and not thoroughly explored elsewhere, and yet given the importance of it, perhaps it should have been paid more attention.

'Agricola, who instantly set out to discharge the duties of affection, was overtaken by the tidings that Vespasian was aiming at the throne. He at once joined his party. Vespasian's early policy, and the government of Rome were directed by Mucianus, for Domitian was a mere youth, and from his father's elevation sought only the opportunities of indulgence. Agricola, having been sent by Mucianus to conduct a levy of troops, and having done his work with integrity and energy.'[18]

The ravaging of the coast would likely have been in late March AD 69, since the fleet was sent forth in early March, and the war was over by mid-April. Otho travelled north with his forces on 14 March, and so when we gaily picture Agricola riding north with tear-stained eyes to honour his mother, arrange her tombstone, put the estate in order and so on, we need to adjust our thinking. Northern Italy is currently a war zone between opposing emperors in one of the most vicious clashes in Roman history. Agricola is not in any official position and is not travelling with lictors or at the head of troops, or any such force. He is a private citizen and the most he could rely upon would be a private force of hired men. Even if he rode north after the decisive battle of Bedriacum and in the wake of the main conflict, the region would be ruined and dangerous for many months. Bearing this in mind and picturing it again, the courage of the man is plain.

The timing here is of interest. Procilla could have died at the latest in early April, just before Otho's fall. Vespasian was proclaimed by his troops in Alexandria on 1 June. The fastest that tidings of Procilla's death could reasonably reach Rome was fourteen days, and news of Vespasian might perhaps reach Italy in roughly the same time. No matter how the numbers are crunched, it seems extremely unlikely that news of Vespasian overtook Agricola on his journey. For the first time, Tacitus seems to be overtly and inescapably wrong.

Our solution might lie in a re-examination of Tacitus and in a passage from the Histories. The most direct translation of 'Igitur ad sollemnia pietatis profectus Agricola' is something along the lines of 'Agricola set out to discharge his pious duties'. Profectus might be translated as 'set out', but also it could be seen as 'proceeded', which would suggest starting a process of events rather than beginning a journey. In that light we might see Agricola reaching Liguria and the family estates and beginning the lengthy process of putting everything in order when news arrives of Vespasian being made emperor. Similarly, 'nuntio adfectati a Vespasiano imperii deprehensus ac statim in partis', which is commonly translated as something like 'was overtaken by news of Vespasian's aiming at the throne', might mean more 'was seized', or even 'was surprised', depending upon the translation of deprehensus.

This is given weight by a passage in the Histories: 'letters were scattered broadcast through the Gallic provinces, and in a moment a great war burst into flame.'[19] The wider context of this extract is that while Vespasian is still in the east with Titus, and Domitian and Sabinus, Vespasian's brother, are in Rome, the legions of the Danube have already declared for the Flavians, have begun to send missives to sister legions in Britain, Spain and elsewhere, and to distribute communications around Gaul in favour of their candidate.

It is therefore easy to see a situation in which Julia Procilla's death is reported to Agricola, he rides north, probably in the direct aftermath of the clashes between the emperors, and begins to put things in order in Liguria only to learn – along with the whole of Gaul – that in the east Vespasian has been raised to the purple. This makes a great deal of chronological, and simply logical, sense.

That Agricola should choose immediately to throw his support behind Vespasian should now come as no surprise. We have noted that the new emperor and Agricola's father had probably served in Rome at the same time, and would likely have known each other. It seems very likely that Agricola and Titus had met in Britain as tribunes. Given his time in Britain, Agricola must have known of Vespasian's part in the conquest and respected his reputation. Moreover, there was the simple matter of choice. The emperors with whom Agricola was 'acquainted' held little in the way of value to him: dangerous Nero, short-lived Galba, Otho whose men had killed Agricola's mother, and Vitellius, who would view Agricola as a Galban man. Vespasian would be a clear choice for support, even without prior personal and familial connections.

We are not told what Agricola does immediately following the news and his declaration for the Flavians. He is next spoken of in Rome after the fall of Vitellius, and so it seems extremely unlikely that he travelled east to join Vespasian and Titus on the other side of the empire and past any trouble in between. Equally, it seems implausible that he travelled to Rome, where Vitellius was still in control, where Vespasian's younger son Domitian had been put under house arrest and the emperor's brother Sabinus walked a fine line, for to do so would be of little benefit and extremely dangerous. The answer is that Agricola probably hurried across northern Italy to join the Danubian forces who were marching on Rome in Vespasian's name, winning the critical second battle of Bedriacum on 24 October AD 69, at which Agricola may even have been present.

As an aside, a similar course of action was pursued at the same time by Petilius Cerialis, whom Agricola had served alongside in the Boudiccan revolt. Of the advancing Flavian army, Tacitus tells us that 'In the mountains they met Petilius Cerialis, who had escaped the pickets of Vitellius by disguising himself as a peasant and using his knowledge of the district. Cerialis was closely connected with Vespasian, and being himself not without reputation in war, was made one of the commanders.'[20]

Whatever the case, once Vitellius was no more and Rome came under Flavian control, Agricola was to be found there. The new emperor himself was still in the east, along with Titus, but the governor of Syria, Mucianus, who had supported Vespasian from the outset, had arrived in Rome and, to Domitian's extreme irritation, immediately took control of Flavian interests in the capital. Clearly Agricola was already acknowledged by the Flavians as an asset, for Mucianus sent him out to levy troops. We do not know where this posting took him, nor how long it took. He is unlikely to have gone further than Gaul or Illyricum, and northern Italy was war-ravaged and probably not a viable location to recruit men to fill the losses of the past year.

It is the end of AD 69. The hell of Nero's reign is over, as is the traumatic year-long civil war that followed. After proving himself in Britain, Agricola has spent his time avoiding trouble under the increasingly dangerous autocracy of Nero, but finally a new dynasty rules in Rome, and Agricola has their favour. It is time for him once more to show his mettle.

The Cursus Honorum for Agricola				
Position	Date	Minimum Age	Agricola's Age	Agricola's Family
Military Tribune	June 58	18	18	No children
Quaestor	June 63	25	23	One son, one pregnancy
Tribune of the Plebs	Jan 66	27	25	One son, one daughter
Praetor	June 68	30	27	One son, one daughter
Legatus Legionis	Spring 70	30	29	One daughter
Governor	78	30	38	

5

THE BRITISH SITUATION REVISITED

Having left Britain in 62, we have concentrated on Agricola's career elsewhere for the following eight years, but now it is time to once more examine that troublesome island and set the scene for Agricola's next assignment. Eight years and three governors has seen a great deal of activity in Britain in our hero's absence.

As previously stated, the run of strong military governors had come to an end with Suetonius Paulinus. Seemingly at the behest of the new procurator, a more peaceable, civilian governor had been assigned. Tacitus tells us 'Meanwhile, things had changed in Britain after the militaristic command of Paulinus. Petronius Turpilianus was sent out to initiate a milder rule. A stranger to the enemy's misdeeds and so more accessible to their penitence, he put an end to old troubles, and, attempting nothing more, handed the province over to Trebellius Maximus.'[1] This summary he reiterates in the Annals, with 'Petronius Turpilianus, who by now had laid down his consulate. The newcomer abstained from provoking the enemy, was not challenged himself, and conferred on this spiritless inaction the honourable name of peace.'[2]

If Tacitus is to be trusted in this characterisation then Turpilianus can only be seen as close to the diametric opposite of his predecessor – precisely what the procurator had suggested was required. We have two other sources to compare this with. Frontinus tells us[3] that Turpilianus was, like Didius Gallus before him, a curator aquarum, one of the commissioners for the aqueducts of Rome, while Plutarch in his life of Galba says that 'Petronius Turpilianus, a man of consular dignity who was faithful to Nero, was ordered to take his own life.'[4] Neither of these two independent references does anything to gainsay Tacitus's painting of a mild governor, and so there is no reason to doubt the veracity of this account. Turpilianus controls Britain from 62 to 63 only, perhaps a short-term appointment to settle the country after the wars led by Paulinus. If we accept Birley's suggestion[5] that he was either the nephew or great-nephew of the renowned Aulus Plautius who first conquered the island, Turpilianus may have appeared a safe bet to follow Paulinus.

As stated above, Turpilianus was replaced in 63 by Marcus Trebellius Maximus. In this time (Trebellius governed Britain from 63 to 69), we might see more than a touch of Tacitus indulging in character assassination. In order to create the impression that Agricola and his friends arrived in Britain to solve a crisis created by a series of weak governors, Tacitus would have to minimize the success of his predecessors. Sometimes an achievement is best highlighted by detailing a series of failures beforehand. As such, we might accept that there was a certain mildness and civilian attitude to this sequence of three governors, but we might want to take Tacitus's picture with a pinch of salt. Having shown us that Turpilianus was a mild governor, we then watch the situation slide with his successors.

Tacitus tells us Trebellius 'was somewhat indolent, and never ventured on a campaign'.[6] Unfortunately we have no other references with which to compare Tacitus's account, but when reading between the lines we can apply different motives to the man's actions other than Tacitus's accusation of indolence. Though there are no recorded wars or campaigns in Britain at the time, it is still a restive province and bordered by tribes outside Roman control.

We might see Trebellius's appointment as something of a parallel to Varus in Germany: a province that the authorities have decided is ripe for full Romanization. Perhaps then what Tacitus attributes to indolence is in fact the official mandate Trebellius was given: 'Do not stir up trouble. Civilize the place.'

Though we have to guess at some of the dating sequence of events, is seems likely that this quiet Romanization is actually working for several years – from 63 until 66 at least – because in 66, Nero has the Fourteenth Legion withdrawn from Britain for a Parthian campaign that never materialises. One could only imagine the emperor withdrawing a quarter of Britain's legions if it was believed that they would no longer be needed. Now, we are perhaps beginning to see Trebellius as just the man for the job and doing precisely what he was told to do. Unfortunately for Trebellius, things were about to go spectacularly wrong, and yet none of it was the fault of the Britons, which once more supports his general method of governance.

We are told of a mutiny among the British troops. It is interesting to note that this mutiny is not mentioned by any other writer covering the time, though since they were almost uniformly writing about the emperors and the civil war that was now about to begin, events in the peripheral provincial regions that did not directly affect the timeline in Rome were perhaps ignored. Legions in mutiny is a very old song to which every senior officer knew the words. Caesar had to return from Egypt deal with the Thirteenth Legion after their mutiny in 47 BC – the ridiculous story of Caligula having his men gather shells as the spoils of war against the sea is almost certainly a spin on his punishment of the mutinous legions who refused to sail for Britain, and such stories go back at least as far as 342 BC with legions mutinying during the Samnite Wars.

The mutiny of the Twentieth in Britain is explained by Tacitus partially as an ongoing enmity between their commander and the governor, but it is also suggested that 'we were sorely troubled with mutiny, as troops habituated to service grew demoralised by idleness.'[7] There is a long tradition of troops becoming restless and rebellious if they are allowed to become idle, from the classical era even to the present day. Even in civil life, landowners in eighteenth- and nineteenth-century England would set their estate workers to building wonderful and entirely pointless follies simply to give them work and keep them busy over the winter. It is not hard to imagine how a legion with a history of war honours might become restive in a period of peace, especially if they are being told deliberately to be as peaceful as possible and not to rock the boat.

That this mutiny had spread beyond the Twentieth is made clear by Tacitus: 'The trouble reached such a point that Trebellius was openly insulted by the auxiliary soldiers as well as by the legions, and when deserted by the auxiliary foot and horse who joined Coelius.'[8]

We can date this event to AD 69 from the fact that it closes Trebellius's governorship and from the emperor to whom he flees in the aftermath. By this time the civil war has begun, Nero and Galba are already dead, and Otho and Vitellius are at war. Bearing in mind that Nero had already stripped the Fourteenth from Britain, we can only marvel in disbelief at Vitellius's decision to withdraw a further 8,000 men for his war against Otho.[9] This is in manpower terms the equivalent of nearly two legions (and though many will have been auxiliaries, there is a later hint that the remaining army of Britain relied heavily upon the auxilia).

Thus, by mid-AD 69, Britain had lost a total of some 12,000 men to the continent, many of them veteran infantry. Given that Wales was still restive, the Brigantes in the north were still in the throes of a civil war of their own, and the Iceni had already rebelled twice, one can only imagine how the remaining officers of the dwindling army felt. Given that no matter who took the soldiers away the direct orders will have come through Trebellius, he cannot have been popular with the army's commanders in Britain. Taking the Fourteenth away because Britain was ripe for settlement is one thing, while stripping a further vast number purely to support imperial claimants weakens the Roman position and encourages the more rebellious elements on the island.

A mutiny, then, hardly comes as a great surprise. Tacitus, still sticking knives in characters, tells us 'The governor of Britain was Trebellius Maximus, whose greed and meanness made him despised and hated by his soldiers. Their hostility towards him was increased by Roscius Coelius, the commander of the Twentieth legion, who had long been at odds with him; but now, on the occasion of civil war, the hostility between the two broke out with great violence. Trebellius charged Coelius with stirring up mutiny and destroying discipline; Coelius reproached Trebellius with robbing the legions and leaving them poor, while meantime the discipline of the army was broken down by this shameful quarrel between the commanders; and the trouble reached such a point that Trebellius [...] fled to Vitellius.'[10]

Boar imagery inscription of the Twentieth Legion from Chesters Museum. (Author's collection)

Most likely Coelius was merely the first of the legionary legates to stand against Trebellius, quite apart from the auxilia. There are two possible causes we might suggest for this mutiny on top of Tacitus's suggestion of idleness. The first is the reduction of strength previously noted, which certainly fits with Tacitus's phrase 'robbing the legions', though the true fault would be with imperial decision-making and not the governor himself. The second is alluded to by Suetonius, who tells us that towards the end of his reign, Nero was 'so utterly impoverished that he was obliged to postpone and defer even the pay of the soldiers and the rewards due to the veterans'.[11] If this is the case, then the imperial treasury would certainly not improve over the next two years of civil war, and may further explain Tacitus's accusations of Trebellius 'robbing the legions', and why his 'greed and meanness made him despised and hated by his soldiers'.

Whatever the direct cause, it is not hard to see how a mutiny might break out, and with none of it being Trebellius's own fault, despite Tacitus's accusations. Indeed, the long-standing enmity he records between the governor and the commander of the Twentieth might have begun in 66 when Trebellius gave the order for a quarter of Britain's legions to leave the island.

The upshot is that by the time Trebellius flees and runs to Vitellius in Gaul, Britain is clearly under-strength, underpaid, under the control of the legionary legates, and ripe for trouble. When Trebellius reaches the emperor, he is promptly replaced by a man at that very meeting who is immediately sent to Britain in his stead.

Vettius Bolanus took control of Britain in AD 69, appointed by Vitellius. He is an interesting character for the odd dichotomies we can uncover in his history and presentation, and the massive questions that remain unanswered about his tenure, for he appears to be the second victim of Tacitus's character assassination in preparing the way for his hero. Bolanus is one of a number of characters whose legacy is being constantly re-evaluated as new archaeological evidence in Britain comes to light, and every change undermines Tacitus's reputation as an historian.

Tacitus begins by presenting Bolanus in similar terms to his predecessors. We are told of the new governor 'Nor did Vettius Bolanus, during the continuance of the civil wars, trouble Britain with discipline. There was the same inaction with respect to the enemy, and similar unruliness in the camp, only Bolanus, an upright man, whom no misdeeds made odious, had secured affection in default of the power of control.'[12] Not precisely a dazzling description, and one underlined by 'Vettius Bolanus [...] governed more mildly than suited so turbulent a province.'[13] With 'Bolanus never enjoyed entire peace in Britain'[14] Tacitus completes a fairly damning picture.

However, once again when we examine this portrait closely enough there are cracks in the paint. Bolanus simply cannot have been the sort of man to shy away from military activity. In the Histories we are told that the governor had served as a legionary legate with the great general Corbulo in Armenia, while Statius goes further, making him Corbulo's second in command. This is a soldier of note, then, and difficult to reconcile with Tacitus's picture. The real opposition to Tacitus's description comes from the poet Statius, who tells us with great overemphasis 'mark in what might he went on his errand to that Thule which beats back the western waves'[15] and in addressing Bolanus's son: 'Rejoice, what glory might exalt Caledonia's plains! Then some aged dweller in that wild land may tell you: "Here your father used to hand out justice, harangue the army from this mound. The forts and watchtowers (there, you can see) he scattered far and wide, and lined these walls with a ditch; these gifts he dedicated to the war-gods (you'll read the inscriptions); this breastplate he wore himself in battle, that he captured from a British king."'[16]

This passage has given historians much to argue over and some take it as evidence that Bolanus was the first governor to campaign in Scotland. The dating evidence, sparse though it is, does not wholly support this notion, since the best undeniable results we have (dendrochronology) put the foundation of Carlisle and Corbridge in his successor's time at the earliest, but a case may yet be made for a northern push by Bolanus, as we shall see.

The simple mention of the word Caledonia might be Statius's poetic licence in trying to evoke the impression of the most northerly bleak lands. After all, Statius never set foot on the island, had no direct connection with anyone involved in the campaigns, and will have reached for whatever imagery impressed most with his poem. The fact that Statius also has Bolanus reaching Thule, a northern island of unknown location but variously attributed to the Shetlands, Iceland, or Smøla in Norway, suggests that at least some of this account is fanciful. That governors while campaigning in northern Scotland might discover Thule is feasible, but when the northernmost action is with the Brigantes in England, this seems very unlikely.

Here, though, we must once more recall that cautionary tale about trusting too much in a single translation. While the majority of translations of Statius render *Thule* directly, Nagle opts for the alternative of 'how great his mission to the British shores which block the waves split by the setting sun'. Much can be altered by the translator. Moreover, attention is due to the line 'these gifts he dedicated to the war-gods (you'll read the inscriptions)'. It was not uncommon for an emperor or general to devote captured prizes to a temple in Rome. Caligula did so with blades that had been used

Triumphal trophies in a relief from the Temple of Hadrian in Rome. (Author's collection)

in attempted assassinations. If Statius is really telling us that the inscriptions could be seen in Rome's temples confirming Bolanus's prizes from Britain, then we are forced to give him at least some credibility in the matter.

The capture of a British king's breastplate is arguable. It may, possibly, suggest that Bolanus actually defeated the troublesome Brigantian king Venutius, but with only the poetic Statius upon which to base this we should be wary, especially given that no other writer tells us of Venutius's end. We might more readily believe that prizes taken back to Rome were the usual haul after conquest (tribal standards, nobles' armour and the like), and yet the defeat of Venutius remains a tempting notion. Since Venutius commanded not only his rebellious Brigantes, but a number of sub-tribes as well as allies he had called in, there would, after all, be a number of kings with breastplates, and not just Venutius himself. The truth about Bolanus likely lies somewhere in the middle ground between the praise from Statius and the disparagement of Tacitus. However, no matter how much we might roll our eyes at Statius, whose work is a song of praise for Bolanus's son, we might also remember the old adage that there is no smoke without fire. For him to create such a vision, it seems extremely likely that he is building upon at least a grain of truth, and the most likely explanation here is that despite the difficulties he faced, Bolanus did campaign against the Brigantes and achieve some success.

In order to do this, Bolanus needed to resolve the mutiny crisis left by his predecessors. Firstly we are told 'the soldiers of the Fourteenth legion were particularly bold [...]. Vitellius decided to send them back to Britain.'[17] Bolanus, then, returns the Fourteenth to Britain. As a Vitellian appointee, he was facing an uphill struggle. Vespasian had now laid claim to the throne in the east. At the same time that those letters of which we earlier heard were being distributed through Gaul, urging the west to support Vespasian, we are told 'the leaders set to work to stir up the discontented throughout the entire empire. They addressed communications to the Fourteenth legion in Britain and to the First in Spain, for both these legions had been for Otho and opposed to Vitellius.'[18] So upon arriving in a province with mutinous armies, even the legion Bolanus brought with him were already being canvassed by the Flavians. Additionally, we know the Twentieth under Coelius were mutinous, and 'In Britain a favourable sentiment inclined toward Vespasian, because he had been put in command of the Second legion there.'[19] We cannot be certain that the Ninth took against Bolanus, but even if they did not, he was left with a rebellion of three-quarters of Britain's military.

The only feasible solution would be Bolanus declaring for Vespasian, and the fact that he remained in office after Vitellius's death suggests that this is exactly what he did, thus securing the loyalty of at least some of the legions. Of Vespasian we are told 'This secured the island for him, but only after some resistance on the part of the other legions, in which there were many centurions and soldiers who owed their promotions to Vitellius, and so hesitated to change from an emperor of whom they had already had some experience.'[20]

We are told by Tacitus that the XX Valeria Victrix continued to disobey Bolanus as they had done with Trebellius: 'the 20th Legion [...] had been slow to take the new oath of allegiance, and the [...] officer [...] was reported to be acting disloyally. It was a trying and formidable charge for even officers of consular rank, and the late praetorian officer [...] was powerless to restrain them.'[21] So Bolanus then seemingly managed to secure the loyalty of some of the under-strength legions, while the Twentieth continued to resist under Roscius Coelius.

Even without the Twentieth, this would give him sufficient strength to deal with a rising problem among the Brigantes. We are told of the Brigantian campaign in the tenure of the next governor, but the initial actions we can place with Bolanus, if not earlier. The Brigantian king and queen, Venutius and Cartimandua, had not been seeing eye to eye since the day she handed Caratacus back to the Romans. The queen was pro-Roman, the king anti, and this tense situation came to a head in 69 when open hostilities broke out once more. The campaign to which Statius was referring, then, in his grand manner, was almost certainly the push Bolanus seems to have achieved against the Brigantes in 69/70.

We are told by Tacitus that Cartimandua 'asked the Romans for protection, and in fact some companies of our foot and horse, after meeting with indifferent success in a number of engagements, finally succeeded in rescuing the queen from danger. The throne was left to Venutius; the war to us.'[22] Bolanus must have achieved success with the Brigantes, rescuing the queen from her enemies and, if there is any veracity to Statius, garrisoning forts within Brigantian territory, or more likely on the periphery of their lands in order to maintain control over Roman-governed Britain. It is not unrealistic, then, to expect prizes of war to be taken to Rome and devoted in a temple. As an aside, the focus on it being 'some companies of foot and horse' involved in the campaign suggests a lack of legionary presence and may once more point to the withdrawal of much of the heavy infantry and a current reliance upon the auxilia across the province.

There is one more intriguing angle suggested by a combination of recent scholarship and open-mindedness concerning Bolanus. If we are willing to see in Statius the possibility that Bolanus truly won the arms of a king, saved the queen and fought the Brigantes ferociously, then it is not hard to imagine Bolanus hammering the Brigantes and pushing them north in retribution, chasing the king even beyond their northern border to where his tribal allies awaited, and there may just be archaeological evidence to support this. Birgitta Hoffman has recently been re-examining the evidence of glassware at the site of Newstead and comfortably dates it to the early Flavian era or even before. As such, it is just feasible that Bolanus pushed as far north as Newstead in the Scottish Borders in his war with the Brigantes. It is thus possible that Statius's attestation of Bolanus campaigning on the 'Caledonian plain' can be explained. Bolanus may have pushed into Brigantian territory with sufficient force, beyond their northern fringe and into what might be considered by less-informed Roman authors as Caledonian lands. Newstead lies in the relatively flat region of north Northumberland and East Lothian, ringed by ranges of hills, which might correspond with Statius's Caledonian plain. It is tempting to see Newstead, then, as evidence of Bolanus being the first Roman in Scotland, albeit during a brief push against the Brigantes. If Newstead had been occupied by Bolanus, then it seems certain it was subsequently abandoned and all manpower withdrawn to the southern fringe of Brigantean lands.

This is important as it would not only marry up Statius with the archaeological timeline, but it would give Bolanus's successors both prior knowledge of, and potential military installations in, the lands north of the Brigantes. What we *can* say is that Bolanus seems in retrospect to have been a vastly different character to the one Tacitus tries to paint in the Agricola. Once again we should remember that, while we might find evidence for Tacitus's veracity, there are times when bias seems to be clearly represented. There is a blurring in our timeline here, for Bolanus was assigned by Vitellius in 69, but continued to command the province under Vespasian until 71. We can be comfortable with these dates, for Bolanus's successor was busy in Germany until the spring of 71. Our story with Agricola, however, picks up once more in AD 70, while Bolanus still governs Britain and a state of war exists with the Brigantes.

6

PARA BELLUM

Britannia seethed. With a legion still in mutiny and, whatever Bolanus had achieved with the Brigantes, clearly a question mark still hanging over the north, the new regime in Rome needed to take control of the island, especially since Vespasian, now emperor, had been part of the initial conquest and had a vested interest in the province. Indeed, Josephus accords Vespasian with procuring Britain for Claudius, such that the emperor might 'have a triumph bestowed on him, without any sweat or labour of his own'.[1] Silius Italicus went so far as to record an ancient prophesy that Vespasian 'shall give Rome victory over Thule, unknown till then, and shall be the first to lead an army against the Caledonian forests'.[2] The ongoing situation in Britain could not be allowed to continue.

Two solutions were required: a new governor had to be found to replace Bolanus and settle the north, and the mutinous Twentieth had to be brought to heel. In fact, though Bolanus was destined to be withdrawn from Britain, his removal does not seem to have been reflected in his career, since he went on to govern Asia, a more peaceable and lucrative province. Moreover, the man chosen to replace him was not immediately available, and so Bolanus was left in control for the time being.

The other problem was more readily solvable. The legate in command of the Twentieth, who had kept his legion in a state of mutiny against the governors for over a year, had to be

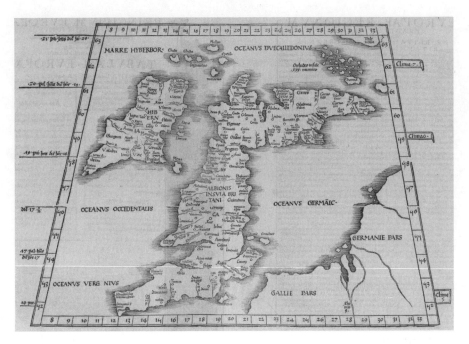

1535 Map of Britain based upon Ptolemy's Geography, marking Thule top right. (Public Domain)

removed from office and a man found at the appropriate stage of his career to replace him. Agricola was now at precisely the appropriate point on the cursus honorum to take command of a legion. He was, we can safely assume, tied closely to the Flavians already, his father to Vespasian and he himself to Titus. He was a man who had proved himself in war suppressing the druids and then defeating Boudicca at the side of Suetonius Paulinus. A man who had come to know Britain and its tribes. Really, there could be few better choices for the job of commanding a British unit.

But this was more than just a legionary command and a war. It was taking control of a *mutinous* legion. This tells us something about how Agricola was seen by the new dynasty in control of Rome. Of course, Mucianus had recently assigned Agricola to the levying of troops, which we are told he did 'with integrity and energy', and likely this influenced the decision to appoint him to such a critical role.

In AD 70, then, Agricola was sent to Britain to take control of the mutinous Twentieth. The troublesome legate Roscius Coelius was recalled to Rome, and yet seemingly not in disgrace. Though he had mutinied, at the time it had been against Vitellius's governor and probably due to imperial policies, lack of pay and the withdrawal of troops from the island. Perhaps Vespasian did not see Coelius as an enemy because of the circumstances, yet he could not be truly trusted. Coelius went on to have a successful career, achieving the consulate, though in four years rather than the customary two, suggesting that some sense of negativity clung to him.

We have only a single line to tell us how Agricola dealt with the critical problem of taking control of the Twentieth: 'Chosen thus at once to supersede and to punish, Agricola, with a singular moderation, wished it to be thought that he had found rather than made an obedient soldiery.'³ This seems odd at first glance, though if we read between the lines there is a great deal of sense to be found here.

Agricola's remit, we are told, was to take command and punish the mutinous legion. Over the past two years, though, legions had been rebelling against emperors more than ever, imperial power being supported or broken by the shifting loyalties of provincial armies. Given the newness of the Flavian reign and the distant, troubled and uncertain position in Britain, no matter what the imperial remit might be, no officer with an ounce of sense would take command of a mutinous legion and immediately impose a harsh, draconian rule upon them, meting out punishments for their behaviour. The legion had already resisted governors after all, and taking a hard line with the Twentieth would as likely drive them further into revolt as bring them to heel, and with wavering loyalties, the other legions in Britain might just throw in their lot with a further mutiny.

On the other hand, he could also not afford to simply let the legion get away with what they had done without acknowledgement. That way he would be seen as weak and would have no better control over the legion than his predecessors. He had to find a different way. There had to be an inventive middle ground. What the above line from Tacitus suggests is a deal struck. It is not hard to imagine Agricola addressing the tribunes and senior centurions of the Twentieth in the headquarters at the legionary fortress of Wroxeter, close to where he had once campaigned with Paulinus. One can picture the glowering faces and surly attitude of men who had seen weak governors come and go and had trusted instead in their commander, only to watch him removed and replaced with this Flavian favourite.

Perhaps Agricola tells them flatly that he will not have a repeat of their behaviour and that they have dishonoured the eagle under which they fight. That he needs the Twentieth in campaigning shape, loyal and true, as the Brigantes need to be dealt with. That he is willing to overlook their mutiny and forego the punishment ordered by the emperor on the condition that they damn well pull their socks up and start acting like soldiers. This way the legion would maintain their honour, there would be no cashiering and loss of pensions, and Agricola might just secure an impressive loyalty among them – the carrot and stick approach as opposed to the rod and flail. History is replete with examples of soldiers being shamed into improvement, after all, this was precisely how Caesar secured the loyalty of the Thirteenth back in his day. This might just explain Agricola's decision – that he reports to Rome he found the Twentieth loyal and ready to serve rather than having to have a hand in it himself. However it is achieved, by the time the fighting season comes about in AD 70, Agricola is in command of the Twentieth in Wroxeter and with no further mention of mutiny.

This is useful timing, since at roughly the same time Agricola takes command of the Twentieth, the Fourteenth is once more transferred from Britain to help deal with revolts in Germany. We are told of Bolanus, who was still in control of Britain, that he was too gentle for the province and that Agricola was forced to restrain himself in line with his commander. Assuming that Tacitus is once more playing down Bolanus's abilities and activity, we might see this 'gentleness' as simply an inability to deal with the warring Brigantes owing to lack of military strength, perhaps initially attempting a political solution. Still presumably down by 8,000 men and with the loss of the Fourteenth, attempting to subdue the largest tribe on the island at this time would surely be a mammoth undertaking.

The likely situation is that Bolanus had begun his campaign against the Brigantes in 69, while the Twentieth remained in revolt, leading a force mainly of auxiliaries and rescuing the queen, but was unable to press home his success, partially due to the end of the season and the onset of winter, and partially due to lack of heavy infantry. Then, in spring, Agricola arrives, Coelius is removed, and the Twentieth is brought back under control. Bolanus would then have the manpower to pick up his campaign once more and push against the Brigantes.

Coin evidence suggests early military activity in Lancashire and the Ribble-Aire corridor which would correspond with a campaign centred on Cartimandua's believed power base around Barwick-in-Elmet. Tacitus tells us that Cartimandua was rescued, but if we are to lend credence to Statius, perhaps Bolanus led the campaign in the next season against King Venutius. In the Histories, Tacitus tells us 'Venutius, calling in aid from outside and at the same time assisted by a revolt of the Brigantes themselves, put Cartimandua into an extremely dangerous position.' Given Roman control to the south, any aid Venutius called on could refer to the Parisi in East Yorkshire or the Carvetii in Cumbria, but it may also refer to the Selgovae and the Votadini in Northumberland and the Scottish Borders. If Bolanus and Agricola were forced to push into their territory to break such an alliance, that would certainly fit with Statius; it would allow for an early date of activity at Newstead and would fit with the logic of the campaign.

Why Bolanus did not press any control in the north could be explained by the uncertainty of his situation. We are already led to believe that Vespasian had selected a replacement early on, and Bolanus, appointed by Vitellius, must have been unsure how long his tenure would last. Thus it is extremely likely that having rescued the queen, put the Brigantes in their place and possibly broken up their alliance with their allies, he settled for forming a line of control on their border.

Roman military operations traditionally took place over the campaigning season, rigidly defined as March to October and marked with festivals at each end. Clearly there were times when winter fighting was required, but it was rare for a Roman general to order a campaign outside the fighting season. As such, we can assume that by October AD 70, whether or not the army had pushed as far north as Newstead, the queen was safe, the Brigantes penned into their lands and the army settled in winter quarters in Bolanus's new line of fortifications across the north.

This entire episode with Bolanus and the Brigantes highlights the danger of taking Tacitus as gospel, for there is a tradition of looking at Statius as a fanciful poet and Tacitus as a historian, and neither is entirely true.

Spring of 71 came around, bringing with it a change in command. Bolanus was finally withdrawn to Rome, and a new governor took his place. The emperor Vespasian was shrewd, having come from humble origins and managed to advance his career throughout the dangerous reigns of Caligula, Claudius and Nero. It should therefore be no surprise that he seems to display a canny knack of assigning the right man for the job at most junctures in his reign, and the new governor of Britain was no exception. The Brigantes were still restive and Rome had at best tenuous control over the north, where they had formerly relied upon the Brigantes as a client kingdom. To actually overcome and subdue the Brigantes would be a huge task, their territory stretching from the Trent to the Tyne and from coast to coast – a massive area. Vespasian had already selected the man for the job, but had to wait while he put down the Civilis revolt in Germany, aided by the arrival there of the Fourteenth. Now, though, in spring 71, said revolt was over and the new man was free to take up his position.

Petilius Cerialis arrived from Germany in the spring of 71. You will likely remember Cerialis, for this is not the first time he has appeared. Tacitus labels him headstrong and rash, a depiction that is seemingly borne out by his record. When Boudicca revolted and attacked Colchester, whereas Suetonius Paulinus sacrificed cities in order to bring adequate forces to bear, Cerialis had attempted to save the Colonia with just part of the Ninth. He had been resoundingly beaten and forced to flee to safety with his cavalry. He had suffered a similarly embarrassing defeat in 69 while the Flavian forces marched on Rome, being utterly overcome with his cavalry by Vitellian forces in the outskirts of the capital. One might wonder what prompted an emperor to entrust an important campaign to a man with such a record.

For the few disasters we can attribute to Cerialis, we must also remember that he is referred to even in 69 as 'being himself not without reputation in war',[4] and that he had just very decisively ended the Civilis revolt in Germany. Whatever rashness he was subject to, and this was also evident in the Civilis episode if Tacitus can be relied upon, his effectiveness was notable. He was dangerous and unpredictable, but he got the job done. Moreover, not only was Cerialis now proven in war, he had been a legate in Britain in 60 and knew the terrain, the geography and the political landscape. Like Agricola, he was a man chosen for both his abilities and his familiarity with the province. And, if one felt jaded, one might note that Cerialis was closely tied to Vespasian, almost certainly related, and probably his son-in-law through Vespasian's daughter Flavia Domitilla.

When Cerialis arrived in Britain, he brought with him a new legion to replace the absent Fourteenth, undoubtedly much to the relief of the various commanders on the island. That new legion was the Second Adiutrix. When the new governor met his commanders it must have been something of a reunion with Agricola, for the two men had both served under Suetonius Paulinus a decade earlier, and had likely both been involved in the Flavian march on Rome a year and a half ago. They must have known one another, both personally and by reputation. Both men were closely tied to the Flavians and undoubtedly wanted to prove themselves in their new roles. Birley suggests an enmity between the two officers based partially on the tone of some of Tacitus's words, identifying a certain grudging quality to any mention of success on behalf of Cerialis. While this remains a possibility, especially given the vastly different characters of the two men, such a division would make it unlikely that the shrewd Mucianus and Vespasian would assign the two men together to such an important campaign, let alone that Cerialis would of the four legates at his command entrust Agricola with the lion's share of the army.

It is worth noting also that there would undoubtedly have been other reunions for Cerialis, for he had commanded the Ninth

Legion a decade earlier, and there would be a number of officers present with whom he had previously served.

Cerialis arrived at the beginning of the campaigning season. Likely Agricola and the Twentieth were already in the north, garrisoning forts on the border of Brigantian territory, and Cerialis brooked no delay. We are told by Tacitus 'in the presence of the great generals and renowned armies the enemy's hopes were crushed. They were at once panic-stricken by the attack of Petilius Cerialis on the state of the Brigantes, said to be the most prosperous in the entire province. There were many battles, some by no means bloodless, and his conquests, or at least his wars, embraced a large part of the territory of the Brigantes.'[5] If we were to apply comparisons to this campaign and its overall commander, it is tempting to see Cerialis as a George S. Patton of his day, while his tactics are reminiscent of the German 'blitzkrieg'.

Cerialis launched straight into war with the Brigantes. We are told that he gave much authority to Agricola, and that Agricola assigned all his successes to Cerialis. This makes sense on several levels. Agricola has been circumspect throughout his career, keeping out of the limelight when dangerous masters ruled. Not only would it be a comradely thing to do with a man he knew of old to allow the senior officer to take the glory, Agricola may also have been wary, knowing Cerialis's reputation and wanting to be sure that, while any glory hung upon Cerialis, any disasters similarly stuck to the senior man. What we are seeing is Agricola playing it safe as he has so often done before.

The authority Cerialis bestowed upon Agricola was 'often by way of trial putting him in command of part of the army, and sometimes, on the strength of the result, of larger forces'. This is a very telling line. It suggests that initially Cerialis tested Agricola's command ability by giving him control of more than just the Twentieth, likely assigning extra vexillations of legionaries and auxiliary units to him, and that when Agricola showed success in this, his forces were increased.

We can perhaps deduce that in addition to the Twentieth Legion, among the other forces at Agricola's call was a unit of Gallic cavalry named the Ala Sebosiana. This unit is attested in several sites in the north-west that have produced Flavian-dated finds, but most importantly among the writing tablet finds in Carlisle was discovered the line '[eq (uiti) al]ae Sebosianae sing(ulari) uacat Agricolae uacat', translated as 'trooper of the ala Sebosiana, singularis of Agricola'. It would appear therefore that this rider was seconded from his unit to Agricola's bodyguard. Whether this dates from the campaigns of Cerialis or from Agricola's later tenure as governor we cannot be certain, but given the confirmed dating of Carlisle to this time, it is entirely conceivable that Agricola led the Ala Sebosiana as part of his force in 72.

We can say with some confidence that Cerialis had at this point transferred a sizeable portion of the army to Agricola's command. There is no mention of any of the other officers in the province being given a similar opportunity, and we must therefore surmise that the army led to campaign in the north had been split into two battle groups, one under Agricola and the other under Cerialis. Once more this makes sense when we remember that Agricola's Twentieth were based in the west and that Cerialis almost certainly took command of the Ninth, who had been his former legion and who were based in the east.

An investigation of the confirmed and the potential sites in the north that date to this period gives us a partial picture of Cerialis's strategy, and given what we have deduced of the army's make-up, it is possible to build a good impression of the progress of the campaign. Bolanus had secured the southern fringe of Brigantian territory, and may have created positions beyond, providing a springboard for Cerialis which he would now use to press north.

Cerialis leads his force from Lincoln, establishing a new base for the Ninth at York, within Brigantian territory and therefore clearly stating his intention to impose Roman control upon the tribe. The legionary fortress at Chester is most commonly assumed to have been constructed around 74/75, partially from ingots dated to 74. It is not impossible, however, that the fortress dates from a little earlier, and could potentially have been begun in 71. This would make Chester Agricola's choice of north-western fortress for the Twentieth, mirroring Cerialis's selection of York in the east, and would give both army groups a solid base for campaigning.

Any advance north through Brigantian lands would inevitably require twin prongs, each moving up the low land on either side of the Pennines. Later Roman roads and series of forts and towns continue to use those two routes, and indeed their arterial nature is still evident now in the form of the A1 and the M6. We can reasonably assume that Cerialis led his force north from York, establishing points of control as he went, while Agricola did precisely the same in the west from Chester.

A look at map 4 shows the sites potentially dated to these campaigns. It has long been assumed, and with some supporting evidence, that the greatest Brigantian stronghold was that now known as Stanwick Camp in County Durham, and a grand-scale battle between Romans and Brigantes at, or close by, Stanwick Camp is highly likely.

If we tentatively date that battle to later in 72, a sequence of events is suggested:

- Spring 71 – Cerialis arrives, settles the II Adiutrix in Lincoln and leads the IX Hispana north into Brigantian territory, involving some clashes and the foundation of York as a new northern base. Agricola does much the same in the west, founding Chester. By the end of the campaigning season, the army is within Brigantian territory and imposing control. The navy begins to deploy ready for further campaigning, and vexillations of the Second are attached to both forces.
- Spring 72 – The army moves north in two groups. Cerialis reaches the area of Stanwick Camp and comes into contact with the Brigantes, some of his force continuing north to the Tyne and founding a fort and harbour at Corbridge Red House on the north-eastern edge of Brigantian lands. Meanwhile Agricola presses on, reaching Carlisle, where he founds a fort, and presumably a harbour also, at the north-western extreme of Brigantian territory.

- Summer 72 – Having effectively boxed in Brigantian lands and sealed the tribe off from their neighbours, isolating them, Cerialis now concentrates his army ready to take Stanwick Camp. Agricola is summoned with his force to join the fight. Agricola heads south-east from Carlisle, forming the Stainmore line as he descends upon the enemy. The two armies meet at Stanwick Camp and the Brigantes are crushed and made to submit.

If we accept that his predecessor, Bolanus, not only defeated the Brigantes but pushed as far north as Newstead, then it becomes reasonable to see how Cerialis might already be aware of the northern fringe of Brigantes' territory, of the potential of the border drawn by the Solway Firth and the Tyne, and Carlisle and Corbridge. It explains how the Romans would be sufficiently aware in advance of the political geography to plan sealing the tribe in. It may even be that Cerialis inherited extant temporary turf installations at Carlisle and Newstead.

Given the above potential sequence in the space of two years, and only one campaigning season of advances, Cerialis (and therefore Agricola) not only managed to cow the Brigantes but, as Tacitus tells us eloquently, 'embraced a large part of the territory'. With a network of forts isolating the tribe and controlling all the major routes, the chances of the Brigantes succeeding in any grand revolt would be minimal, perhaps suggesting a lesson learned by both commanders from their experiences with Boudicca.

It is highly probable that the Classis Britannica, the fleet that had been created for the invasion and had been based in the English Channel near Kent ever since, took part in the campaigns of 71–73. We have seen earlier a noted lack of naval activity in the Welsh campaigns of Suetonius Paulinus, and while we are not told of any here, there is a great deal more logic to it, and no specific evidence against it. There would be sufficient access for the fleet to supply the army now at Chester, York and Corbridge, and likely Carlisle would have had a local harbour opened for the campaign. Other sites such as Wilderspool and Piercebridge would almost certainly be reachable by navigable waterways. If the army on both sides of the country could be confident of resupply by ship, then the reliance upon supply lines running through hostile territory would be avoided and, since the British tribes had a negligible naval capability, the supplies would be truly safe.

Moreover, it is of note that the legion Cerialis has brought with him to Britain was II Adiutrix. The Second was a new legion, only formed in AD 70 as the Flavians sought to impose control over their new empire, and had been formed from the marines of the Ravenna fleet. As such, the Second would have an unparalleled understanding of, and familiarity with, all things naval. The navy was considered by many military men as something of a lower class of force than the legions, and that an important campaign might have been given as a quarter of its force a legion of newly commissioned sailors seems an odd decision, unless there was a specific reason for their selection. The army's reliance upon the navy in the campaign could explain it. After all, Britain was an island, and Cerialis must have realised the importance of water transport during his campaign with the Second against Civilis, along the River Rhine.

The scale of the campaign's conclusion might be hinted at by the physical evidence. We can readily conjecture about an early fort at Piercebridge, possibly including the site at Holmes House Farm, but a single fort would not be sufficient for the force Cerialis and Agricola could bring to bear on the Brigantes, even if both sites were in use. However, the existence of a local temporary camp at Sandforth Moor suggests that there may be an ensemble of sites (possibly even a ring of them) around Stanwick Camp, forming the Roman assault line, and mostly still waiting to be identified.

The remains of the Stanwick Camp fortification survive to impressive heights, and the complex is massive, giving some idea of the power of the Brigantes. However, arguments have persisted over the past century as to its precise place in Romano-British history, whether it was the seat of Cartimandua or Venutius, and even whether it was the site of a siege or not. Although a section of the defences has been slighted in the period, there has

Defences of the Brigantian fortress of Stanwick Camp in County Durham. (Author's collection)

been no archaeological evidence turned up for a siege. The most likely answer is that the Brigantes marshalled here, as did the Romans, but the two forces met on an open field of battle, as was the preferred tactic for both peoples. Perhaps in the future some greensward around the area will suddenly turn up the evidence of Cerialis's victory.

The blitzkrieg nature of this campaign is clear from the scale and the timeline. Even if the sequence of events above is incorrect, the longest the campaign could take was from the spring of 71 to the autumn of 73, a grand total of three seasons to break the strongest tribe in Britain and secure a territory of some 10,000 square miles. Compare this with other campaigns of similar scope and the achievements of Cerialis become apparent.

Agricola's western advance route	
Chester (1)	Founded sometime between AD 71 and 75, with ingots dated 74 and Vespasianic inscriptions discovered on site.
Middlewich (2)	Believed to pre-date the Flavian fort at Northwich based on proximity to each other and to King Street.
Wilderspool (3)	No fort or camp identified, but military production centre has yielded Flavian-dated fittings and fort may yet be found.
Ribchester (4)	Earliest fort shows two pre-Trajanic phases interpreted as both Flavian based on finds. High probability that the second is Agricolan, suggesting the first is earlier.
Kirkham (5)	Flavian pottery dating the earlier of two fort phases.
Lancaster (6)	Finds of early Flavian period indicate a possible date for the first phase of the fort. Inscription of the Ala Sebosiana gives an Agricolan link.
Burrow in Lonsdale (7)	Turf and timber defences found beneath stone fort, with first-century pottery located, suggesting a possible early Flavian foundation.
Low Borrowbridge (8)	Post holes and pottery evidence suggest an early Flavian date for the first phase of the fort.
Plumpton Head (9)	Tentatively dated to Cerialis based on similarity to and geographical relationship with Rey Cross.
Carlisle (10)	Dendrochronological dating to 72. The existence of a cluster of temporary camps nearby (Watchclose, Grinsdale, etc.), given the early dating of Carlisle fort, suggests a possible military staging area like Rhyn Park for the Welsh campaigns.
Cerialis's eastern advance route*	
Rossington Bridge (11)	Vexillation fortress interpreted as pre-Flavian.
Castleford (12)	Two tile stamps of LEGIO IX and a wealth of Flavian pottery suggest an early date for Castleford.

Newton Kyme (13)	Marching camp undated, but probably pre-dates the foundation of a full fort at Newton Kyme.
York (14)	Founded 71 by Legion IX Hispana.
Roecliffe (15)	Potentially pre-dating Dere Street, and with pottery suggesting an early Flavian date.
Breckenborough (16)	Undated, but suggested as Flavian.
Catterick (17)	Finds suggest a Flavian origin. Additionally, an undated marching camp may have an early date, and the local archaeological society are investigating the possibility of an earlier, perhaps Neronian, fort at nearby Richmond.
Piercebridge (18)	Flavian finds in the vicus indicate it may pre-date the extant fort, suggesting an undiscovered earlier site, or perhaps the nearby Holmes House site. Proximity to Stanwick Camp supports a date of 72–73.
Corbridge Red House (19)	Early Flavian site, generally attributed to Agricola but with earlier potential.
Stainmore Pass	
Kirkby Thore (20) **	Spread of eight pre-Vespasianic coins suggests early Flavian presence.
Crackenthorpe (21) **	Tentatively dated to Cerialis based on similarity to and geographical relationship with Rey Cross.
Warcop (22)	Marching camp. If Plumpton Head, Crackenthorpe and Rey Cross are considered a sequence, then Warcop fills an obvious gap.
Rey Cross (23)	Positioning suggests it pre-dates the forts at Brough and Bowes (both c. AD 80) and that it also pre-dates the road across the pass.
Greta Bridge (24)	A single sherd of Flavian pottery is minimal evidence, but Greta Bridge also stands almost halfway between Rey Cross and Piercebridge.
Parisi ring sites	
Brough on Humber (25)	Earliest phase believed to date to early Flavian period on the site of an earlier native settlement. Nearby pre-Roman Redcliffe seems to go into decline at this time, suggesting a new river crossing at Brough.
Hayton (26)	Dated by finds as a short-lived early Flavian fort.

Malton (27)	Flavian finds usually attributed to Agricolan establishment, but earliest fort could pre-date this.
Wath (28)	Undated, but suggested as Flavian.
Thirkleby (29)	Dated to the Flavian era on coin find evidence.
Lease Rigg (30) ***	Pottery dated from the early Flavian era suggests a fort of that period.
Carvetii ring sites	
Papcastle (31)	Flavian coins suggest an early date for the fort.
Blennerhasset (32)	Dated to early Flavian period based on pottery finds.
Troutbeck III (33)	Suggested as a Flavian stage of the Troutbeck ensemble.
Ambleside (34)	Collingwood reported an earlier fort beneath the first phase of extant site, which was dated c. 90.

* The large gap between Piercebridge and Corbridge when compared with Agricola's advance in the west (which are roughly a day's march of 20 miles apart) suggests that there are others missing from the sequence.
** The proximity of these two sites makes the use of both within the same campaign unlikely, though I have included both due to the evidence in favour of Kirkby Thore and the common attribution of Crackenthorpe.
*** Lease Rigg is dated to the period, though its positioning is of little use in surrounding the Parisi. Possibly it relates to an as yet undiscovered site at or near Whitby, which may be the 'Dictum' mentioned in chapter XL of the Notitia Dignitatum.

In addition to the sites shown on the campaign map, if dating evidence is ignored and the simple presence of temporary camps is examined, certain lines stand out. One such is the Stainmore Pass and the continuation from its western end to Carlisle (map 5). It is tempting to attribute the entire line to this Cerialian campaign, since we are unaware of any later war that would engender such a line, and with the existence of the Stainmore fort system from the later Flavian period there would be little need for such a profusion of temporary camps thereafter.

There is a growing belief among historians that Cerialis was the first governor to campaign in Scotland (brushing aside the possibility of Bolanus, based upon the poetry of Statius). As I have previously stated, the dating evidence in Scotland, based largely upon temporary camps, is difficult to interpret with any level of confidence, and so it is difficult to prove or disprove this theory. If the war against the Brigantes was completed by the end of the campaigning season in 72 then, since Cerialis did not leave the island until the close of 73, he could potentially continue to campaign further north for a season. There are arguments both for and against the idea.

A fresh push would certainly be in keeping with the personality we have seen in Cerialis. He was clearly not a man to rest upon his laurels, and the tribes of the Votadini, the Selgovae and the Novantae would be tantalisingly close and comparatively easy targets after the Brigantes. Moreover, if Bolanus had already established some sort of northern outpost at Newstead, then at least part of the infrastructure of advance was already in place. It is hard to imagine Cerialis looking north at an installation left by his predecessor and not wanting to surpass it.

On the other hand, even for a headstrong man like Cerialis, conquering the Brigantes, the remit with which he had been sent to the province in the first place, and then immediately pushing north without taking any time to consolidate his gains would be dangerous, risking the Brigantes regrouping and turning on him. A thorough governor would undoubtedly have spent the following season settling his military infrastructure and beginning the process of Romanising his conquered terrain, incorporating it into the province.

Another factor against Cerialis campaigning in Scotland is suggested by Shotter,[6] even as he contemplates just such a campaign. He ascribes to Cerialis a 'divide and conquer' attitude derived from a speech in Tacitus, and such an attitude could be seen in the handling of the Brigantes noted above. The Brigantes were more a confederation of peoples dominated by one power rather than an individual tribe. They were bordered to the east and west by the Parisi (occupying what is now the East Riding of Yorkshire) and the Carvetii (occupying Cumbria), though the latter may have been subject to the Brigantes. Given the position of these two tribes, it would be advantageous to make sure they were secured and incorporated at the same time as the Brigantes, and from the map of the campaign (map 4) it is possible to see a ring of forts in place about each of these tribes.

The most likely answer is that 73 saw a number of activities, including the consolidating of the network of forts and routes that held down the Brigantes, the isolation and subjugation of the Carvetii and the Parisi, and quite possibly some form of initial mission into the north. That Cerialis might involve himself in the divide and rule of the occupied territories while sending Agricola to size up the Votadini is a tempting notion – that the first man to fortify positions in Scotland is the man commonly said to have conquered the place a decade later would be a satisfying conclusion. Some indications of multiple Flavian periods have come to light in the excavation of the Gask Ridge system across Fife, and it may even be that Cerialis (or Agricola on his behalf) created a system of advance installations as far north as Perth. It is possible that the rebel Brigantian king Venutius had survived the war in his own territory and fled north to his erstwhile allies. We know nothing of the man's last days and his death, but it seems highly likely that Cerialis put an end to him, advancing north of Brigantian territory in pursuit. There is a tempting link to be made just north of Newstead, for the Ravenna Cosmography notes a Roman installation to the north of that fort named Venutio, leading to the possibility that this place (probably modern Oxton) was the site of Venutius's final defeat at the hands of Cerialis. This would also put the man already halfway between Brigantian lands and the River Tay, supporting the notion that he advanced into Scotland. Indeed, if Venutius had fled to the Selgovae, Cerialis would have to have overcome that tribe and, with the relatively quiet Votadini to the east, that would give Rome tentative control as far north as Fife. So the possibility of Cerialian structures between the Forth and the Tay seems much more feasible. It is possible that Venutius was originally from a tribe allied to the Brigantes (possibly even the Selgovae) and, if so, fleeing to them would be logical. It is quite possible, then, that some form of advance into Scotland was undertaken during the closing days of Cerialis's tenure as governor, whether it be he or Agricola responsible. If the two tribes were indeed ringed in with forts and overcome at this time, the conclusion would be that Cerialis handled the Parisi from his new fortress in York, while Agricola handled the Carvetii from the fort in Carlisle, and then one or both commanders led a first push into Scotland proper, perhaps establishing a centre for control over the new lands at Newstead, either as a fresh foundation or utilising a site already created by Bolanus.

While we cannot confirm any northern push or action against the secondary tribes, we also cannot suggest that these events did not occur simply because Tacitus makes no mention of them. Until Agricola takes on the governorship of Britain, Tacitus's account is somewhat brief and in the form of bullet points, giving us only what he considers important and pertinent. Moreover, since Tacitus will have heard the tales of this campaign primarily from the mouth of Agricola himself in later years, it may be that the storyteller glossed over any Scottish advances under Cerialis in order to focus attention more upon his own successes.

In any event, the end of AD 73 sees the north of England secured under Roman control. The Brigantes have been put down, the threat to Rome neutralised and her territory expanded. Cerialis must have left for Rome towards the end of the year with his head held high, his reputation not only intact but enhanced, his future career looking ever more secure. Agricola, ending his three-year command of the Twentieth, must have been similarly pleased as he returned to the capital and the Flavian court to see what the emperor had lined up for him next. Cerialis would secure the consulship for the next year, while Agricola anticipated his first full governorship.

Agricola has now served in Britain twice, first as a tribune and then as a legionary legate. He has spent six years on the island, mostly campaigning. He has travelled extensively across Wales and the south of England, and now the north of England and possibly even the borders of Scotland. He has experience of British tribal warfare in most terrains, and against several different tribes, having also fought two of Britain's most infamous tribal leaders, Boudicca and Venutius. He is becoming familiar with hill and mountain warfare, with campaigning strategies and political manoeuvring. He has fought alongside two very different generals, both with their own style, both ultimately very effective in their time. Few Romans could, by the age of thirty-three, be as conversant with Britain.

7

GOVERNORSHIP

Passing along the cursus honorum, a man of senatorial standing would typically govern a minimum of two provinces, once after he had served as a praetor, and then again after he had secured a consulship. There are good reasons for this.

Rome's provinces were divided into two pairs of groups, one based upon assignment of governor and the other upon that governor's seniority. In the imperial period one group of provinces became known as the 'Senatorial Provinces', and the other the 'Imperial Provinces'. The senatorial provinces are typically the older regions that were more settled, more Romanized, required less direct intervention and more or less ran themselves. The governors of these provinces were assigned by the senate. The imperial provinces were more commonly the border provinces or the more dangerous or important ones, filled with legions and adjacent to enemy nations. The governors of such provinces, the control of which was vital, were selected directly by the emperor.

Moreover, a second division existed, consisting of 'praetorian provinces' and 'consular provinces'. You will undoubtedly have already worked this one out: yes, the praetorian provinces would be governed by a former praetor and the consular provinces by a former consul. Needless to say, the praetorian provinces were on the whole the less critical ones requiring a lesser governor, while the consular provinces were the most important and thus merited a more senior man, one who already had gubernatorial experience in the former role. Clearly there is a great deal of correlation between imperial/consular provinces and senatorial/praetorian ones.

In effect, one might see the praetorian governorship as something of a dry run for a more important province.

Agricola, then, has served as a praetor, and then commanded a legion (an optional step on the ladder). Now he has returned to Rome aged thirty-three to seek a new appointment. The next four years pass swiftly in a single passage of Tacitus, and it is possible upon reading of the events of those years to see it as the unfolding of a Flavian plan. Indeed, Agricola may even have been recalled from Britain with foreknowledge of what was coming next. Agricola (along with Cerialis) had achieved Flavian goals in Britain with speed and decisiveness. Perhaps Vespasian already had plans to send him back to the island in due course. It might even be that the emperor would have liked to promote Agricola to the governorship of the province immediately, to continue the good work there, but the cursus honorum was not *that* flexible. Britain was a consular province, and assigning an inexperienced governor there would not be a popular decision.

Therefore Agricola would have to be assigned to a praetorian province at this point. With the recall of Cerialis, Vespasian assigned a man named Frontinus to govern Britain, of whom we will learn more, and had another province in mind for Agricola. Tacitus tells us: 'As he was returning from the command of the legion, Vespasian admitted him into the patrician order, and then gave him the province of Aquitania, a pre-eminently splendid appointment both from the importance of its duties and the prospect of the consulate to which the Emperor destined him.'[1]

The duration of a governorship was a variable thing, though three years seems to have been the expected standard at this time. That the emperor had some kind of long-term plan for Agricola is intimated here by the suggestion that Vespasian had already vouchsafed the consulate for his young friend. In 73, when Agricola returned to Rome, Vespasian and Titus together shared the position of censor, the duties of which included revising senate membership and the membership of the equestrian order. As such it would be perfectly acceptable and understandable for the censors to grant a place in the senate to a former praetor who had distinguished himself in military command. Indeed, Vespasian raised the senate membership to 1,000 during his time in the role, and so a number of new senators would need to be found.

Though consuls were selected in the new year, it was not unheard of for a man to be promised the consulship, even officially, in advance. We see the phrase 'COS DES' in epigraphy, meaning Consul Designate. It seems highly likely that Vespasian as a patron, and Titus as a friend, vouchsafed the consulship for Agricola even at this early stage, before he had governed a province.

Agricola, then, is selected directly by the emperor to oversee Gallia Aquitania (the region of south-west France still known as Aquitaine, along with part of the Pyrenees and land up to the Loire Valley). This is a praetorian province and therefore well within Agricola's political means, and an imperial one, so Vespasian himself could appoint the governor. Why Aquitania? This being one of the more peaceful and easy provinces, perhaps Vespasian was giving Agricola the chance to hone his gubernatorial skills.

If we continue with our notion that Vespasian and Titus were already planning out Agricola's career, though, and were already preparing to send him back to Britain, for which a case can certainly be made, then Aquitania becomes an interesting choice. We can see it as maybe more than mere gubernatorial experience.

Aquitania had been a province of Rome for roughly a century, prior to which it had been part of the Gaulish world conquered by Caesar. Its people had been Celtic, led by chieftains and druids. It had worshipped those well-known Celtic Gods such as Taranis and Toutatis, and they were still revered alongside Roman deities. Its language was still inflected with Celtic elements, as were the names of people and places. It had a length of good coastline, with flat plains that provided excellent agricultural land, leading to rolling hills and then high moors and deep valleys like the Dorgogne and the Lot. To the south rose the foothills and then the mountains of the Pyrenees, providing abundant minerals. Even the older settlements of the area had been Celtic oppida – hill fort settlements with defences.

Sound familiar? Read through the last paragraph again and think this time not of Aquitania but of Britain. Every element of that land corresponds rather comfortably with the island Agricola had just left. In an odd way it must have felt like being transported to a conquered and settled version of Britain. Perhaps he was being shown what was expected of Britain? Indeed, the links between Aquitania and Britain can still be found the twelfth century, when Queen Eleanor and her sons Richard the Lionheart and John rule over both lands simultaneously.

We are told of Agricola's governorship of the province in more detail than one might expect in Tacitus's usually rapid-fire manner. 'Many think the genius of the soldier wants subtlety, because military law, which is summary and blunt, and apt to appeal to the sword, finds no exercise for the refinements of the forum. Yet Agricola, from his natural good sense, though called to act among civilians, did his work with ease and correctness.'[2]

One might wonder why Tacitus feels the need to tell us that Agricola managed not to bring the martial attitude of the soldier to such a civic role. Rome had no standing military high command structure. Despite the professional centurionate and infantry, senior commanders were by and large politicians assigned to command by the senate or the emperor, and few exhibited any kind of real military skill. Few commanders could really be said to be soldiers. In this Agricola was unusual, falling into that rare category that contained men like Caesar, Pompey, Scipio and Corbulo. This martial attitude of military men is pointed out in other cases. Paterculus tells us that the conqueror of the Achaean League and destroyer of Corinth, Mummius, 'was so uncultivated (*rudis*)',[3] and Livy that 'The untrained tongue of the soldier was unable to express the freedom of his sentiments; as words failed him.'[4] Given this Roman attitude to the military figure, it is not surprising that Tacitus goes to great lengths then to tell us that his father-in-law is more than just a soldier.

There is an intimation in the text that a commander is not used to having his orders questioned, which would happen in a civil administrative post, and the governance of Aquitania would be far removed from military command. Indeed there is no record of a military presence in the province at all, let alone that of a legion. How Agricola handled such a civil posting is noted by Tacitus, and it is interesting to compare his words to those of Paterculus's description of the great Scipio in a similar situation.

Tacitus gives us 'besides, the times of business and relaxation were kept distinct. When his public and judicial duties required it, he was dignified, thoughtful, austere, and yet often merciful; when business was done with, he wore no longer the official character. He was altogether without harshness, pride, or the greed of gain. With a most rare felicity, his good nature did not weaken his authority, nor his strictness the attachment of his friends. To speak of uprightness and purity in such a man would be an insult to his virtues. Fame itself, of which even good men are often weakly fond, he did not seek by an ostentation of virtue or by artifice.'[5]

Gushing with compliments for his father-in-law, we might compare this with Paterculus: 'Scipio was a cultivated patron and admirer of liberal studies and of every form of learning, and kept constantly with him, at home and in the field, two men of eminent genius, Polybius and Panaetius. No one ever relieved the duties of an active life by a more refined use of his intervals of leisure than Scipio, or was more constant in his devotion to the arts either of war or peace. Ever engaged in the pursuit of arms or his studies, he was either training his body by exposing it to dangers or his mind by learning.'[6]

In fact, I am grateful to Church & Brodribb's above translation of Tacitus, for it neatly skirts a difficult piece of text, but it would be remiss of me to ignore it. Their somewhat sympathetic translation of 'when business was done with, he wore no longer the official character. He was altogether without harshness, pride, or the greed of gain'[7] fits the picture of the man we have been given much better than most. Birley gives us 'When he had completed his official duties, he no longer wore the mask of power. Sullenness and arrogance and greed he had cast aside.' Yikes. Could this be the same Agricola? Mattingly and Handford give us 'When duty had been discharged, he completely dropped his official air. As to sullenness or arrogance, he had long overcome any tendency to such faults.'[8] Once again, then, we should always be aware of the potential differences in a passage's meaning achieved by choices of translation. In the original text, *tristitas* (melancholy, sourness, etc.), *adrogans* (arrogance, presumption, etc.) and *avaritia* (rapacity, stinginess, etc.) are uniformly negative traits, but the way in which the sentence is handled makes all the difference.

We could perhaps compare this with Plutarch's treatment of Cato: 'on the tribunal and in the senate he was severe and terrible in his defence of justice, but afterwards his manner towards all men was benevolent and kindly.'[9] It was apparently the norm for a Roman governor to display a façade of severity and austereness, and to have almost entirely separate personalities for public and private life. Ogilvie and Richmond suggest that this 'mask' worn in public by governors had in effect been relieved of these specific three negative values by Agricola, and that this may have been the effect for which Tacitus was striving.

Whatever the case, we are given a clear picture of Agricola governing Aquitania with a fair hand and in a composed and reasonable manner. Before we leave Aquitania, though, I would like to draw attention to the line 'He avoided rivalry with his colleagues, contention with his procurator, thinking such victories no honour and defeat disgrace.' Again, we might wonder why Tacitus draws our attention so specifically to this, but we should note that there is a long tradition in Rome of conflict between a province's governor and its procurator. After all, a governor was often a corrupt politician intent on creating a nest egg from his position (as we have seen in the case of Salvius Titianus in Asia). It is said of Verres, when put on trial for corruption, that he claimed a governor had to make three fortunes: one to pay his debts for getting there, one to bribe the authorities on his trial afterwards and a third to retire upon. The job of a procurator, on the other hand, was to oversee the financial viability of a province. The two could only realistically coexist without friction in the case of both men being honest and true (or both not). And we have already had an example of this friction at work in the case of Classicianus, who came to Britain at the end of Paulinus's governorship and immediately launched into a campaign to have the governor removed.

That Tacitus tells us Agricola made pains to work with his procurator and his peers and to avoid conflict with them is therefore noteworthy. With less than three years in office, Agricola was recalled to Rome. We can assume that he had taken up his governorship of Aquitania in the new year of 74, having returned from Britain in 73. Tacitus tells us that he was 'recalled with an immediate prospect of the consulate', which suggests that he left his position mid-76, having served two-and-a-half years, to return to Rome and take on the suffect consulship later that year. He may have been consul designate since January and have been wrapping up his affairs in Aquitania ready for a mid-year recall.

Upon his recall, we are told 'A general belief went with him that the province of Britain was to be his, not because he had himself hinted it, but because he seemed worthy of it.'[10] If this is true, and again we have no real reason to doubt it, then it hints once more at a grand Flavian plan. It might be suggested that when Agricola was assigned to Aquitania, it was already on the understanding from Vespasian and Titus that he would return to a consulship and then be given Britain as his major province. Such a thing would be a normal outcome of the relationship between patron and client. From this deal, Agricola would have a preferential career path offered to him in the coming years, while Vespasian could be content that he had a workable plan for the completion of Britain's subjugation.

This sort of planning is perfectly in line with Vespasian. A simple glance at the events of the year of the four emperors shows evidence of such 'thinking ahead'. Galba, Otho and Vitellius all reacted to events. There were small measures put in place by them all, but mostly they were struggling to react to pressures. In the case of Vespasian, though, he managed to secure the support of legions all along the Danube and as far as Britain and Spain before he even left the east. He had a right-hand man in Mucianus advancing his cause on Rome, a brother in a position of power in the city, and a son there too. By the time Vespasian deigned to descend upon Rome his control was a foregone conclusion.

His dealing with a province in such a way is also in evidence in Judea. He had been busy conducting a war there when he achieved the purple, and his son Titus continued it thereafter. Where Judea had previously been controlled by a procurator and overseen by the governor of neighbouring Syria, Vespasian now had a praetorian governor installed directly in Judea with his own legion, the Tenth Fretensis. When Titus was withdrawn, Vespasian put in his place Sextus Vettulenus Cerialis, who had led a legion throughout that war and was cognisant of what needed to be done. Lucilius Bassus was next, a former prefect of the fleet, though he died in office. The

Spoils from the sack of Jerusalem in AD 70, which would help fund the Colosseum, as shown on the Arch of Titus in Rome. (Author's collection)

man who ended the war for the Flavians with the infamous siege of Masada, and governed Judea thereafter, was Lucius Flavius Silva, a former legionary legate who had served as a tribune in Syria and would be familiar with both the army of the region, the terrain, and the people. We know that from AD 72 construction had begun on the Colosseum and that it was paid for by the spoils of the Judean war. Silva would almost certainly be relied upon to supply a steady flow of funds to the capital for the work. The list of men assigned to Judea is another example of Vespasianic planning.

So Agricola had spent two-and-a-half years honing his skills governing a land and its people that bore a resemblance to Britain. He was recalled to Rome, seemingly already expecting Britain as his next province, to the suffect consulship later in 76. Under the normal rules of the cursus honorum, a man would have a two-year break between his governorship and taking on the role of consul, but with that customary flexibility, since a three-year stint leading the Twentieth Legion had put Agricola over the required age for the consulate, he was smoothly lifted from the one to achieve the other.

Thus in late 76, Agricola became suffect consul and during those months of consulship he betroths his thirteen-year-old daughter. Her husband tells us 'He was consul, and I but a youth, when he betrothed to me his daughter [...] After his consulate he gave her to me in marriage, and was then at once appointed to the government of Britain, with the addition of the sacred office of the pontificate.'

Agricola would have laid down his consulship at the end of the year, and then at some time in 77 he married his daughter to Tacitus, and from here on, the writer has a direct connection to his subject. As Britain's previous governor packs his bags to return to Rome, Agricola sets forth to Britain once more, this time as a consular governor, very likely with a remit from Vespasian to complete the conquest of the island. Moreover, having served two years of the vigintiviri, Tacitus was now ready for his first outing as a military tribune. It is difficult to believe that he did not join his new father-in-law in making for Britain.

8

THE BRITISH SITUATION, REPRISE

Agricola had left Britain in 73 along with its governor, Petilius Cerialis. During the four years of Agricola's absence, his governorship and consulship, the man Vespasian had selected to control the island is better known now for his writings than his politics: Sextus Julius Frontinus. Like two other governors we have previously mentioned, Frontinus also later served as a *curator aquarum*, overseeing the water supply of Rome. Unlike the other two, Frontinus wrote a treatise on the subject which remains to this day one of the academic mainstays of the entire field. In fact, it is only through his work that we know that those other two ever held the position.

Frontinus's career before his tenure in Britain is largely unknown. We can assume a Flavian connection and favour since it is clear that the imperial governorships bestowed by Vespasian were almost uniformly given to men who had supported him in his bid for the throne. We can also assume a level of competence both expected from and realised by the man, for Vespasian had also continually assigned to posts the right men for the job.

What we do know of him provides a partial reflection of Agricola in the years preceding their governorships. Just as our main subject had been granted an extraordinary commission by Cerialis during the Brigantes campaign, Frontinus had led a similar special force during the Civilis revolt in Germany at roughly the same time. Both men were therefore clearly highly qualified commanders. Of Frontinus, Tacitus tells us only: 'Indeed he [Cerialis] would have altogether thrown into the shade the activity and renown of any other successor; but Julius Frontinus was equal to the burden, a great man as far as greatness was then possible, who subdued by his arms the powerful and warlike tribe of the Silures, surmounting the difficulties of the country as well as the valour of the enemy.'[1]

A short entry in *Agricola* then, but a worthy one. Given how Tacitus appears to have been downplaying the achievements of other governors, and even possibly assassinating their characters, this is more or less an encomium. Once again, we're told of a governor forced to deal with the Silures. Scapula had almost put them down, and then it seemed as though Suetonius Paulinus had finally subdued them. Not so. The Silures were on the rise once more as Frontinus took control.

Tacitus tells us that Frontinus campaigned against the Silures, and we can only assume that he did so with the utmost efficiency, since this is the last time history relates trouble with that tribe, suggesting that whatever Frontinus did during his four years it was sufficient to conquer the tribe for good. What we do know is that during his tenure the II Augusta was transferred from its extant base in Exeter and created a new full-scale legionary fortress at Caerleon, the remains of which can still be seen. The siting of the Caerleon fortress, along with other existing fortifications, was designed to put a stranglehold on the Silures. Moreover, whereas until this date we have no clear evidence of the Classis Britannica operating around Wales, now we see our first indication of their presence.

In recent years a site to the south-west of the fortress of Caerleon and close to the River Usk has been excavated and has revealed the remnants of a port of impressive dimensions. Dr Peter Guest of Cardiff University believes that 'the port dates to the period when the Legions were fighting and subduing the native tribes in western Britain', and that implies not only a strong naval presence in the area, but a solid level of control over Silurian territory.

Clearly the scale of the operation against the Silures under Frontinus is far grander than anything previously attempted. The

Copper alloy image of victory from Caerleon, possibly forming part of ceremonial armour. (Author's collection)

fortress of Isca at Caerleon is dated to 74/75, and therefore gives us a good idea of the dating of the campaigns of Frontinus. It is possible, then, that by 75 or 76 the campaign was over and that Rome was simply settling the area and creating the infrastructure required to keep the Silures under control and gradually Romanise them, much as was now happening in Brigantian lands courtesy of Cerialis's blitzkrieg.

If this is the case, then we can consider two possibilities: that Frontinus spent the last year or two of his tenure imposing control over the Silures and undertaking civilian government projects, or that there was a secondary campaign not mentioned in Tacitus's brief treatment.

The idea that as well as the Welsh campaign, Frontinus may have also expanded to the north is not new, and has been espoused now for decades, and the more that archaeological discoveries help us rewrite the history of the north, the more we are forced to consider this a real possibility. Gone are the days of Tacitus's word being law and all students of Roman Britain accepting that Agricola was the first man to attack Scotland, as we have already seen in our study of Bolanus and Cerialis.

Under Frontinus, while the Second Augusta is relocated at Caerleon, the Twentieth Legion remain at Wroxeter, or possibly Chester. This general shift northwards would now put two legions on the Welsh border and, with auxiliary forts in control of Brigantian lands, two more legions (the Ninth and the Second Adiutrix) are available to move north.

We have already considered the possibility that Vettius Bolanus pushed into the lowlands and founded a site at Newstead, based upon a reconsideration of glassware finds from the site. We have considered the possibility that Cerialis formed his control grid over the Brigantes based on knowledge gleaned from Bolanus's time in the north.

We have even then considered the possibility that under Cerialis Newstead was reoccupied and that perhaps new sites were constructed in the north, even as far as the Tay. The simple undeniable fact is that some sites in Scotland have begun to turn up evidence that points more and more to pre-Agricolan occupation, and work done on the Gask Ridge sites by the Roman Gask Project is forcing historians to reconsider its place in British history. It is therefore more than just possible that Frontinus continued this northward trend upon securing the Silures.

There has been a tendency throughout scholarship of Roman Britain to see certain systems of forts, camps, roads and signal stations as frontiers, but I have already mentioned that at this stage Rome has no real notion of a permanent frontier. All such systems were temporary structures to hold in or hold out hostile forces until Rome was regrouped for the next advance.

Additionally, some systems might be seen as being designed to block off an area, but a view from another angle suggests something much different. The later Roman road north known as Dere Street (now the A1/A68) is dotted with forts a day's march apart, and yet it is clear that this is a highway with intermittent control points rather than a frontier. Much the same can now be said of the Stainmore Pass with its forts and signal stations. Why then assume that the Gask Ridge, which runs from north of Stirling up to Perth, was ever designed or used as a frontier? Running in a north-easterly direction, it is far more likely to have been intended as a monitored and garrisoned route into the north than any kind of defensive border.

If we look at the evidence of dating from the Gask Ridge and several other sites, a new narrative emerges, giving us a possible 'lost' campaign of Frontinus.

Blackhill Wood tower	Evidence of structural rebuilds
Bochastle fort	Flavian. Marching camp present might pre-date fort
Broomholm fort	Earlier ditches noted beneath Flavian installation
Camelon fort	Flavian phase believed beneath later fort
Cardean fort	Evidence of rebuilds
Cargill fort	Early Vespasian coin in good condition suggests early occupation
Dalginross fort	Flavian. Adjacent camp shows two phases of occupation
Dalswinton fort	Four noted Flavian phases
Drumquhassle fort	Dated 75–95 by pottery

Fendoch fort	Early Flavian, possibly even late Neronian Samian
Glenbank fortlet	Ditches recut twice, suggesting long-term occupation
Glenlochar fort	Rubbish pit alignment beneath Flavian phase suggests an earlier fort
Greenloaning tower	Evidence of rebuilding with replacement timbers
Huntingtower tower	Evidence of rebuilding
Midgate tower	Tower and fortlet so close that one must surely predate the other
Milton fort	Two noted Flavian phases
Raith tower	Possible close presence of a fortlet and camp suggest multiple phases
Shielhill South tower	Evidence of rebuilding
Strageath fort	Coin finds suggest an early Flavian date

With reference to the dating of these sites, the numerous phases of rebuilding are important. At the absolute outside, given current notions of Romano-Scottish dating, sites with more than one phase of building might mean a Flavian site reconstructed during the Antonine or Severan pushes north. Indeed, some of the timber fragments found at these sites are oak, which has an expected outdoor durability of roughly 15–25 years. This might correspond to a site built by Agricola in 80, reoccupied in 140 and reconstructed, and then the same in 208.

But while oak has been found, it has only been discovered in relatively small quantities, and oak was not a local timber for the area in the period. The vast majority of trees available in this area were softwoods, such as alder and willow, which have a rough durability of less than five years. Barring the possibility that the legions shipped in timber from elsewhere, it seems highly likely that most of the timbers used in these sites would need to be replaced at least once a decade. If this is the case, it creates the possibility that these sites had been around long enough before Agricola's push that they required reconstruction – say from AD 80 going back to somewhere around 75.

As with all dating for Roman Scotland, this is largely conjecture based upon a combination of logic and archaeological evidence, and what I am suggesting is not a bold, new, factually based rewriting of the canon, but the exploration of possibilities beyond what has been accepted now for centuries.

In addition to the examination of timber rebuilds, other factors here cited include finds and geographical logic. I shall not explain the dubious value of coins and pottery in dating sites, as I've covered this, but there are incidences when seemingly newly minted coins are found which can reasonably date a site. And in some cases two sites either overlap or are too close to have been simultaneous, which leads us to consider multiple periods of occupation. Hoffman[2] suggests multiple phases at Cardean and even cites the discovery of early ditches at Inchtuthil as indicative of a possible earlier phase at this most Agricolan of sites. Wooliscroft[3] notes that the fortlets so far identified on the Gask Ridge seem to belong to a different phase to the signal stations and camps. He suggests, based upon the size of fortlets and their placement and general make-up, that they belong to a second-century phase. As such it is possible that the Gask Ridge was revitalised in the Antonine era by the replacement of signal stations with more solid fortlets. What we have, then, are sites that just might be connected with a campaign of Frontinus.

The Roman route along the Gask Ridge. (Author's collection)

Such a campaign is perhaps even alluded to later in the Agricola. Without wanting to jump ahead of ourselves too far, when Tacitus references the isthmus later defended by the Antonine Wall he claims that Agricola garrisons the line, but the words he uses are 'quod tum praesidiis firmabatur atque omnis propior sinus tenebatur'. This has been variously translated by Church & Brodribb as 'This Agricola then began to defend with a line of forts' (the most commonly quoted variation), by Birley as 'This was now being securely held by garrisons', and by Mattingly and Handford as 'This isthmus was now firmly held by garrisons.' All three of these translations are perfectly viable, but all three gloss over something pertinent to pre-Agricolan activity: the Latin word *firmabatur*, from the verb *firmo*. Firmo can be translated as 'fortified', and therefore by extension as 'garrisoned', but a more direct translation of firmo is 'strengthen'. What Tacitus is quite possibly telling us then is that later Agricola *strengthened* the fortifications on the Forth/Clyde line and, if this is the case, then there must have been something there for him to strengthen. We might here be seeing the written evidence that one of Agricola's predecessors actually penetrated Scotland to the extent that they had placed fortifications at least along the future Antonine Wall line, if not the Gask Ridge to Perth. This is in turn supported by finds at several forts along the Forth/Clyde that suggest a Flavian phase (Old Kilpatrick, Bearsden, Balmuildy, Cadder, Mollins, Castlecary, Camelon, Mumrills).

To further support the fact that Tacitus may have been telling us that Agricola's predecessors had paved the way, we can look to another phrase later in the text: 'The third year of his campaigns opened up new tribes, our ravages on the native population being carried as far as the Taus, an estuary so called.'[4] Logic tells us that if the Roman force advances to the Tay and this opens up new tribes, then those south of the Tay cannot have been new tribes and must therefore have already been familiar to Rome. Beyond the Tay lay the Caledonii, occupying mainly what is now the Scottish Highlands; the Vacomagi along the eastern coast land; and the Taexali, covering Aberdeen and Speyside.

It is possible, then, based upon the find evidence, site structure, multiple phases, etc. that Frontinus not only pushed into Scotland, but built the first line of fortifications along the Forth/Clyde isthmus, and even continued it onto the Gask Ridge all the way to the River Tay at Perth. Currently, there is no evidence of a connection between the Gask Ridge and the Forth/Clyde line, with a lack of sites located between Glenbank and Camelon, but the likelihood is that the sites do exist and are yet waiting to be found. The terrain the line would follow is almost uniformly low farmland, and most signs may well have been ploughed out. While a conjectured site at West Plean has now been disproved (ironically just off Roman Road, south of Stirling), an enigmatic possibility remains Stirling itself, which lies exactly on the route between the two systems, roughly 10 miles from each, halfway along. Stirling has no recorded Roman settlement, but a stone was found on the hill in 1707, which has since sadly disappeared, inscribed with the legend IN EXCU AGIT LEG II, and in 1757 Maitland referred to a local Roman fort. A partially excavated Roman road in Stirling assumed to be Agricolan takes a route from the south to the lowest crossing point of the Forth. It may be that this road pre-dates Agricola. Stirling has ever been a critical crossing and so a Roman fort on the site might well be expected. It is thus possible that the Gask Ridge and the Forth/Clyde system were always meant to be one line, hinging at Camelon.

A quick glance at the map of the British tribes (map 7) will help reveal the lay of the land here. Rome already has control of the island as far as the northern edge of the Brigantes. Cerialis may have subdued the Selgovae as part of his conquest of Venutius's allies; the Votadini seem to have dealt favourably with Rome and there is no record of a campaign against them. The Novantae were somewhat peripheral and may have been ignored at this point, the Damnonii seem never to have been involved in a conflict, and the Venicones are quiet even when we learn of campaigns in their region. It may be that in the aftermath of the Brigantian war, Frontinus finds that the tribes to the north are far less belligerent than he expected. Rome does have a history of conquest by commercial and political annexation where possible, and perhaps treaties and agreements were all that were required for Frontinus to advance as far as the Tay. It is notable that the Forth/Clyde and Gask Ridge line, if they date to this time, neatly seal in those peaceful tribes behind a Roman frontier, with the fierce Caledonii and the unknown Taexali and Vacomagi on the far side. Perhaps Frontinus had in his tenure expanded Roman influence to cover the entire area up to the Forth/Clyde isthmus and the Tay, a massive accomplishment that, if true, history has forgotten, courtesy of Tacitus's glossing over in favour of his father-in-law.

Frontinus, then, departs the island in 77, having done more than most of his predecessors, leaving a highway into the north prepared for his successor. He goes on to a watery destiny writing his famous texts and overseeing aqueducts.

We have reached the end of our pre-Agricolan British journey. We have seen governors both military and civil, successful and less so. The fearsome Aulus Plautius, the cunning Ostorius Scapula, the quiet Didius Gallus, the evanescent Quintus Veranius, the druid-smashing Suetonius Paulinus, the nonentity Publius Turpilianus, the troubled Trebellius Maximus, the unsung Vettius Bolanus, the lunatic Petilius Cerialis and the surprising Sextus Frontinus. We have covered every incumbent in the rule of Britain from its invasion to the day we've been waiting for: Agricola's governorship.

But there remains one thing to be said before we move on. If one follows the Tacitan line of the governors of Britain, there is a hotchpotch of men of different capabilities, seemingly selected at random and with little connection among them.

If we now look back along the line we have explored you will hopefully see a growth, a plan, or even a domino effect taking place. Plautius invaded, Scapula subdued south Wales and created a border there so that Gallus could consolidate those gains. Veranius would press the Welsh advance based on the work of his predecessors, and Paulinus would use all of that to bring the whole of Wales under the Roman boot, though his achievements are a little cut short because of Boudicca. Turpilianus is ineffective due to the political and military situation in which he finds himself, but his successor, Trebellius, despite everything, hammers the Brigantes and begins the first moves into the north of Britain. Bolanus moves further north and lays down the foundations for the conquest of the north, Cerialis conquers the Brigantes using Bolanus's groundwork and sets out into Scotland. Frontinus creates a line of fortified advance into Scotland, and by the end of his tenure Rome can be fairly sure of peace and security all the way to the Forth/ Clyde corridor.

The conventional historical view is that the governors before Agricola gradually expand imperial control over Britain with varying degrees of success, but that it is under Cerialis that the Brigantes are subdued, and that it is not until Agricola that the real conquest of the north of Britain happens. Based on written and archaeological evidence it is looking increasingly likely that what we have examined thus far is closer to the truth: that Agricola may have conquered Scotland, but he was far from the first Roman there, and his achievements seem to have been based upon foundations already in place. He was, as they say, standing on the shoulders of giants. Map 6 illustrates the proposed sequence for the securing of territory by each successive governor.

For now, Frontinus is heading back to his aqueducts, and Agricola is bound for Britain.

9

VENI, VIDI, VICI

It was, according to Tacitus, midsummer when Agricola took ship for Britain to govern the unruly and troublesome island. Whatever our opinion of Tacitus's veracity, I think we can safely assume that he had left Rome with a remit from the emperor Vespasian to complete the conquest of Britain. This has to have been a cause close to the emperor's heart, given his personal associations with the island, and everything hints that Vespasian had personally selected Agricola for his military skill, his loyalty to the Flavian family, his old-fashioned and steady attitude to governance, but most of all for his now unparalleled (among his class, at least) familiarity with Britain and its peoples.

Opinion on Agricola's assignment is divided even now. Hoffman is of the opinion that he was an unlikely choice for governor of Britain, telling us 'Up to this point his mainly civilian career had been somewhat lacklustre,'[1] and 'the governorship [...] almost always went to one of the leading generals of the day. Yet this is something which Agricola, most emphatically, was not.'[2] Yet Grant, a scholar of the subject to rival Wooliscroft and Hoffman, disagrees, saying 'There is no doubt that Gnaeus Julius Agricola had excellent credentials for the post of governor of Britain.'[3]

For my part, I agree with Grant. Logic suggests that even if there were more appropriate choices for the position by rank or record, there was certainly no one *better* for it, and we might remember that Vespasian was himself far from a traditional patrician Roman, having come from a relatively low-born family in a rural area. His decisions as emperor are generally based upon need, logic, and expedience, rather than tradition and precedent. Hoffman's statement in that same passage that 'Cerialis (Governor 71–74) was possibly the most able general of his day' belies Cerialis's history of charging rashly into situations and as often incurring disaster as victory (though he had a reputation for getting the job done).

We know from later in Tacitus's account that Agricola brought his family with him, as he had done when posted as procurator to Asia, and probably also had as governor of Aquitania. We have already discussed the likelihood that Tacitus came with him, bound for a tribunate in the legions, most likely either the II Augusta or the Twentieth, both of whom Agricola would now have a personal connection with. The party would have arrived in Britain on the south coast and made for the capital, which has now been identified as London. Colchester had been the capital until the city was razed by Boudicca, and Museum of London Archaeology, investigating the recently discovered remains of a fort in the heart of London, have concluded that it was constructed immediately in the aftermath of the Iceni's defeat, and based upon this find, the reappraisal of a now-lost inscription from the city,[4] and the simple logic of commerce and positioning, suggest that London had by this time supplanted Colchester as the capital.

If Agricola set sail 'about midsummer', meaning towards the end of June, the best time a governor could realistically hope to make in reaching London would be just short of a month, and it is therefore likely that he arrived some time in July or August. The campaigning season had perhaps two or three months left at most, and with Frontinus's departure the legions and the auxilia would have returned to their winter quarters and taken up their garrison positions. Tacitus, in his more disparaging manner, tells us 'Our soldiers made it a pretext for carelessness, as if all fighting was over, and the enemy were biding their time,' though it seems likely they had done nothing more than retire for the end of the fighting season as usual. Tacitus is a master of spin, after all, and anything he can criticise to make Agricola look good he will, presumably as

The Ninth in York were too far away, as were the Second Augusta in Caerleon and the Second Adiutrix in Lincoln. By the time the message to march reached them and they moved, they would be too late to be of immediate use. So Agricola rode for his old unit, the Twentieth, who were based either in Wroxeter on the border of mid-Wales (which is current accepted wisdom) or just possibly at an early base at Chester (if my hypothesis of Agricola's foundation there under Cerialis and the archaeology of Deva proves correct). Either way, the Twentieth lay between Agricola and the Ordovices. Undoubtedly, numerous other auxiliary units were garrisoned close enough to call up, and we can safely assume based on material yet to come that Agricola gathered to his standard units of German cavalry. Tacitus tells us that 'He collected a force of veterans and a small body of auxiliaries'[5] which would correspond comfortably with the Twentieth and the local auxiliary garrisons. If Tacitus was assigned to Britain as a tribune at this time, it seems highly likely that he would have mirrored his father-in-law's history and been appointed to the general's staff. We will never know whether Tacitus was in Wales for this campaign or not, but the possibility cannot be ignored.

It is interesting to note that in 77 Agricola marched, newly arrived and late in the season, unexpectedly, against a Welsh tribe, and the man upon whom he may have modelled his self, Ostorius Scapula, had done exactly the same thirty years earlier, giving us yet another parallel between the two.

Of the campaign, Tacitus tells us only 'as the Ordovices did not venture to descend into the plain, he led his men up into the hills, marching in front himself so as to impart his own courage to the rest by sharing their danger, and cut to pieces almost the whole fighting force of the tribe'.[6]

Not precisely a detailed description. Tacitus seems to be telling us that Agricola led his troops out for a grand field engagement, couldn't get the Ordovices to come out to fight, and so had to lead his men into the Welsh uplands against them. Traditional Roman military wisdom was to attempt to draw the enemy into a grand pitched battle in the open, where Rome's tactics could be employed to the full. The Ordovices were having none of this, and who could blame them, having been so brutalised at the hands of Paulinus's army less than two decades earlier? We can perhaps identify the plain that the Ordovices would not descend to as the flat lands of the Deceangli, between the Ordovices and the Romans in Cheshire, or perhaps the Severn Valley in Shropshire, close to the fortress of Wroxeter. Thus we can see in either case how the Roman advance proceeded into the hills. If the Twentieth were still based in Wroxeter, then he arrived there from London, gathered the legion and the local auxiliary units and tried to lure the Ordovices down to battle. Then, with the enemy probably reeling at the unexpected arrival of this general and the beginning of a surprise campaign, and refusing to come down from their hills, he would have marched through Forden Gaer and Caersws up into what is now Snowdonia, conquering as he went. If the legion was already based at Chester, then the same situation would occur, but with the advance across the north of Wales instead and into the hills beyond the Conwy River.

Tacitus tells us that Agricola led his army from the front, something generals did not do, with odd exceptions like Caesar, and that he was truly successful. Some translations suggest that the tribe was almost exterminated, which have led to descriptions of 'genocide' by Agricola, and which sound like hyperbole, but it is worth recalling once again that stalwart in our tale, Ostorius Scapula, who had already said of the Silures that it might be better if they were exterminated right down to their name. While it seems unlikely that Agricola managed to exterminate an entire tribe, it is notable that the Ordovices disappear from written history at this point with no further mention, and so it is in fact possible that Tacitus is giving us the absolute truth. Certainly it seems likely that what Agricola did was to exterminate an entire generation of war-capable tribesfolk as in Handford and Mattingly's translation, leaving sufficient populace to continue the Ordovices but removing any possibility of them rising against Rome for generations. This is a faint echo of Caesar in Gaul, who is variously estimated to have killed over a million Gauls, or perhaps two-thirds of the population, resulting in such a disaster for the land that it took generations for the population and the economy to become viable once more. The severity of Agricola's campaign against the Ordovices is supported by the following line: 'The almost complete absence of relics of the 1ˢᵗ or 2ⁿᵈ centuries A.D. is characteristic of all sites in Caernarvonshire save of course Roman military works, and could be regarded as indicating a complete punitive clearance of the area.'[7] Moreover, the apparent rise of fortifications in North Wales, simultaneous with the diminishing signs of occupation, gives Tacitus further support.

'Well aware that he must follow up the prestige of his arms, and that in proportion to his first success would be the terror of the other tribes, he formed the design of subjugating the island of Mona, from the occupation of which Paulinus had been recalled.'[8]

Tacitus tells us, then, that having annihilated the Ordovices on the mainland, he knew he could not leave the job unfinished, and that if he wanted other tribes to fear rebellion enough to stay in line, he needed to make a further example of the Ordovices. Seventeen years earlier, Agricola had fought across these hills and mountains with Paulinus's army, probably alongside some of the older veterans in the Twentieth Legion with whom he now travelled. With that great general he had reached the coast, crossed the Menai Strait and conquered Anglesey. Unfortunately, the Iceni's revolt prevented them from garrisoning and consolidating Roman power in the region, which is perhaps what had led to this last gasp of Welsh rebellion. (Welsh friends of mine are now cursing me for the phrasing and citing Llewellyn and Owain Glyndwr, but I am referring to the period of Roman Britain here!)

To be able to leave Wales as a settled part of the province and move on to the north, Agricola needed to impose total control. The first step for this, then, was the renewed conquest of Mona, which was always to some extent the spiritual heartland of tribal Wales. Tacitus, for once not eulogising, tells us 'as his plans were not matured, he had no fleet.'[9] Tacitus is suggesting that lack of planning had left Agricola without ships to get to Anglesey, which seems highly unlikely. Agricola knew the area and precisely what he would need. However, there are several very good possible reasons for the fleet being unavailable at this juncture. Firstly, Agricola arrived in Britain, raced for North Wales picking up what troops he could as he went, and carried out a blitzkrieg campaign in the ensuing two months. It is more than possible that with the Classis Britannica being deployed around the south of the island, marshalling the navy and getting it to North Wales would have taken too long, and he simply did not have the time to do this before winter, so was forced to rely upon his land forces. Secondly, anyone who has sailed the Irish Sea in autumn (for instance to the Isle of Man on a ferry) will be fully aware of how wild and treacherous it can be. When combined with the dangerous rocky nature of the Welsh coast, this would be enough to put most sailors off attempting the voyage. A third possibility is that Agricola only intended to fight the Ordovices on the mainland, and that the attack on Mona was an afterthought, a direct consequence of his victory, and therefore what he had originally planned had not required naval support.

It may be that what Tacitus is actually telling us is that Agricola had planned for the fleet to be in the area but either he had moved too fast in his conquest or the fleet had moved too slowly and not arrived in time. Either way, Agricola arrived on the same stretch of land upon which he had stood seventeen years earlier, and once again had to cross without ships. It is tempting to imagine in this uncharacteristically negative line that this is Tacitus now talking from personal experience rather than second-hand accounts; that Tacitus the tribune found himself standing on the beach in North Wales with his father-in-law, kicking at pebbles while Agricola hurriedly put things into place to cross the water.

He goes on to tell us 'He carefully picked out from his auxiliaries men who had experience of shallow waters and had been trained at home to swim carrying their arms and keeping their horses under control, and made them discard all their equipment. He then launched them on a surprise attack; and the enemy, who had been thinking in terms of a fleet of ships and naval operations, were completely nonplussed.'[10]

There can be little doubt, given the description, that the auxiliaries Agricola took across the water are the same German cavalry units who had done so almost two decades earlier in the suppression of the druids. Our evidence for cavalry units in this era is scant, but in 103, just twenty-six years later, cavalry units attested in the area around Chester include the Ala Gallorum Petriana (from north-east Gaul and first attested in Germany) and the Ala I Tungrorum (formed of the Tungri from Germany).

As an interesting aside, in AD 103, a cavalry unit noted under the Caerleon command is that same Ala Gallorum Sebosiana that we know was connected with Agricola in Carlisle, and it may be that they also were part of Agricola's Mona invasion. Moreover, it is generally believed that eight cohorts of Batavian cavalry were part of Aulus Plautius's initial invasion force, and while some are attested in Germany during the Civilis revolt, we know that Agricola had four cohorts of them with him later, so it is reasonable to assume that there were at least four cohorts of Batavian cavalry stationed somewhere in Britain at this time.

An interesting alternative translation is provided by Birley, who says of Agricola's chosen auxiliaries that they were 'specially selected from those who knew the fords and whose national practice was to swim while carrying their weapons and controlling their horses'. This not only suggests those German cavalry units, but also intimates that they were familiar with the area. Ogilvie and Richmond note that 'It is in fact possible to ford the straits on foot over Caernarvon Bar at certain conditions of low tide [...] but not at Bangor or elsewhere.'[11] Tacitus continually thrusts at us huge events tied up in bundles of just a few words, such as the entire campaign against the Ordovices on the mainland in one short sentence, and yet here we are receiving details on an unexpected level that have no great effect on the narrative, and I am once more inclined to take these small details as potential proof of Tacitus's personal presence during the events.

So, leaving his legionaries on the mainland and using only auxiliaries (something we might remember Scapula doing against the Iceni), Agricola crossed to Anglesey and conquered the island with seemingly little effort. Certainly, Tacitus does not regale us with a bloodthirsty blow-by-blow account.

The archaeology and history of Roman Anglesey is thin, but a recent discovery might point to the aftermath of Agricola's campaign. Having once again conquered Wales, Agricola set about doing what Paulinus had been prevented from doing by the revolt of Boudicca: setting up a military network to maintain control of the area (see map 8 and the listing below).

Caernarfon	Dated to 77 or shortly thereafter based on finds evidence
Caerhun	Dated to 75 of after based upon finds, inc. many coins
Cefn Gaer	Tentatively dated to the era based upon pottery and small finds
Tomen Y Mur	Dated to the era based upon Samian ware finds
Pen Llystyn	Finds suggest an occupation of *c.* 78–88
Caer Gai	Turf bank dated *c.* 75–80, supported by finds
Brithdir	Early polygonal enclosure dated to *c.* 75
Bryn Y Gefeiliau	Pottery dating to *c.* 90, but positioning on road between other sites suggests contemporaneity
Cemlyn Bay	Unexcavated and only recently discovered, but currently the only pre-third/fourth-century site yet found on Anglesey

In several areas of Britain the late Flavian era sees the foundation of a network of forts, supply sites, roads, ports and signal stations that forms the basis for the infrastructure of Roman Britain right through to the fifth century, and this network in North Wales is a prime example of that first step.

Tacitus goes on to hurl compliments at his father-in-law at a stomach-churning pace, all revolving around Agricola's modesty and his lack of pomp and glory over his victory. Once more we are reminded that this is a eulogy and a political statement at least as much as a history or a biography, and it sets the modern scholar's teeth on edge to watch earth-changing events pass in a brief sentence only to be followed by an entire paragraph on what a humble victor the man was.

Still, the sudden half-season of war was now over, and the army would be settled once more into winter quarters with sufficient garrison left across the newly controlled region of North Wales to prevent any recurrence of revolt. With no further threats to the peace of the province, Agricola would be free to return to London and see to the civil administration.

Tacitus tells us 'Next, with thorough insight into the feelings of his province, and taught also, by the experience of others, that little is gained by conquest if followed by oppression, he determined to root out the causes of war.'[12] There can be little doubt that this is a reference not only to his own recently completed campaign, but also to the Boudiccan revolt. Agricola would have seen first-hand the revolt, would have known how the entire disaster had unfolded, and seen the after-effects. Moreover, he had served under a corrupt governor in Asia, and had later controlled his own peaceful province. His 'experience' and 'insight' must have been impressive. Clearly Agricola was concerned that having arrived and immediately suppressed a tribe, teaching a lesson to all those who might consider violence against the Roman garrisons, he needed now to temper the lesson by showing the people what there was to be gained by accepting the Pax Romana.

The 'causes of war' we have already considered, in the possible identity of the cavalry unit the Ordovices had destroyed, but there may be another cause, linked to the grain supply, which we will examine more closely. Agricola was new to the province and needed to take the reins immediately, stamping his own style of governance on Britain. That winter, Tacitus tells us in the form of another river of praise: 'he kept his household under restraint [...] He transacted no public business through freedmen or slaves; no private leanings, no recommendations or entreaties of friends, moved him in the selection of centurions and soldiers, but it was ever the best man whom he thought most trustworthy. He knew everything, but did not always act on his knowledge. Trifling errors he treated with leniency, serious offences with severity. Nor was it always punishment, but far oftener penitence, which satisfied him. He preferred to give office and power to men who would not transgress, rather than have to condemn a transgressor. He lightened the exaction of corn and tribute by an equal distribution of the burden, while he got rid of those contrivances for gain which were more intolerable than the tribute itself. Hitherto the people had been compelled to endure the farce of waiting by the closed granary and of purchasing corn unnecessarily and raising it to a fictitious price. Difficult byroads and distant places were fixed for them, so that states with a winter-camp close to them had to carry corn to remote and inaccessible parts of the country, until what was within the reach of all became a source of profit to the few.'[13]

Keeping his 'household under restraint' applies to more than merely his own house. What we are being told is that Agricola kept the provincial administration under restraint, a lesson learned from the errors of Catus Decianus in the case of Boudicca. We are told that he does not give away commands for bribes and favours, which is above and beyond the simple cause of decency, since almost certainly not only he, but everyone upon whom he relied, had been granted their position through some form of nepotism or purchase. Likely this is glossing over the truth, especially if Tacitus was present as a tribune because his father-in-law had taken him along to Britain. Here, I think we need to use common sense to divine whether Tacitus is giving us the 'straight dope' or embellishing to make his subject look good. However, there is something telling here in that Tacitus clearly states Agricola selected the men most trustworthy for the job, an echo of that we have already seen in the Flavian emperor who assigned him to the province.

We are told that Agricola prefers the carrot and stick approach to the whip; that he prefers to reward success rather than punish failure. The truth of this is hard to divine, but we have no real reason to doubt it, especially given that this is exactly what we have seen in the conquest of Mona followed by a carefully just administration. The attitude fits with the man who settled the mutinous Twentieth seven years earlier.

There is next an intimation that something was wrong with the grain supply and distribution in the province, something that is often cited as a cause for dissent in the provinces, and even in Rome itself under the reign of Commodus. Perhaps this, then, is the result of Agricola's rooting out the causes of war. We are told in the text that some areas of the province were remote and were not receiving sufficient grain, and that one of the things Agricola set to in his first winter was building and repairing roads to these remote parts to ease the problem. Road construction was one of the regular tasks of soldiers over their garrison time. It is just possible that what we are being told here is that the original cause for the Ordovices rising and massacring a garrison was because they were starving. The Ordovices occupied the Welsh highlands and their arable land was scarce, barring newly ravaged Anglesey. Likely they had earlier traded with the Deceangli on the Cheshire plain, but with the wars, the installation of Scapula's fort line

Roman soldiers clearing forest for a road, image from Trajan's column. (Author's collection)

keeping them from the flat lands, and the imposition of troops, perhaps their earlier systems were no longer adequate.

It is not hard to imagine the Twentieth Legion out of either Wroxeter or Chester spending their winter constructing the known Roman road across North Wales from Chester to Caernarfon via Caerhun. This would be a prime example of the sort of road that would grant access to 'inaccessible parts'. The removal of corruption in the sale and distribution of grain and a reorganisation to ensure sufficient food reached all the population would go a long way to ensuring ongoing peace and preventing any further risings. After all, Agricola had been sent to complete the conquest of Britain, and he knew how easily such plans could be derailed by unexpected revolts.

An interesting find might shed some light upon the sort of corruption of which we are speaking. A modius, or bronze grain measure, was unearthed at Carvoran on the Stanegate in 1915. It dates from the reign of Domitian, some time just after Agricola's tenure, in the 90s, but it is a fascinating insight into the Roman grain system, for the capacity of the modius is different to the measure inscribed upon it. There are various theories as to the reason for this, but the most clear and likely one is that this official military measure, which would probably have been used in the gathering of grain from locals, was designed to cheat the populace into paying higher grain taxes. Was this the sort of institutionalised corruption that Agricola sought to put a stop to?

His first winter as governor is summarised by Tacitus thus: 'Agricola, by the repression of these abuses in his very first year in office, restored to peace its good name.'[14]

10

HOC EST BELLUM

'But when the summer came he concentrated his army and took the field in person. He was present everywhere on the march, praising good discipline and keeping stragglers up to the mark. He himself chose sites for camps and reconnoitred estuaries and forests; and all the time he gave the enemy no rest, but constantly launched plundering raids. Then, when he had done enough to inspire fear, he tried the effect of clemency and showed them the attraction of peace. As a result, many states which till then had maintained their independence gave hostages and abandoned their resentful attitude. A ring of garrisoned forts was placed around them; and so skilfully and thoroughly was the operation carried through that no British tribes ever made their first submission with so little interference from their neighbours.'[1]

Agricola wastes no time, then, in his first full campaigning season in Britain. We have no direct geographical indications of where these campaigns take place, but the clues are there in the text nonetheless. Tacitus tells us that this campaign involves tribes which 'till then had maintained their independence', and we have seen the conquest so far of every tribe as far north as the Brigantes, and more than a little contact has been suggested with the tribes north of them.

The Brigantes' lands extended into Northumberland and the southern reaches of the Scottish Borders, and we have evidence that Roman installations were in place at Carlisle and probably therefore on the future Stanegate line to Beaufront Red House near Corbridge by at least AD 73. We can safely assume on this basis that Agricola's campaigns in 78 took place north of this line.

Without wishing to skip ahead, Tacitus tells us in the next year's narrative that Agricola reaches the Tay, and so we can be fairly certain that wherever he campaigned in this year, it was sufficiently south of the Tay to not include that river in the text. A quick glance at the disposition of the British tribes (map 7) gives us a clue as to perhaps where the campaigns reached.

North of the Brigantes, the land is divided into three roughly even tribal groups: the Votadini to the east, the Selgovae in the centre and the Novantae to the west. North of them all lay the Damnonii, occupying the narrow isthmus of the Forth/Clyde line. Any tribal conquests north of the latter would bring Agricola to the Tay, and so it can only realistically be these three tribes to which we must turn, and perhaps the southern reaches of the Damnonii.

Tacitus is likely being careful here with his descriptions. At no point in the above quote does he tell us that the lands, nations and tribes to which Agricola turns are *new* to Rome, which is how the text is often viewed. He tells us only that these nations had 'maintained their independence'. This does not necessarily deny Roman dominion or even the presence of garrisons. After all, the Brigantes had spent decades being independent as a client kingdom of Rome, even when Scapula and Bolanus had campaigned among them. The Iceni had been nominally a client kingdom even with legions based on their borders. Thus we cannot rule out a campaign against the Votadini, the Selgovae, the Novantae and the Damnonii simply because they had already been encountered during previous governorships.

Did Agricola simply begin to conquer north because his remit was to complete the conquest of the island? The answer is, of course, probably yes. Tacitus does not tell us anything of the sort, since he is in the business of eulogising the man, but a conquest-based motivation is too likely to be ignored. The island to the south of these tribes was now settled. Under Cerialis, they had initiated a network that had kept the Brigantes quiet for the first time in decades, and Frontinus and Agricola had, between them, done the same to Wales. There was precious little chance of a revolt across the province, and so Agricola would feel free to concentrate his advance north, as his predecessors had done.

Tacitus only obliquely gives us any reasoning for the campaign. He tells us they displayed a 'resentful attitude', and infers that there was 'interference' from their neighbours. Sounds like a flimsy excuse for war, in truth, yet even in the modern world wars have been fought over less. After all, just over a century earlier, Julius Caesar had used the Helvetii's journey west into Gallic lands as an excuse to begin an eight-year campaign of conquest that would leave the whole of Gaul in Roman hands.

Of the four tribes mentioned above, the general assumption is that the Votadini (in Northumberland, Berwickshire and East Lothian, with a suspected capital at Traprain Law) remained at peace with Rome throughout the period – they likely accepted the usual deal of maintaining their tribal nature in return for the status of client kingdom. There have been no signs of warfare found within Votadini lands, and there are hardly any Roman installations, notably only Learchild fort, temporary camps at Norham and East Learmouth, and a suspected fort and harbour that has never been located at Berwick-upon-Tweed. Only two roads have been identified in their lands, and Roman coinage of good quality has been found at native sites suggesting a level of trade and contact. Simply, there is no sign that the Votadini were ever campaigned against.

A similar story emerges for the Novantae, isolated in the Galloway region. There are signs there of Roman occupation, but they remain few and far between, and are almost certainly connected with events further along in Tacitus's narrative. What we might infer, then, is that the Novantae were of little bother or interest.

Given the apparent absence of trouble with either of these tribes, it seems highly likely that in earlier years it *had* been the Selgovae in the centre who had supported Venutius and his rebel Brigantes and had been trampled in response by Roman reprisals. The simple number of temporary camps (which cannot easily be dated) surrounding Selgovae lands is suggestive of more than one season of campaigns. Would the Selgovae fit the bill for Tacitus's description? Yes, they would. On the reasonable assumption that they had been the allies of the Brigantes to whom Venutius had fled and whom Cerialis had made war against in the aftermath while bringing down the king, there are more than adequate grounds for a certain resentment among the tribe. Given that there is reasonable evidence to suggest that as well as the temporary camps that had been created in their lands, the fort at Newstead, on their eastern fringe, had been occupied either intermittently or constantly ever since, we can perhaps understand said resentment.

It is not unreasonable to suggest that the Selgovae had in recent years begun to impose their will by force upon their neighbours to either side, and possibly the edges of the now-settled Brigantes to the south. This would certainly be adequate excuse for Agricola to lead his armies north. Despite the usual lack of detail in Tacitus's account it is reasonable to assume that Agricola, now leading a gathered army, made war primarily upon the Selgovae. Of the army he led we can perhaps identify three legions and assume sundry other auxiliaries.

At this stage the Second Augusta was installed in Caerleon and from there was capable of controlling Wales and the south-west. The south-east and central England were peaceful and no legionary presence would be expected to be needed there. The Ninth remained in York, so it is highly probable that this legion, or at least a sizeable portion of it, was involved in Agricola's push north. The evidence suggests that the II Adiutrix was based in Chester at this time. There is a strong belief that the Second were the original constructors of Chester's fortress and that this occurred *c.* AD 75. However, given that they were only a decade old as a unit and had been raised from sailors and marines, their construction skills might not be expected to be as good as the other legions, and so it seems reasonable to assume that the Twentieth constructed the fortress from their nearby base at Wroxeter, and the Second came in to garrison it later, perhaps building the associated port, the remains of which can be seen on the Roodee racecourse. The II Adiutrix, then, was now based at Chester, the perfect place for a major military harbour and the presence of a legion with maritime experience. We can assume that at least part of the II Adiutrix was also taken along to the northern campaign. Finally the Twentieth, Agricola's old legion: they may have been nominally based at this time in Wroxeter, but the likelihood is that the Twentieth formed the core of Agricola's army in the north, supported by the Ninth, and with the Second acting as a liaison unit with the fleet as the ships kept pace with the northern moves along the coast. It is worthwhile noting here that there is no reason to expect a full legion to remain in garrison. Though the common image of the Roman army is of full legions on the march to war, evidence suggests a much different picture, that it was common for legions to be split into vexillations most of the time, and so it is not unlikely that a few cohorts of the Ninth, Second and Twentieth remained in their home fortresses as a constant reminder of Roman authority for the locals.

It is more than likely that Agricola took some of his favoured German cavalry auxiliaries with him also. We know they were present in the coming years, and so there is no reason to doubt their active participation in this period.

What of the campaign itself? All we know from Tacitus is that the army raided the natives repeatedly, built camps, and moved through terrain with forests and estuaries. This neatly sums up the landscape between Carlisle and the Clyde/Forth and supports the idea of a campaign here. Forest still does cover large swathes of land, and estuaries are numerous on the north coast of the Solway Firth and in coastal Northumberland.

The fort sites indicating potential Agricolan occupation and the number of temporary camps located in Northumberland and the Borders is huge. A look at any map of Roman Britain (I have provided one – map 9 – specifically aimed at this campaign, but for a large and detailed map for further study, I highly recommend the Ordnance Survey Map of Roman Britain for the task) helps us identify the possible progress of the campaign. The heart of Selgovae lands consists of the hard terrain of the Cheviot Hills, and understandably signs of occupation are rare. To either side, though, running along the edge of Selgovae territory, are parallel sequences of Roman activity, clusters of camps, forts, fortlets and roads, following more or less the modern routes of the A68 and the M74.

While it has to be recognised that these two lines form the main corridors from south to north, and would therefore naturally be

Swine Hill temporary camp in Selgovae territory, possibly dating to Agricolan campaigns and giving an impression of the terrain involved. (Author's collection)

maintained and controlled throughout all future periods of Roman occupation, it is of interest that they coincidentally also follow the borders that separate the Selgovae from their neighbours to both east and west. It is possible that beneath the centuries-old strata of activity on those two routes, in the early days of Roman Britain their purpose was to separate the tribes.

This hints at a continuation of Cerialis's purported policy of 'divide and rule'. Separating the troublesome Selgovae from the largely untouched Novantae and the allied Votadini would be an important step in controlling the region. We are told, though, that the campaign involved *states*, or *tribes*, in the plural, and so we can perhaps see some raiding into the lands of the Novantae here. Most likely the action of 78 pressed on north of the Selgovae and involved the Damnonii. Evidence of campaigns in the region are sporadic, but it is hard to be certain what might have occurred in early days, since the area was to later host the Antonine Wall and all its support installations, and so Antonine and Severan use might have obliterated numerous signs of Agricola campaigning here.

We are also told that once the campaigns were completed as autumn came around, the tribes had been subdued and were about as ready as any tribe in British history to accept Roman control and pay their taxes. We are told, moreover, that Agricola does precisely what Cerialis is believed to have done with the Carvetii and the Parisi. He rings them with garrisoned forts to maintain peace and control. This would be the last activity of the campaign season before winter set in.

The evidence lends a great deal of support to the notion that Agricola's campaign of 78 reached the Forth/Clyde line and divided up and ringed in the tribes between there and civilised Carlisle. A look at map 9, in conjunction with the following table, shows the installations for which there is at least some kind of evidence that they were were occupied at this time by Agricola's army, along with the known temporary camps that lie between Hadrian's Wall and the Antonine Wall. It is easy to see the rings of forts surrounding the Selgovae and their neighbours, and the evidence of what we have discerned of the year's campaign.

Ambleside	Collingwood reported an earlier fort beneath the first phase of extant site, which was dated c. 90
Beattock	Dated Agricolan through presence of 'Stracathro' gateways
Binchester	Early turf rampart dated c. 75
Birrens	'undisturbed stratigraphy' (RCAHMS Eastern Dumfriesshire) under Hadrianic layer suggests Flavian occupation
Blennerhasset	Dated to early Flavian period based on pottery finds
Bowes	Early timber phase dated to Agricola
Broomholm	Two noted Flavian phases
Brough	Pottery indicates a possible Flavian origin
Brough on Humber	Earliest phase believed to date to early Flavian period on the site of an earlier native settlement.
Brougham	Collingwood suggested the presence of a first-century phase beneath the later fort
Burrow in Lonsdale	Turf and timber defences found beneath stone fort, with first-century pottery located, suggesting a possible early Flavian foundation

Cappuck	Two Flavian phases noted in excavation
Carlisle	Extant now for five years
Castle Greg	Fortlet dated to Flavian era on coins
Castledykes	Dated Agricolan through presence of 'Stracathro' gateways
Catterick	Coin and pottery evidence for Flavian date
Cawthorne	Flavian dates have been attached to the fort and one of the temporary camps here
Chester	Extant. Now occupied by II Adiutrix
Corbridge Red House	Early Flavian site, generally attributed to Agricola
Crawford	Dated to early Agricolan by finds
Dalswinton	Four noted Flavian phases
Ebchester	Flavian phase noted beneath Hadrianic fort
Elginhaugh	Dated to 78/79 based on finds, especially mint condition coins
Eshiels	Dated Agricolan through presence of 'Stracathro' gateways
Glenlochar	Two early phases, including Flavian, noted
Greta Bridge	Single sherd of Flavian pottery
High Rochester	Two Flavian phases noted in excavation
Ilkley	Coin finds suggest Agricolan date
Kirkby Thore	Dated to Flavian era on coins
Kirkham	Flavian pottery dating the earlier of two fort phases
Lancaster	Finds of early Flavian period indicate a possible date for the first phase of the fort. Inscription of the Ala Sebosiana gives an Agricolan link
Lanchester	No evidence as yet discovered for first-century construction, but Claudian coins found suggest potential early occupation, and positioning between Binchester and Ebchester supports that. Possibly an earlier site lies somewhere nearby, as yet unidentified
Learchild	Dated as Flavian on pottery finds
Lease Rigg	Pottery dated from the early Flavian era suggests a fort of that period
Low Borrowbridge	Postholes and pottery evidence suggest an early Flavian date for the first phase of the fort
Malton	Flavian finds usually attributed to Agricolan establishment
Manchester	Assumed Agricolan based on coin finds
Milton	Two noted Flavian phases

Nether Denton	Evidence currently places it *c.* 84, but positioning in relation to Carlisle and Corbridge Red House suggests a slightly earlier date
Netherby	No evidence but assumed to be Agricolan from river crossing position
Newstead	Confidently dated now as extant with possible Agricolan occupation phase
Northwich	First phase determined as Flavian
Oakwood	Dated Agricolan based on form of gateways and ditches
Papcastle	Flavian coins suggest an early date for the fort
Piercebridge	Flavian finds in the vicus indicate it may pre-date the extant fort, suggesting an undiscovered earlier site, or perhaps the nearby Holmes House site
Ribchester	Earliest fort shows two pre-Trajanic phases interpreted as both Flavian based on finds. High probability that the second is Agricolan
Roecliffe	Extant from the campaigns of Cerialis
Slack/Outlane	Dated c.79 by finds during excavation
Vindolanda	Evidence currently places it *c.* 84, but positioning in relation to Carlisle and Corbridge Red House suggests a slightly earlier date
Whitby?	While no Roman site has yet been identified at Whitby, it sits at the assumed terminus of a road linking Flavian forts and would be a natural harbour. It may be the noted installation of Dictum
Woodhead	Dated Agricolan through presence of 'Stracathro' gateways
York	Extant. Occupied by IX Hispana

In addition to the campaign area north of the Solway/Tyne line, the map also shows the network of forts by this time in existence across the lands of the Brigantes, for there is evidence of new Agricolan foundations throughout this region also. This would suggest that as well as ringing the newly conquered lands to the north, he also refurbished and reworked the network of forts controlling Brigantian territory initially put in place by Cerialis while Agricola served with the Twentieth.

It is perhaps at this time that Dere Street (aka the 'Great North Road' or the A1/A68) is first begun, as well as the Stanegate.

Davies suggests that since 'Agricola was campaigning north of the River Tay by AD 80, so it seems likely that both east and west coast roads were under construction, at least through Northern England, and probably into Scotland, by this date.'[2] His statement is, of course, thoroughly dependent upon Tacitus giving us accurate information, and Bishop disagrees, dating the road to some time after AD 85 based largely upon its relationship to the site at Corbridge.[3] Of course, this assumes that the route remained in the same form throughout the period, and Bishop does also postulate a 'proto-Dere Street' that would connect such sites as Red House and Roecliffe, possibly even as far back as Cerialis. The upshot is that given the level of campaigns we may now have identified north of York and Chester in the space of eighteen years, the notion that there had never been an attempt to install an arterial road system to the north is difficult to credit.

The campaigning season over, Agricola retires from the war zone. In a year and a half on the island, if our appraisal of Tacitus

The 'Devil's Arrows' at Boroughbridge, which likely mark the line of a pre-Roman trackway that Agricola could have re-used to found his 'proto-Dere Street'. (Author's collection)

is correct, he has finally put to rest the trouble with Wales and imposed the Pax Romana there, and extended full control of territory from the Solway/Tyne isthmus to the Forth/Clyde line. No small achievement.

Winter for a governor of a province like Britain brought an end to hostilities and an opportunity to concentrate on the civil administration. Tacitus tells us: 'The following winter passed without disturbance, and was employed in salutary measures. For, to accustom to rest and repose through the charms of luxury a population scattered and barbarous and therefore inclined to war, Agricola gave private encouragement and public aid to the building of temples, courts of justice and dwelling-houses, praising the energetic, and reproving the indolent. Thus an honourable rivalry took the place of compulsion. He likewise provided a liberal education for the sons of the chiefs, and showed such a preference for the natural powers of the Britons over the industry of the Gauls that they who lately disdained the tongue of Rome now coveted its eloquence. Hence, too, a liking sprang up for our style of dress, and the "toga" became fashionable. Step by step they were led to things which dispose to vice, the lounge, the bath, the elegant banquet. All this in their ignorance they called civilisation, when it was but a part of their servitude.'[4]

It is interesting to note in his treatment of this year how Tacitus's description of the campaign is brief and uninformative, yet his explanation of the events of the winter are much more detailed. If we were to assume that Tacitus was in Britain still, then perhaps he spent the year of 78 engaged in more civil duties in the province, rather than campaigning with his father-in-law in the north.

We are told, then, that Agricola spends his winter in an effort to essentially Romanise the peoples of Britain; that building projects abounded, encouraged by him and with official aid, which might refer to funding, or possibly the aid of the legions who were experts at construction.

Evidence of building projects at this time is more readily available than one might think. One of the few pieces of clear written evidence of Agricola outside of Tacitus is the inscription discovered in shattered pieces at Verulamium (St Albans). The inscription refers to the rebuilding of the Forum and has been reconstructed to read:

[IMP TITO CAESARI DIVI] VESPA[SIANI]
F VES[PASIANO AUG]
[P M TR P VIIII IMP XV COS VII] DESI[G VIII CENSORI
PATRI PATRIAE]
[[ET CAESARI DIVI VESPASIANI F DOMITIANO COS
VI DESIG VII PRINCIPI]]
[[IVVENTVTIS ET OMNIVM COLLEGIORVM
SACERDOTI]]
[CN IVLIO A]GRIC[OLA LEGATO AUG PRO] PR
[MVNICIPIVM] VE[RVLAMIVM BASILICA OR]NATA

Which translates as:

> For the Emperor Titus Caesar Vespasian Augustus, son of
> the deified Vespasian, Pontifex Maximus, in the ninth year
> of tribunician power, acclaimed Imperator fifteen times,
> having been consul seven times, designated consul for an
> eighth time, censor, Father of the Fatherland, and to Caesar
> Domitian, son of the deified Vespasian, having been consul
> six times, designated consul for a seventh term, Prince of
> Youth, and member of all the priestly brotherhoods, when
> Gnaeus Julius Agricola was legate of the emperor with
> pro-praetorian power, the Verulamium basilica was adorned.

The inscription can be very firmly dated. It names Titus as the
emperor, which narrows the time to between AD 79 and 81, but
it also tells us that Titus had been designated consul for an eighth
time, which suggests the inscription was made early in the year 80,
after the consuls had been decided but before Titus had taken it up
(he had been consul for the seventh time in 79).

While this puts the inscription early in AD 80, up to a year
and a half after this building spree we are considering, it must
be remembered how much work would be required to rebuild
something on the scale of a city forum. St Albans had been
destroyed by Boudicca eighteen years earlier, and was clearly still
being rebuilt and enhanced. Likely the forum had already been
being reconstructed for some time before Agricola's governorship,
over a period of several years, but now the work was almost

finished. There is further evidence of building in the period at St Albans. Niblett has a refurbished baths dating from this period, as well as a macellum (market) and a large number of private and public buildings.[5] A large temple occupying an entire insula of the city dates to the Flavian era.

Given that there is evidence of massive construction in St Albans in the period, we can perhaps assume that in addition to the remit to conquer the island, Agricola had also been given specific instructions to rebuild the cities that had been destroyed during the revolt (an instruction that may also have been given to Frontinus earlier). As such it is likely that Agricola also oversaw work on both Colchester and London.

Construction was not restricted to these needy cities, though. Mazurek notes that the civitas capitals of Dorchester, Exeter, Leicester and Wroxeter seem to date from the Flavian era.[6] Niblett also notes that at Braughing the road network seems to have been overhauled in this period, as well as seeing the construction of fine masonry buildings and baths.[7] Later first-century structures have also been identified at Caerwent, Cirencester, Exeter and Wroxeter among others. From the period of 75 onwards she also notes the foundation of a number of modest villas in Hertfordshire, including Latimer, Northchurch, Boxmoor and Kings Langley, which is indicative of a move to a more Roman way of life in rural areas as well as in the cities.

There is little we can look for beyond the archaeology of constructions to confirm or deny what Tacitus tells us of this winter. Statues and images of people from the period in Britain are extremely rare and are often Celtic images that are far more stylised than illuminating. Statues of lumpy, misshapen people in formless smocks, often with demonic eyes and clubs, are hardly likely to clear up to what extent the toga was becoming a garment of choice.

It is telling that Tacitus describes the natives as preferring the Roman language and the toga. The toga was, of course, only worn by officials and the upper classes, and so what Tacitus is actually telling us is of a shift in favour of Roman style among that level of native who was going to benefit most from it, rather than Johnny farmhand who would have to work his whole life just to afford a toga. Tacitus, if he was there at the time, would have socialised with the upper classes during that winter, and so he can only tell us what they favoured. There was, of course, a long tradition of Rome currying favour among powerful natives to help in annexing an area. Caesar did much the same. There is nothing new in Tacitus's description, then, just what had been happening with native tribes for centuries. Moreover, the Romanised education for chieftains' sons was an old ploy, training the future leaders of tribes to think like a Roman. This does occasionally backfire, of course, as with the case of the German prince Arminius who betrayed his Roman patrons and led three legions to their doom in the Teutoburg Forest. Still, the policy was generally sound.

Another point of interest in connection with this policy of Romanisation comes from the impressive collection of the Vindolanda tablets. These written records were discovered in 1973 outside the eponymous Roman fort. They date from the late first century into the second and cover a vast variety of topics from official to personal, from demands for missing cartloads of leatherwork to requests for mum to send more socks. Lying preserved under a charred heap, they had been part of the common disposal of documents by the fort's staff, but the conditions had preserved the lower strata and for forty years now they have been being painstakingly translated. Of interest to us is the high number of names among them that include the element 'Flavius'. Given the tablets' dating, this indicates a large number of auxiliary soldiers that were enfranchised during the Flavian era, which points to an explosion of settlement and Romanisation of the region.

One thing of note here is how disparaging Tacitus becomes. He pours scorn on the natives for how easily they are swayed by the comforts of Roman life away from their native pride. Indeed, his last line 'All this in their ignorance they called civilisation, when it was but a part of their servitude' is thoroughly damning, and other translations use slavery instead of servitude. This perhaps once again hints at a touch of personal involvement for Tacitus.

The year of 78 ends, then, with successful campaigning in the north and a major push for the Romanisation of the province. This follows what we have seen in Agricola more than once already: the iron fist of the general laying down Roman dominion followed by the velvet glove to smooth things over.

II

AD VICTORIAM

The year AD 79 brings new challenges in Britain, but while we concentrate on Agricola's activity on the island, it is worth taking a moment to recall that there is a greater empire at work beyond the Channel, for events in that empire inevitably influence the island's history.

Since AD 69, for a decade the Julio-Claudian dynasty has been over, and the empire has settled once more from civil war into the steady and advantageous reign of the Flavian dynasty. While Vespasian has ever been held up as one of the best of Rome's crop of emperors, history is written by the victors, and there are hints visible through the cracks in the veneer of benevolence that indicate Vespasian was not only shrewd but sometimes draconian in his handling of dissent. In fact, Vespasian seems to have been the best master of 'spin' since Augustus. Still, there can be no comparing him with what came before, he had clearly been a breath of fresh air after the reigns of the Julio-Claudians. Agricola had served his political and military career under Nero and Vespasian, and all the senior posts under the latter. He was tied to the Flavians as closely as many who were related to the dynasty.

For two years now Agricola had pursued a policy of conquest and expansion in Britain that was fitting with what Vespasian undoubtedly wanted for the island. AD 79, though, brings momentous events. Not just the eruption of Vesuvius and the burial of Pompeii under ash, of course, though that likely had an oblique effect, but more particularly, the change of emperors. On 24 June, Vespasian, now an old man, died from a protracted illness, and as everyone expected from this dynasty, Titus, the eldest son, successful general and heir groomed for the position, took the throne. One might not immediately see why this matters, since they were of the same family it was a peaceful succession, and Agricola was close to both men, but there are factors that influence the events in Britain that year.

The campaigning season came around in March, and Agricola prepared for another year of warfare. It seems reasonable to assume that the core of his force was the Twentieth Legion, probably with the bulk of the Ninth and the Second Adiutrix. The first two of those legions were at this point likely split for winter between installations around the northern fringe of Roman territory, in Northumberland and the Scottish Borders, perhaps with a command centre at Newstead or Carlisle. The Second Augusta could maintain peace in the south easily enough.

Of this season Tacitus tells us firstly 'The third year of his campaigns opened up new tribes, our ravages on the native population being carried as far as the Taus, an estuary so called.'[1] This 'ravaging' is confirmed by Cassius Dio, who says 'Meanwhile war had again broken out in Britain, and Gnaeus Julius Agricola overran the whole of the enemy's territory there.'[2]

A strong start, then. Dio tends to blur his chronology and condense information, most of which would be based upon Tacitus anyway, and his phrasing likely takes into account more than one season, but still between the two sources we are given a straightforward impression. The campaigning season begins, and Agricola gathers his legions and auxilia and pushes on, conquering, ravaging and battling the peoples outside imperial control.

Specifically, Tacitus tells us that Agricola ravaged as far as the Taus, which has been convincingly identified as the River Tay. If we consider the line of Roman garrisons and control over the winter to have been somewhere in the Scottish Borders, this is a significant increase of territory. It is not new land to Rome, if earlier estimations based upon archaeology are correct. Cerialis may well have campaigned in these lands before and even built outposts, and if not he, then very likely Frontinus. A system of watch stations and posts along the Gask Ridge was almost certainly in existence by this time. But there is a difference. Earlier governors, if they had reached the Tay, had done so as part of temporary campaigns with specific purposes. Agricola is here to conquer. Rome is now here to stay.

We know of only two tribes between that region in which Agricola must have campaigned the previous year and the Tay: the Damnonii, occupying the lands around the Forth/Clyde isthmus, and the Venicones, who dominated the region of Fife. The Venicones seem to have enjoyed a relatively peaceful relationship with Rome, from the lack of military archaeological evidence and scarcity of sites, and if there was any 'ravaging' done against them, it must have been on a minor scale to secure their lands within the province. What Agricola may have done, then, is to spend the first part of the campaigning season of 79 conquering the Damnonii which, if he also now had control of the lands of the Venicones, gave Rome all the good arable land and easy terrain as far as the Tay and the edge of the Highlands. Two more tribes had been brought within the empire and Tacitus tells us then that reaching the Tay opened up new tribes.

Beyond the Tay and the natural border of the Highlands lay the Caledonii, the Taexali and the Vacomagi, and it seems likely that the new tribes referred to here are the first two of those, the Caledonii to the east in the Highlands and the Vacomagi in the flat lands north of the Tay. It may be that the Taexali and the Vacomagi were to some extent part of the Caledonii, who seem to have been more of a confederation of tribes, much like the Brigantes. The fact that Tacitus uses no tribal names and simply refers to them as the tribes of Caledonia supports this notion, and it is only from Roman geographers that we get the individual names of such peoples, so forgive me if I often lump these all together as the tribes of Caledonia. (Caledonia's been everything I've ever had...)

Tacitus goes on to tell us 'This struck such terror into the enemy that he did not dare to attack our army, harassed though it was by violent storms.'[3] Since Agricola is 'ravaging' the tribes to the south of the Tay, we can naturally assume that they are attempting to defend themselves, even if the result is defeat, and so the enemy he must be referring to here are the tribes of Caledonia beyond that line. Seemingly the ferocity of the conquest of Damnonii lands puts the newly encountered tribes on their guard. More of this ferocity shortly.

It seems odd here that Tacitus also tells us that the army was harassed by violent storms. Such storms have no effect whatsoever on the story he tells beyond this brief mention, and so one wonders why mention them at all. Is it to provide tension and local colour to his tale? As a writer of historical fiction myself, I know that it is more the job of a fiction author to entertain than to inform, after all. It seems pointless to have lied about them when they are of such insignificance, though, and yet this is the campaigning season, from March to October, the traditional season of better weather. Not that bad storms don't occur. The Berwickshire storm of 1881 killed 189 people, Glasgow's 1968 storm destroyed 300 homes, and Cyclone Friedhelm in 2011 caused damage and disaster across the Cairngorms and down to Edinburgh; but still these are rare events, and even rarer in the summer months.

If there was such a freak season of storms, then it is as likely that which keeps the Caledonian tribes in their fastnesses over the season at least as much as fear of Agricola's legions. It would also seriously hamper naval capability, and prevent any activity along the enemy coastline.

Reading between the lines, it is possible to see a few short months of savage conquest reaching the Tay before a sudden and unexpected storm hits and prevents any further advance, keeping both sides busy within their own lines. This is not to say that Agricola simply put his men in fortresses and pulled the duvet over his head for the duration, setting the teasmaid for August. We are told 'there was even time for the erection of forts. It was noted by experienced officers that no general had ever shown more judgment in choosing suitable positions.'[4]

If the timeline of governors' activity upon which we are now working is correct, then Agricola would already have been provided with the bones of a system. The Gask Ridge would exist in some form, and what this excerpt would refer to, then, is a reworking of the system. Forts may have been added at this time, a few crumbling signal stations replaced with fortlets, and other extant installations rebuilt. This would neatly explain the timeline of the Gask Ridge which is now revealing more than one phase of construction, and certain sites along its line being repurposed at a second stage.

Likely what had been a fortified line of advance under Cerialis or Frontinus has now been turned into a solid defendable system by Agricola. There is a notion that the Gask Ridge's role was to protect the favoured Venicones from raids by hostile tribes to the north-west, though Grant notes that with Agricola's arrival and campaigns, the era of the client kingdom in Britain is over, replaced by a policy of straightforward conquest,[5] and since this seems to be the case, the purpose of the Gask Ridge in protecting the Venicones seems unlikely. That it is meant to form a defensible border for a season is considerably more likely.

Tacitus also goes to some lengths to tell us once again how good Agricola was at the siting of forts (he had mentioned this the previous year too). I am inclined to believe Tacitus in this, for since he had cited senior officers in their approval, there is a very good chance that those senior officers were still around at his time of writing and would be able to gainsay him, were this a fiction. Certainly a glance at some of the purported Agricolan sites across Scotland and northern England seems to support Tacitus. It is interesting to read in Hyginus of the desired siting of forts and then apply it to such locations. Hyginus tells us: 'Now, as far as the choice of terrain in setting up the survey is concerned, those sites that gently rise to a height from the plain have first place, in which the Deciman Gate occupies the highest spot, so that the region is dominated by the camp. The Praetorian Gate must always face the enemy. Those sites that are located on the plain have second place, those on a hill third, those on a mountain fourth [and] those in an unavoidable position fifth, from which they are called "unavoidable camps".'[6]

A Roman fort was planned such that the front third of the camp, facing the enemy (as mentioned by Hyginus) held the porta praetoria (praetorian gate), and the praetentura (the accommodation of the more senior or veteran troops and officers). Behind this came a road that linked the two side gates, onto which opened the entrance to the headquarters building. The remaining two-thirds of the camp (the retentura) hosted the command

and logistics structures and more barracks (see map 10 for a standardised plan). In an attempt to apply the words of Hyginus, I examined four of the forts concerned with our story.

Ardoch remains one of Scotland's most impressive remains, and from the profusion of temporary camps surrounding it, may have been used as a muster point for Roman forces more than once. An examination of Ardoch shows that it appears to fly in the face of Hyginus, with its praetentura facing south towards the river and the decuman gate facing the Caledonii to the north. However, since the fort visible now is a later construction, and the earlier fort was considerably longer – the northern quarter having been abandoned and later cut through by defensive ditches – it is extremely difficult to identify the form of the earliest fort on the site, and this orientation may be a later one. Its siting above a curve in the river, though, is solid.

At Cargill, the ground is flat, and the praetorian gate faces the river crossing and the Caledonii to the north-west in a manner perfectly acceptable to Hyginus. This fort shows two phases of construction but displays no sign of reuse after our period, and so it is safe to assume that this form is the original Agricolan orientation. The presence of a defended annexe to the north-west, between the praetorian gate and the lands of the Caledonii, might call into question its acceptability, but we cannot be certain of the purpose of the annexe. If it was to accommodate cavalry and their steeds, the annexe being closest to the enemy makes a great deal of sense.

Strageath also lies on relatively flat ground in a loop of the river. Its form is extremely difficult to determine due to the lack of surface signs of the site and a complex series of phases with an eye-watering collection of crossing and colliding ditches. It seems likely that the visible markings are of a later small fort upon the site of an earlier larger one, reusing ditches. Still, the fort conforms with Hyginus, the praetentura facing west, the retentura protected by the river. To the west, outside the praetorian gate, lies what is likely one or more phases of annexes or potentially remnants of an earlier iteration.

Inchtuthil is an odd case, in that its porta praetoria faces south-west while its side gate, the porta principalis dextra, actually

Above left: 1. Tombstone of standard bearer Lucius Didius Rufinus of the Ninth Legion, dated between AD 71 and 120 and found in York. (Author's collection by permission of the Yorkshire Museum)

Above right: 2. Tombstone of cavalry trooper Insus, found in Lancaster and dated to *c.* AD 100. He likely served in the Ala Augusta during Agricola's tenure and was recruited from among the Germanic Treveri tribe. (Reproduction by permission of Lancaster City Museums)

Above left: 3. Tombstone of Caius Castricius Victor, a standard bearer of the II Adiutrix found in Budapest and dated *c.* AD 90. He would almost certainly have served under Agricola a few years earlier. (Image by Carole Radato)

Above right: 4. Tablet from Carlisle naming one of Agricola's bodyguard from the Ala Sebosiana. (Author's collection by kind permission of the Tullie House Museum)

5. Portrait of the emperor Gaius Caligula in the Carlsberg Glyptotek in Copenhagen. (Author's collection)

6. Portrait of the emperor Vespasian in the British Museum. (Author's collection)

7. Portrait of the emperor Titus in the Museo Archeologico Baglio Anselmi, Marsala. (Author's collection)

8. Portrait of the emperor Domitian in Naples Archaeological Museum. (Author's collection)

9. Modern statue of Gnaeus Julius Agricola in his hometown of Frejus, France. (Author's collection)

10. Governors of Britain portrayed at the complex of Roman Bath. From left to right: Ostorius Scapula, Suetonius Paulinus, Gnaeus Julius Agricola. (Author's collection)

11. Lead water pipes from the elliptical building in Chester, dated AD 79 and identifying Agricola as governor of Britain. (Author's collection by permission of the Grosvenor Museum, Chester)

12. Inscription from the Forum of Saint Albans, ancient Verulamium, dated 79–80 and naming the governor Agricola. (Image with kind permission of St Albans Museums)

Above: 13. Trimontium fort site at Newstead, with the Eildon Hills in the background. 'Those sites that gently rise to a height from the plain have first place, [...] those sites that are located on the plain have second place, those on a hill third, those on a mountain fourth, those in an unavoidable position fifth, from which they are called "unavoidable camps"' – attributed to Hyginus, *De Munitionibus Castrorum*. (Author's collection)

Below: 14. Maiden Castle fortlet and the Stainmore Pass. (Author's collection)

Above: 15. The defences of Raedykes camp. 'A rampart cannot be heaped up except with an abundance of loose stones or a ditch dug so that the sides will not collapse' – Hyginus, *De Munitionibus Castrorum*. (Author's collection)

Below: 16. The eastern defences of Ardoch fort. (Author's collection)

17. Watch towers as depicted on Trajan's column. (Author's collection)

18. Fort building as depicted on Trajan's column. (Author's collection)

Above: 19. Lands of the Caledonii viewed from the Gask Ridge. (Author's collection)

Below: 20. Fendoch 'glen-blocker' fort. (Author's collection)

Above: 21. Bochastle 'glen-blocker' fort, sited at the point where the Eas Gobhain and Garbh Uisage converge into the River Teith. (Author's collection)

Below: 22. Kirkhill signal station on the Gask Ridge. (Author's collection)

23. Gourdie quarry, source of the stone for Inchtuthil fortress. (Author's collection)

24. The site of Dun fort, a possible Agricolan harbour, with the Montrose Basin in the background. (Author's collection)

Above: 25. Domitian prepares for war against the Chatti on Frieze A of the Cancellaria Reliefs in Rome. (Public domain, image by Rabax63)

Right: 26. Officers and men of the 20th Legion in the late first century as portrayed by Deva Victrix reenactors of Chester. (Image courtesy of Paul Harston of Deva Victrix)

Above left: 27. Batavian auxiliary of the first century AD. (Image courtesy of the Roman Military Research Society)

Above right: 28. Reconstruction of a timber fort gate. (Image courtesy of Park in the Past)

29. Roman cavalryman of the Principate era. (Author's collection)

30. Carving of a horned warrior god of the Carvetii, now in the Senhouse Museum, Maryport. (Author's collection)

Above: 31. Anglesey from the presumed point of the Roman invasion at Llanfair-Is-Gaer. (Author's collection)

Below: 32. Roman siege works as reconstructed at Alesia. (Author's collection)

33. *Above left:* Bronze horse mask of the Brigantes from Stanwick Camp, replica in Richmondshire Museum of an original held by the British Museum. (Author's collection)

34. *Above right:* Ritual/theatrical mask of the Brigantes, found at Catterick. (Image from author's collection by permission of the Yorkshire Museum)

35. *Above left:* Modius, or grain measure, of the Domitianic period bearing false measurements found at Carvoran fort on Stanegate. (Author's collection, by kind permission of the trustees of the Clayton Collection)

36. *Above right:* Image of Victory from the triumphal arch of Domitian in Rome, Museo della Civilta Romana. (Author's collection)

Above: 37. Mons Graupius 1: A view across Carey/Abernathy Camp at the Hill of Moncrieff. 'The plain between resounded with the noise and with the rapid movements of chariots and cavalry' – Tacitus: *Agricola*. (Author's collection)

Below: 38. Mons Graupius 2: A view from Raeykes Camp in the direction of Kempstone Hill. (Author's collection)

Above: 39. Mons Graupius 3: A view across Muiryfold Camp at Knock Hill at the Pass of Grange. 'The enemy, to make a formidable display, had posted himself on high ground; his van was on the plain, while the rest of his army rose in an arch-like form up the slope of a hill'– Tacitus: *Agricola*. (Author's collection)

Below: 40. Mons Graupius 4: A view from Logie Durno Camp at the slopes of Bennachie. (Author's collection)

faces the lands of the Caledonii to the north-west. The decuman gate still occupies the high point of the plateau, though, some 50 feet above the plain, and the River Tay protects the east and the south. The terrain is extremely advantageous in terms of natural defences.

The simple fact is that despite Hyginus and the common conception that every fort across the empire follows exactly the same pattern, there is no real hard and fast rule. Roman forts were adapted to the terrain and to requirements, and despite the traditional 'playing card' layout, the existence of forts and camps like Bewcastle (an oddly almost hexagonal site), Whitley Castle with its diamond shape occupying a high plateau, and from our own campaigns Raedykes, which is an amorphous shape in order to take advantage of the high ground, make clear just how adaptable the Roman camp could be. See Map 10 for comparisons.

Why do I, and indeed Tacitus, seemingly attach such importance to this aspect? Simply because the ability to effectively site military installations seems to have been one of the benchmarks of a good general in the Roman world. Indeed, throughout the ages, terrain has been very much the concern of the successful general. In the movie *Gettysburg*, more than once we hear the refrain 'Damn good ground.' Writing of Hannibal, Livy says he 'selected Pyrrhus; saying that he had been the first to teach the art of castrametation; besides, no one had chosen his ground or placed his troops more discriminatingly',[7] and, of course, as we saw earlier, while Statius was praising Bolanus for his son, he told us 'The forts and watchtowers (there, you can see) he scattered far and wide, and lined these walls with a ditch.'[8] Agricola, then, is being praised along the lines of other great tacticians here. Grant places a re-siting of Dalswinton fort in this season, as well as the construction of other sites in Dumfries and Galloway,[9] which would support once again this view of Agricola's talent, since the re-siting of Dalswinton removed the prior danger of flooding. While I am happy to accept that particular site as an example of Agricola's military nous, the dating here does not sit so well. The sites in this region would fit more comfortably later in the campaign.

So after a few months of hammering the Damnonii and annexing the Venicones, Agricola has renewed the redundant Gask Ridge fortifications and turned them into an effective system, keeping the Caledonian tribes at bay, while storms ravage Scotland.

Tacitus goes on in his usual manner to then laud Agricola. We are told that 'No fort on a site of his choosing was ever taken by storm, ever capitulated, or was ever abandoned. On the contrary, the garrisons could frequently venture upon sallies; for they were secured against protracted siege by having supplies sufficient for a whole year.'[10]

Tacitus is referring to forts built under Agricola's governorship, beginning in 77, and the Scottish system would be abandoned by around 87. A decade is, in the grand scheme of things, not a huge window for disaster. This piece of praise, however, flies in the face of events to come, when Tacitus relates how the tribes storm a Roman camp. Nitpickers might try to draw a line and suggest that the site in that case is a temporary camp, while Tacitus's praise refers to forts, but there is, in the early stages of conquest, little difference between the two in terms of defences. The main difference would be the presence of barracks rather than mere space for tents, but of the defences, which would be the enemy's main obstacle, Agricola's

Turf and timber defences being reconstructed at Vindolanda, showing the materials involved. (Author's collection)

forts of the period were of turf ramparts and timber fortifications surrounded by ditches, and not a great deal more permanent than the temporary camp with its fences of wattle or sudis stakes, so this argument falls flat. The original text uses the word Castellum, rather than Castrum, which suggests smaller installations such as fortlets or towers, and tells us they are stocked with a year's supply suggesting that these are permanent forts. It is possible that the fort and annexe at Strageath was part of Agricola's rework of the Gask Ridge system, and there is a suggestion by Grant that Strageath was intended as a form of military headquarters for the entire system, sitting as it does at the north-west corner of the angled line and therefore closest to the enemy (see map 11). It is possible that Carpow dates from this year, as well as a postulated early site at Cramond, and if that is the case, then these two sites, one at each end of a long, angled line, would make perfect harbours for the supply of a system with Strageath at its centre. *If*, of course, storms do not make sea transport impossible! It seems likely that the storms were brief (they could not have raged all summer and autumn, after all), and that in their aftermath sea transport would be used to stock up and supply this entire system for the winter, which accords perfectly with Tacitus's words.

Two things remain to be noted about this year, both of striking importance. The first is a change in the general nature of the campaign. At the start of this year, Agricola is marching to the Tay, conquering and frightening the life out of the northern tribes, and then suddenly he is developing a defensive system and placing forts that are prepared for a siege. It feels as though there is something missing from the middle of this chain of events; something that robs the campaign of its forward momentum. Indeed, as we shall see, this period of consolidation extends beyond 79. So what happened to change the pace?

The answer comes in two forms, and our other thing of note about the year is the first of them. While Tacitus's phrasing of 'ravaging' creates images of lesser strikes, Dio's picture is one of grand war and conquest. There *is* perhaps something we are missing. There is an intimation that this fighting northward culminated in a hard contest that was notable enough to accord it the title of a victory. Perhaps Agricola crushed the Damnonii in a major clash in the north of their territory, or even came up against the Caledonii for the first time. What evidence do I have to support this theory? There are, in fact, several hints that suggest this. Firstly, the placing of forts bordering Caledonii territory and stocking them to withstand a siege. If they had not encountered this tribe before and not waged war against them this year, why would Agricola expect to be besieged by them, unless it was perhaps in reprisal? But that is conjecture.

What is not conjecture is that back in Rome, Vespasian had died during the summer, only three months into the campaigning season, and Titus was now on the throne. Cassius Dio tells us that 'As a result of these events in Britain Titus received the title of imperator for the fifteenth time.'[11] We know that Titus received this honour in late 79, and while Dio cites a circumnavigation of the island (to which we will return presently) and a strange story of deserters in that same passage, it can only be to how Agricola 'overran the whole of the enemy's territory' that he is referring with regard to the honours for the emperor. This suggests a major victory, and dates it to this very year, 79. Moreover, in both Ptolemy's geography and the Ravenna Cosmography there is a fort in this area by the name of Victoria/Victorie which has been tentatively linked with Strageath (also with Cargill based upon mileages between sites). Whether the name Victoria belongs to either of these sites, both of which may well have been founded in this year by Agricola, it points to a major victory being celebrated as this system was being created. It is looking increasingly as though Agricola had won a major engagement in 79.

Why, then, would Tacitus not describe it? There are two very good possible reasons. Firstly, given that this entire tale of his reaches a satisfying crescendo with the Battle of Mons Graupius, his set piece for Agricola's glory, he would rob his finale of some power by reporting a similar victory much earlier in his text. Secondly, that Titus was the one who received the glory for this while no triumphal honour seems to have been accorded to Agricola might lead a bitter son-in-law to omit a victory that had been accorded to the emperor instead of his leading general. Or perhaps he even omitted it out of respect for the emperor's reputation and not wishing to sully it.

Based upon the apparent change in Agricola's policy in mid-79, Titus's honours, and the founding of Victoria, I am inclined to suggest a hidden battle of note somewhere in this year, likely in the northern territory of the Damnonii.

Tacitus goes on to tell us 'So winter brought with it no alarms, and each garrison could hold its own, as the baffled and despairing enemy, who had been accustomed often to repair his summer losses by winter successes, found himself repelled alike both in summer and winter.'[12] We have to examine this. He suggests that the enemy (which after the founding of these forts can only refer to the tribes of the Caledonii) had commonly lost out in summer and recouped their victories in winter. There is no hint of this happening over the previous two years of campaigning. Of Agricola's first winter, Tacitus had said Agricola 'restored to peace its good name', and of the second, 'winter passed without disturbance'. Perhaps we are meant, then, to understand that this was the standard give-and-take of the Caledonii in troubles with their neighbours, but now that Rome was here with well-stocked forts, this was no longer the case.

The year in Tacitus's account once more ends with a slew of enthusiastic praise for his father-in-law. He is presented as firm but fair, as straight-talking, as wearing his heart on his sleeve. One telling thing here is a comparison subtly drawn by Tacitus between Agricola and Domitian. Of Agricola he says 'He thought it better to show anger than to cherish hatred,' while of Domitian later in chapter 35 he says 'with joy in his face but anxiety in his heart'. Polar opposites. The perfect contrast with which to both praise the one and damn the other.

Here ends Tacitus's treatment of the year 79. Not ours, though. There remain aspects to examine. Firstly, why precisely the pace of conquest seems to change at this point, for as I mentioned above, this pause in the northward advance of conquest is not limited to the latter half of 79. What might cause a change in Agricola's policy? It can only have come from one of two sources. Either Agricola identified problems that needed addressing before the advance could resume, or a command came down to him from Rome.

Given what we have seen of Agricola and the very strong likelihood that this successful year of campaigning had culminated in a major victory, it seems unlikely that Agricola would be happy to draw a line in the sand and then garrison it while resting on his laurels. The order, then, most likely came from Rome, from the mouth of Titus himself. Reasons for this are somewhat nebulous, but can be unearthed with a little logic in light of imperial history.

Titus was new to the throne. A new emperor, no matter how straightforward his succession, had to secure his reputation with a military victory. This was by now a standard formula. Augustus had his Actium, Tiberius and Caligula their Germanies, Claudius his Britain, Nero his Armenia and Vespasian his Judea. Titus was, of course, one of the architects of that Judean victory, but he needed one within his regnal period, and it seems likely that Agricola provided that in 79 on the plains of Scotland. If Agricola had then been permitted to immediately continue his war north in the following season, it would rob that important victory of meaning and undermine the achievement. It may therefore be simple politics that lie at the root of this policy change. Titus needed his victory and Agricola handed him it, but was then forced to endure a lull in the campaign so as to allow the emperor his glory.

This would neatly explain a year or two of halting in the northward advance, as well as the fort named Victoria. It might also be worth mentioning here that at the end of the campaigning season of 79, Titus had to deal with the aftermath of the eruption of Vesuvius, and the political and financial fallout of this would require a great deal of attention. It may be that British conquest was sidelined by necessity.

There seems to be a focus late in 79 on the subject of victory, grandeur and Roman propaganda. It has been postulated that the great legionary fortress of Inchtuthil was begun in 79. The similarity between the stonework of Inchtuthil and that of Chester has been noted, and since it is possible that the Twentieth Legion built both, then there might be a good reason for this. Their joint dating to 79 cannot realistically be connected through this, though. Chester's construction works have been dated in this context through lead pipes which bear Agricola's name, but this seems to be a later addition to the fortress rather than part of the original plan. While a grand system that included the Gask Ridge, a command post at Strageath, and supply ports at Cramond and

Carpow (which is often identified with the place name Horrea Classis, translating helpfully as 'Granaries of the fleet') seems highly likely at this time, the construction of Inchtuthil, which lies some distance north, on the far side of the Tay, cannot easily be subsumed within it. Refer once again to map 11 for a good view of this possible system.

Might we accord to Agricola construction projects in the civil sphere during that winter? After all, Tacitus had gone to great pains to tell us of the governor's projects in his first winter. There is evidence of an increased push to civil construction during the second winter, and yet it seems almost certain that Agricola was in Scotland throughout the year, well into winter and possibly even *over* the winter and into the spring. While he concentrated on war, then, who was building in the south?

The answer might lie in the vague provincial position known as the *iuridicus*. This role seems to have been a praetorian position with authority province-wide alongside the governor and the procurator, with work purely in the civil sphere. It is only rarely attested in Britain, leading Birley to suggest[13] that the role was an ad hoc position appointed when the governor was busying himself with war and had insufficient time to turn to the works of the civil world. One of only two known iuridici for Britain, Gaius Salvius Liberalis, can be dated to AD 78–81 and so it seems extremely likely that with Agricola focussing on campaigns in the north, this secondary official had been assigned to assist him with civil matters. As such, Liberalis seems to have done an excellent job.

The elliptical building in Chester, which can be attributed to Agricola from the magnificent evidence of having his name on the lead pipes, is an enigmatic structure. Its purpose is unclear and it has no parallels in any other legionary fortress across the empire. It was clearly a structure of importance, and some have even taken it as an indication that Chester was intended to become a provincial capital. The role of this building, now lost forever to modern construction, will likely never be discerned, but it is possible, given its position at the heart of the fortress and next to the headquarters building, that it was linked with the imperial cult. Could this be a further indication of an unrecorded victory in Scotland in 79? While Titus is granted his fifteenth *imperator* in Rome, Agricola has a magnificent new cult centre erected to the glory of the Flavians in the fortress of the Second Adiutrix, one of the Flavians' most loyal and personal legions?

Other building works that seem to have been completed during the winter of 79 hint at a province-wide push for recognising the glory of Rome, the Flavians and the emperor Titus. Fishwick suggests that the rebuilding of the temple to the imperial cult at Colchester, previously burned down by Boudicca, may well have been completed in this year,[14] and that undoubtedly on its re-dedication it would have been applied to Titus rather than the deified Claudius. Grant also cites the possibility that the grand triumphal arch that once stood at Richborough, the Roman 'Gateway to Britannia', may also have been completed around this time. She notes the discovery of marble fragments at Dover referring to the son of a deified emperor, which may have come from the arch and clearly do not refer to Claudius. They must realistically refer to either Titus or Domitian, and size and possible placing of the words on the inscription suggest Titus.[15]

One of the most fascinating structures we can perhaps date to this season is the enigmatic ruin known as 'Arthur's O'on'. This strange monument that once rose like an enormous pimple upon a hill near Falkirk was the subject of various theories, though the most common description of this Roman work has been as a temple. Destroyed in 1743 to reuse the masonry, it has now long since gone, though drawings of it were made and descriptions recorded. Archaeology around the site has produced the intriguing find of a brass finger from a statue among the rubble, which suggests the possibility that it was in fact a victory monument of the sort raised by Trajan in Romania, by Hadrian at Tynemouth, and by Augustus in the hills above Monte Carlo.

It may just be that Arthur's O'on was Titus's monument of victory over the Damnonii. Its location, close to the line of the Antonine Wall and near the fort of Camelon, links it with the Roman presence there, and no victory in the area is recorded under Antoninus Pius, Septimius Severus or Constantius. Sadly, we will almost certainly never know the truth of it, but it remains an intriguing possibility.

Arthur's O'on from the Itinerarium Septentrionale of
Alexander Gordon, 1726. (Author's collection)

A last thing worth noting here is that in the following year, after about a decade of construction work, the Colosseum was finally inaugurated by Titus with over a hundred days of games. These lavish spectacles were recorded by the poet Martial, who tells us, tantalisingly, 'so did Laureolus, hanging on no sham cross, give his naked flesh to a Caledonian boar.'[16] If a Caledonian boar was used in the games in AD 80, there seems little doubt that it had been supplied by Agricola as one of the prizes of a successful campaign in 79, bearing in mind thay it would have taken some time to reach Rome. This is perhaps just another small hint at a victory that has gone unrecorded and yet was celebrated at the time. What we seem to have, then, in this strangely under-reported year, is a season of warfare, a major victory, and then a winter in which Agricola oversees the construction of an impressive system of control on the border of conquered lands in Scotland, while his deputy in the south raises monuments recording the greatness of Titus and the Flavians across the settled province.

There remain a few small points to mop up before we move on. The first is a weird story from Cassius Dio, about the mutiny of an auxiliary cohort who steal three ships and try to go home only to get lost, be carried by the winds around the entirety of Britain, and then get dumped right back where they started. This is almost certainly a retelling by Dio of a story Agricola gives us later on, and so we can safely disregard it in 79. And it is a very silly story, more reminiscent of Monty Python than of Roman history. '*He's a very naughty navigator...*'

He also then goes on to tell us that in this year Agricola has the island circumnavigated, proving that it truly is an island, but again Tacitus tells us similar stories much later, and so once more this appears to be a case of Cassius Dio conflating the events of several years into a short narrative. And, of course, Britain was wracked by storms, wasn't it? Not conducive to circumnavigation.

We can safely assume that the navy's only real role during this particular year was in the support and supply of the army in the north and the provisioning of Agricola's new system there. Our last note for 79 is one of importance not related by Tacitus, but concerning the man himself. We know from his own words in other works that Tacitus was appointed to the position of quaestor by Titus. Quaestors were traditionally appointed in January, and the age limit for the role was twenty-five. If we accept AD 56 as the year of Tacitus's birth, that would make him the right age to hold the quaestorship in 81. Also, Titus, to whom he owed the role, died in 81, and so Tacitus has to have been back in Rome at some point in 80. Given that he would be unlikely to leave mid-season if serving as an officer in the north, he likely departed the island over the winter of 79 and before the campaigning season of 80 began in March, which would mean that from this point on we cannot realistically expect Tacitus to be giving us a first-hand account anymore, but from now he would be working from conversations with his father-in-law and other figures variously involved.

For now, the war has paused, and Agricola digs in across Scotland while his man in the south glorifies the new emperor.

12

FIRMABATUR

AD 80 is dealt with by Tacitus in the briefest of all his treatments.

'The fourth summer he employed in securing what he had overrun. Had the valour of our armies and the renown of the Roman name permitted it, a limit to our conquests might have been found in Britain itself. Clota and Bodotria, estuaries which the tides of two opposite seas carry far back into the country, are separated by but a narrow strip of land. This Agricola then began to defend with a line of forts, and, as all the country to the south was now occupied, the enemy were pushed into what might be called another island.'[1]

He tells us nothing of the events in the winter to follow, something he usually does illustrate, and nothing of the civic provincial world. This entry is just a brief note on how the campaign was going. Had Tacitus been in Britain from 77 to 79 with his father-in-law as postulated, and returned at the end of that campaigning season ready to move on to the next post on the cursus honorum, then this would be the first year of the British campaign that he had not witnessed, and that may explain his brevity. Still, there are things to be gained from his text.

The first is that the forward momentum of the invasion that had halted the previous year remains absent in 80. This is a time of consolidation, and there are various possible reasons for that. Potentially, Titus may have called a halt to the advance as previously noted, having had his triumph, and with other pressing matters demanding imperial attention. In 80, the aftermath of Vesuvius would still be shocking, but in this year both fire and plague swept through Rome, causing innumerable deaths and great damage, and all at a cost to the imperial treasury. This was not a conflagration on the same scale as the massive Neronian burnings, but would still occupy the administration and the imperial purse. It may be that Titus simply drew a line under Britain for now, and told Agricola not to advance any further north on costly conquests. This is the angle that Birley prefers, and it is a seductive one.

There may be another, less permanent and more prosaic reason for this extended pause in conquest, which is raised by Maxwell. He suggests that there would be necessary pauses in expansion once certain tracts of territory had been added to the province, for 'assessment'.[2] That the governor would need to pause to carry out a census to determine population numbers and centres, to plan the infrastructure it would all require, to re-form his forces and set garrisons. That this would take time, and there would be no further advance until what had already been taken had been fully brought under control.

It is, of course, possible that both these explanations are applicable. Late in 79, Agricola had already been noted as building forts. Here we are told that he creates a defended line from the Forth to the Clyde, which confirms that the forts he built in 79 could not be those ones. That lends a great deal of credence to the notion that late 79 had been spent reconstructing the Gask Ridge with new forts and fortlets.

Now, in 80, the Forth/Clyde (*Bodotria/Clota*) is garrisoned. Once again, a look at map 11 shows how the system would now work. A solid defended line from the west coast, along the isthmus, turning northward around Camelon and then turning again, east-northeast along the Gask Ridge to the Tay. The fort of Bertha was probably begun in 79 and completed in 80, sited on the near bank of the Tay at its confluence with the Almond, the point furthest north yet garrisoned. Tacitus makes no mention of anything north of the Forth/Clyde in the fourth season, but given that Agricola had reached the Tay the year before, had built forts, and was unlikely to give up his new territory, it seems inconceivable that the line did not remain extended to the Tay. This would include the land of the settled Venicones, which would be a natural decision.

Agricola's army would need to be spread thin over such a long line, and that might be why many installations can be regarded as small for the period, and many sites were held by fortlets rather than full-sized forts. This rings true with Tacitus using 'castellum' rather than 'castrum' to describe sites. It seems likely that units were split up into subdivisions to create the garrisons.

Tacitus seems to be suggesting that the creation of a permanent frontier at the isthmus, something hitherto unknown in the Roman world, had been considered but had been brushed aside by the more military minded. In a later passage there is the suggestion of a division of opinion at a command level as to the viability of further conquest or the notion of a permanent frontier. It does foreshadow the creation of the Antonine Wall, suggesting such a thing half a century early, and it is not hard to imagine the emperor Antoninus Pius reading Tacitus and taking his cue from the text. Regardless of having suggested the possibility of such a thing, in all three translations of the Agricola used in this book, the result is the same. For the honour of Rome and the pride of the army, the idea of a permanent border was cast aside.

Thus, no matter how long this pause in the northward advance lasts, it can be seen that it was never intended to be a permanent end, and was simply a period of consolidation. Titus probably intended Agricola to pick up the conquest at a later date.

We have already examined the case of the Gask Ridge, with its multi-phase constructions and fortlets built almost abutting signal stations, thereby rendering them unnecessary, so in this we can see Agricola's constructions of late 79, which would continue throughout 80, forming a well-defended route from south of Ardoch as far as Bertha (the northern outskirts of modern Perth) on the Tay. We now know that he fortified the Forth/Clyde isthmus. There is no evidence the two defensive lines meet, though earlier under Frontinus I postulated a link between them. Stirling seems certain to be a missing fort that would connect Ardoch to Camelon. With the potential site at Cramond and that of Carpow, the line could be supplied from the east coast at both ends.

The Firth of Forth as seen from the fort of Cramond. (Author's collection)

What of the Forth/Clyde, though? In the above translation, Church and Brodribb tell us of the isthmus that Agricola began to 'defend with a line of forts', which suggests the creation of forts, while Mattingly and Handford give us 'This isthmus was now firmly held by garrisons,' and Birley 'This was now being securely held by garrisons,' both of which do not imply construction, but rather infer simply the *manning* of sites.

Here, in the Latin text we finally encounter that word *firmabatur* that I mentioned earlier while postulating that Frontinus was responsible for the earliest phase of the Gask Ridge system. We are told, if we take the more direct translation of firmo, that Agricola *strengthened* the Forth/Clyde line, which would mean that the line already existed. What we are likely looking at, then, is a line of fortifications that had already been in temporary use at some earlier date, possibly under Frontinus, or possibly when conquering the Selgovae in 78. Agricola then reoccupies these forts with new garrisons, probably adds a few forts or fortlets to the line to 'strengthen' it, and thereby creates his new barrier. Examining the various sites on the line of the Antonine Wall and extending beyond its eastern and western termini, a number stand out as very likely being originally Flavian.

Based upon pottery and coin finds, sites along the isthmus that can be dated to Agricola are (west to east): Barochan, Old Kilpatrick, Bearsden, Balmuildy, Cadder, Mollins, Castlecary, Camelon, Mumrills, Cramond and Elginhaugh. Many of these sites would later be incorporated into the Antonine Wall, which only confirms the strategic value of the original sites, once more in line with Tacitus's assessment of his father-in-law's strategic cunning. The stretch of the Firth of Clyde from Greenock to Glasgow was originally too shallow and apt to silting to allow shipping upriver, and no early Roman sites have been identified west of Barochan that might have served as a Roman harbour, so it seems unlikely that the fleet could have supplied the system from the west.

It is difficult to read of these two phases of construction and consolidation over 79 and 80 without drawing the conclusion that the Forth/Clyde and the Gask Ridge were part of one and the same system, encompassing all the currently controlled territory and preventing raids into it by the Caledonian tribes.

It has been argued that Tacitus's statement that all the country to the south of the isthmus was now occupied is not only erroneous, but a blatant untruth. Certainly there is no reason to assume at this stage that Rome had any control over the Novantae in Galloway. Still, given that this is a text intended to extol the abilities of Agricola, it would be acceptable for the author to go with a generalisation, rather than qualifying it with tribal exceptions that would mean nothing to an audience in Rome.

So in AD 80, Agricola continued his work of consolidation, probably utilising sites that had been initially created under Frontinus but had been abandoned for some time, likely adding new forts and fortlets of his own, using his apparently excellent strategic skill. The line would connect the Tay to the Clyde, keeping the tribes so far untouched away from those that were now in the process of being Romanised and settled, it could be supplied by sea from the east coast at two locations, by road from the south at both ends of the isthmus, and manned by a well-spread-out force of small garrisons rather than sporadic large units. And yet we are given the impression by Tacitus that this was only ever a temporary measure. Agricola was pausing for a reason but intended to continue his northward advance, perhaps once the emperor gave him the go-ahead.

Winter, then, would be spent in these garrisons, probably constructing roads and ancillary structures, while back in the south of the island Agricola's iuridicus, Gaius Salvius Liberalis, continued to enhance and expand the urban fabric of the province to the greater glory of the Flavians.

All hail Titus.

Briefly.

As we move on into AD 81, the Flavian dynasty faces another change, for Titus will not live to see the end of that year. Sadly in the scheme of long-reigning emperors, Titus is but a short, despondent squeak. Still, as the campaigning season of the year dawns, Titus is still on the throne, there is still seemingly an embargo upon northward expansion, and Agricola's system is now complete. What would the man naturally do at this juncture? We have conjectured already that the Novantae were the one tribe south of Agricola's line that were as yet uncontrolled by Rome, almost cut off from the main advance as they were in Dumfries and Galloway, and so Agricola's gaze perhaps now turns west. For the rest of this chapter, map 12 should be of use.

'In the fifth year of the campaigns he crossed in the leading ship and defeated peoples up to that time unknown in a series of successful actions. He lined up his forces in that part of Britain that faces Ireland, an expression of hope rather than of fear. For, in fact, Ireland, which lies midway between Britain and Spain, and is also within easy reach of the Gallic Sea, would have united the strongest parts of the empire with great mutual advantage.'[3]

I have selected Birley's translation here because his wording is closest to the source text. In the original Latin the wording is 'nave prima transgressus', which is perfectly translatable as 'crossed in the leading ship', as Birley chooses. Other translations make an attempt to fill in the blank in Tacitus by adding what it is that he crosses. In fact, this is not made clear by Tacitus, and that fact remains one of the most argued points of the Agricola, especially since the sequence of events for the year is based partly upon the answer to that question.

Church and Brodribb tell us in their translation that he crossed the Clota (the Clyde), which persists as a common belief and is the best of the translation alternatives. Since Rome controlled the land south of the Forth/Clyde line, the natural image of this is of a fleet of boats crossing the Firth of Clyde from somewhere around modern Glasgow and carrying the war into the northern lands beyond. There are a number of problems with this, though. Firstly, no evidence of a campaign north of the Clyde has ever emerged. Two forts could be said to be located in the region, but they are part of something we shall explore later and therefore almost certainly not connected to this year. Moreover if, as the evidence suggests, the forts of Old Kilpatrick, Bearsden and Balmuildy were part of Agricola's line at this time, then his garrisons were already based north of the Clyde, making such a crossing nonsensical. Thirdly, and the nail in the coffin of the theory is that, as previously mentioned, the part of the Clyde from Greenock to at least Glasgow was in places as shallow as a metre and subject to silting, and so a shipboard crossing of it would be impossible anywhere upstream of Greenock.

Birley does not tell us what waterway was crossed, in his translation or in his notes, but as he suggests that the army went to campaign against the Epidii on the Mull of Kintyre, which is the closest point on the mainland coast to Ireland, and also mentions the isle of Arran, he implies that the water crossing would be the outer reaches of the Firth of Clyde, off the Ayrshire coast, more or less part of the Irish Sea. Of the solutions offered, this is the most comfortable, at least supporting the idea of a campaign against hitherto unknown tribes. The army would have to rendezvous with the fleet in Damnonii lands, somewhere between Greenock and Ayr for the trip, and the crossing to the Mull of Kintyre from there would be almost as far as sailing straight to Ireland. While Birley's theory cannot be discounted there is no archaeological evidence to support Roman campaigns on Arran, Bute, Kintyre or the mainland between them. If Ireland was Agricola's target, attempting to conquer a collection of lands in an arc to the north-west on the way seems an overambitious choice.

Mattingly and Handford in their translation name the crossed body of water as the Annan, a river that rises in the Moffat Hills of the southern uplands and flows in a more or less southerly direction to empty into the Solway Firth. This is a possibility and fits on several counts, with the Galloway coast almost as close to

Ireland as the Mull of Kintyre and more properly facing it, the entire region being south of the current limit of Roman territory. Only the lowest mile of the river, as far as the town of Annan, is navigable, though, and so this makes the use of ships extremely unlikely. The upper stretch of the Annan, which a soldier could walk across in places, comes within a few miles of the upper reaches of the Clyde.

When one thinks of the Clyde, one automatically pictures the shipbuilding Glasgow area and the region of the western Antonine Wall, but the Clyde in fact turns in a southerly direction fairly quickly and cuts across Lanarkshire, heading south-east, almost meeting the Annan, the two between them nearly cutting Ayrshire and Dumfries and Galloway off from the rest of Scotland. Once again, though, the upper Clyde could realistically be crossed by an army without rafts or canoes, let alone ships. If Agricola was based at this time somewhere on the Forth/Clyde isthmus, and the mentioned location that faces Ireland was the Galloway coast, then the most direct route would cross the Clyde in these wider reaches. Still, though, the crossing in ships makes little sense here.

Another hiccup with the latter two hypotheses, and the major point that commends Birley's theory, is the lack of unknown tribes to engage south of the Forth/Clyde line. Ogilvie and Richmond attempt to resolve this problem by comparing the text with another line of Tacitus, with similar wording, where he refers to the Orkneys. The Romans were already aware of the Orkneys, and yet Tacitus describes them as being unknown until being discovered and subjugated by Agricola's fleet. The suggestion raised is that Tacitus is using *unknown* (in this case *incognitas*) to refer to the islands before being subjugated and explored fully. If this same logic can be applied to the events of the fifth season, then we do not necessarily have to be looking for a tribe that was entirely new, just for one that had yet to feel the full weight of Roman conquest. It so happens, of course, that the only tribe in Britain south of Agricola's fortified line that fits that description is the Novantae of Galloway, lying across the line of the Clyde and the Annan from the encamped army and between them and the coast that faces Ireland. The way this piece fits into the puzzle is simply too neat to ignore.

The wording of Tacitus, though, is a seemingly unsolvable problem. Crossing the Annan or the upper Clyde would not require ships, crossing the tidal Clyde estuary is impossible due to the conditions, and crossing the Firth of Clyde all the way to the Mull of Kintyre seems to be too distant to make strategic sense. One possible answer to all of this is that Tacitus either embellished the tale with conflicting details since he did not have first-hand knowledge of it, or perhaps became muddled with what Agricola had told him of the campaign and conflated events. It is easy to blame Tacitus here, and this is one of the most glaring instances that suggest fiction in his work. Fortunately, in the grand scheme of things, the crossing and the attacks on the tribes thereafter has no bearing on the rest of the tale, and so we can happily write it off as Tacitus rambling if we like. It is more entertaining to theorise, so let us look at two other possibilities before we move on.

It is possible that this campaign was a nearby and very brief thing, taking ship somewhere around Wemyss Bay down the coast from Greenock and attacking the inhabitants (the Epidii again?) of the Cowal Peninsula just 2 miles across the water, only 15 miles from the fort at Barochan and, thanks to Scotland's complex coastline, actually partially lying south of the Forth/Clyde line. With no Celtic written history, our knowledge of the island's ancient tribes relies upon Roman authors, and there is a high probability that there were many lesser tribes that never made it to the history books. We are unlikely to ever learn the truth, and will have to decide among ourselves whether Tacitus is making it up or mistaken, or whether some advance was made for which no archaeological evidence has been found.

So onto the the next step. 'He lined up his forces in that part of Britain that faces Ireland.' We can safely discard the idea that this happened anywhere south of the Solway Firth, as the entire military, barring local garrisons, was now based north of that line. We can also safely rule out anywhere north of the Forth/Clyde line, since this is currently Agricola's fortified limit. I am inclined to rule out Kintyre, as the army would have to travel over a hundred miles through unknown, mountainous and unfriendly territory to get there, or to cross by ship, which brings us back to Birley, of course. The most accessible land that directly faces Ireland would be the Galloway coastline, between Ayrshire and the Solway Firth, the only problem being that the Novantae occupy that region. Agricola has seemingly left the Novantae alone thus far, given that they are peripheral, tucked away in a corner and far from his north-south routes of conquest.

I suspect that, given his vaunted personality, Agricola was struck by a sense of incompleteness in that he had subjugated and begun the Romanisation of the entire island south of the Forth/Clyde, with the sole exception of the peninsula of the Novantae. Having his northward advance curtailed would grant him the time to attend to this issue.

Moreover, at this point Agricola's army has spent almost two years engaged in building fortifications and provincial infrastructure, their military activity limited to a few raids or skirmishes. Only a decade earlier Agricola had been appointed to the Twentieth Legion to bring them back to order after their mutiny, and one major contributing cause of their mutiny seems to have been a lack of military focus for the legion, frustration and dissatisfaction spreading through the men at the lack of a campaign which offered booty and promotions. Agricola had to be well aware of the danger of leaving legions in garrison for protracted periods and would not want to risk them becoming bored and irritable. He would need a campaign for his men, and if he had been ordered not to advance north, he may have taken advantage of a loophole to turn on the one tribe to the south as yet untouched. This issue may have been the impetus for any separate seaborne assault on other tribes, too.

These are good reasons why Agricola might take a force (albeit a diminished one given the number of men he must have left garrisoning the line of fortifications from the Clyde to the Tay) into the lands of the Novantae. It does not explain where the unexpected focus on Ireland comes from though. Fortunately, Tacitus, following a short tour-guide section on Ireland that tells of its geographical and commercial advantages and its main harbours but stops short of listing the best pubs, goes on to give us a clue as to the reason: 'One of the petty kings of the nation, driven out by internal faction, had been received by Agricola, who detained him under the semblance of friendship till he could make use of him. I have often heard him say that a single legion with a few auxiliaries could conquer and occupy Ireland, and that it would have a salutary effect on Britain for the Roman arms to be seen everywhere, and for freedom, so to speak, to be banished from its sight.'[4]

This is an old story, the ousted tribal leader calling upon Rome's help and, perhaps unwittingly, opening the door to conquest. Much the same had happened less than half a century earlier and had led to the invasion of Britain. Verica, king of the Atrebates, had gone to Rome for aid, and aid had come in hobnailed boots and then refused to leave. Such an opportunity as an exiled Irish king would be too good for Agricola to miss. If he invaded Ireland with this king at his side, ostensibly to reinstate him, Agricola could be confident of support from at least some of the tribes he encountered.

It could be that Agricola had been focused on the subjugation of the Novantae and had had the good fortune to meet this king in the process, though the wording suggests that the king had been with Agricola for some time, and this implies that the decision to move against Ireland in support of the king was the initial reason for moving into the Novantae's lands.

In the previously quoted passage, we had been told that Agricola 'lined up his forces in that part of Britain that faces Ireland, an expression of hope rather than of fear'; a curious phrase. It is perhaps best explained if Titus had, as I have suggested, given Agricola orders to curtail his campaign for a time. As such, despite aiming west rather than north, Agricola would need to seek permission from the emperor to accept the king's plea and invade Ireland. His troops could be marshalled on the coast ready, waiting for word from Rome, with hope of being unleashed rather than fear of crossing.

There is a possible substantiation of Tacitus's exiled Irish king in AD 81. In Irish legend, recorded by monks in the Middle Ages, one Túathal Techtmar, the son of a deposed Irish high king, went into exile and later returned with an army and retook the throne in a great battle. Some versions of the legend place Túathal's exile in Britain.[5] The *Annals of the Four Masters* gives us the dates for these events (spurious as they may be, even for a vague legend), telling us that he was exiled in AD 56 and returned in 76. The fact that these dates come within five years of Agricola theoretically having an exiled Irish king at his side is a coincidence hard to ignore. As with all legends, the story of Túathal Techtmar should be treated with a great deal of caution, but it remains an intriguing possible link.

In the second of the two Tacitus extracts covering these events, Agricola expounds on the value of Ireland's conquest, a subject I have heard discussed many times among Roman and Irish historians. If the island could be taken and held, along with finishing the conquest of the mainland, then the British Isles would be under no threat from outside, and nothing would lie to the west of the Roman empire but open sea. That control would free up many troops who could be of use elsewhere (for Britain hosted more legions than any other province). Of course, Tacitus would have ample opportunity to hear his father-in-law's views over the six years they would later spend in close contact.

We can tentatively reconstruct at least one possible sequence of events then for this year.

Having been largely inactive for a season and a half, and prevented from northward expansion, Agricola crosses an unknown body of water and takes it out on small, unrecorded tribes, keeping his troops content and up to scratch. He then receives a plea for aid from an exiled Irish prince. He draws together a diminished force, leaving a substantial garrison along the Forth/Clyde line and the Gask Ridge and sets out to garrison Novantae lands with a view to using them as a point of departure for Ireland.

It is possible that Agricola set out to conquer the Novantae in a two-pronged attack. This tactic is a Roman norm of the era, which Cerialis had used to conquer the Brigantes, and which Agricola had likely used in 78 against the Selgovae. Two forces could penetrate the Galloway peninsula, making the most of the low terrain, skirting the southern uplands. One may have marshalled at the Agricolan-era fort of Castledykes, close to modern Lanark, where there is a multi-phase fort and a cluster of camps of varying eras, suggesting its use as a base from time to time. From there Agricola could cross the Clyde and advance around the northern edge of the hills, building and garrisoning the known fort of Loudoun Hill (where a recognised Roman road has been traced back towards Castledykes), and on to the coast near

Ayr. Signs of Roman occupation and campaigning in south-west Scotland are few, but in 2015 excavations at Ayr revealed evidence of a temporary camp. Here, Agricola and his force would have reached the coast overlooking Ireland. Simultaneously, if the army were employing a twin-pronged assault, a second force could have mustered at Birrens (Roman Blatobulgium), around which there lies another cluster of temporary camps. From there, they could cross the Annan and advance along the southern coast of Dumfries and Galloway, meeting up with Agricola's force on the western coast.

By the close of the season it seems likely that a rudimentary network of control was in place around Novantae lands (see map 12), including known camps and forts at Loudoun Hill, Ayr, Girvan, Glenluce, Gatehouse of Fleet, Glenlochar, Ward Law and Dalswinton, and a postulated and very probable fort at Stranraer. Perhaps, while Agricola waits and ponders a campaign in Ireland, his forces are busy fortifying and garrisoning Galloway and Ayrshire.

As Mason notes, there must have been a sizeable fleet off the western coast if an invasion of Ireland was being considered, and of course if the army had used them to descend on some hitherto unknown island tribe and suppress them. Possible harbours that could accommodate parts of the fleet include Ayr, Stranraer and Glenluce, spread along the western coastline from the Irish Sea to the Solway Firth. Moreover, that same fleet must have reconnoitred coastal Ireland for Agricola, and through him Tacitus, to be familiar enough with the place to hold such opinions of it.

The notion of an invasion of Ireland, even a failed one, can largely be discounted through lack of evidence. Continued attempts to prove the coastal fortification of Drumanagh near Dublin to be Roman fail to prove anything. Roman finds there stretch over two centuries and are probably the result of trade. So there is no evidence of an invasion, but then there is no evidence for a seaborn campaign of destruction in early 81 either.

The campaigning season of 81, then, ends with Roman domination established over south-west Scotland, completing the conquest of all lands and tribes south of the Forth/Clyde line. Forts and networks are being constructed, and the army remains in the region awaiting confirmation from Rome that they are permitted to initiate an invasion of Ireland. No doubt Agricola's tame Irish

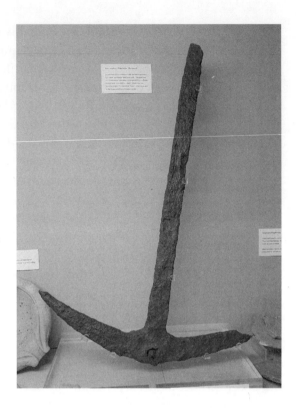

Roman anchor found at Ruthwell near Dumfries, close to the Solway Firth. (Author's collection)

king remained by his side throughout the season, ever hopeful that the fleet would soon sail and put him back on his throne, short-sighted as that would be, given that it would also sound the death knell for kingships in Ireland entirely.

The order for Ireland's conquest would never come. On 13 September, still within the campaigning season, the emperor Titus fell ill and died of a fever, his younger brother Domitian taking the throne. It is possible that Agricola and Domitian were never on the best of terms. Of course, Tacitus is writing in retrospect and blames Domitian for most ills, so there is a bias in the described relationship, but certain facts suggest a dislike regardless. His brother Titus had enjoyed prestige, responsibility and favour throughout their father's reign, while Domitian had been somewhat side-lined and kept in the shadows, given sinecures and empty titles. Agricola's presumed connection to Titus, then, would not necessarily stand him in good stead with Domitian. Further, in the aftermath of the civil war, while Vespasian and Titus were still in the east, Domitian was in Rome, but his responsibilities were clamped down upon by his father's representative, Mucianus, who in turn granted Agricola roles first in recruiting troops, and then as a legate in Britain. A connection to Mucianus would stand him in no better stead than a connection to Titus. That being said, there are also moments towards the end of the work that hint at a far less inimical relationship than Tacitus would have us believe.

Agricola must have greeted the news of his friend's demise and the elevation of the second brother with trepidation, wondering, as many across the empire might have done, whether he was to remain in position. Orders likely came from Domitian in due course over the winter. Clearly the new emperor refused Agricola's request, denying him the opportunity to launch some crazy invasion of Ireland. After all, why initiate a new invasion when the first one was not yet complete? Agricola had been governor for five years, which is the longest standard term for the post, and was probably half-expecting to be recalled now anyway, and perhaps the looming end of his governorship was behind his call for a new invasion, which could grant him an extension. In the event, when the orders come, he is surprisingly not recalled. Domitian extends Agricola's tenure, probably by one year, given the new emperor's plans for his own campaign in Germany. It is not hard to imagine Domitian's words to Agricola.

'You've been at this too long. You should have finished it by now. Have another year, but get the damn island conquered sharpish, so that I can tax them and have my legions back for other campaigns. Get to it. Conquer, or else.'

Domitian giving him an extension and the specific remit to finish the job would perfectly explain the next about-face in policy, as two-and-a-half years of consolidation and immobility are now cast aside and momentum returns once more to the northward advance.

The winter of 81 passes and brings us to a new stage in the conquest.

13

THE EAGLE OF THE NINTH

It is odd to think that the events of Agricola's sixth season as governor, in AD 82, are remembered more for a work of fiction by Rosemary Sutcliff than for the writings of Tacitus. That the Ninth Legion were massacred in Northern Britain is up there with the most infamous events in Romano-British history. Indeed, the 'destruction' of the Ninth Legion is a seemingly unending theme in fiction. The truth behind that tale, as given to us by Tacitus anyway, is still a tense and gripping story, notwithstanding the fact that archaeology tells us a different tale to Sutcliff's.

The campaigning season opens once more on this new year, Agricola's first year of extended governorship under the new emperor, with the promise of conquest. Domitian has his own military plans, too, however. While Agricola may have been given an extra year to complete the conquest of Britain, Domitian has no intention of simply sitting back and claiming Agricola's victory to militarily justify his reign. Titus may have done just that, but the army would still have respected the man even if he celebrated a victory won by proxy, since he had been a successful general in his own right in Judea before he took the throne. The same with their father Vespasian, who had a glorious military career of his own. Domitian had been raised in a more bookish manner and had no military background to call upon. If he wanted the trust of the army, he needed to make a name for himself, not to have someone do it for him.

Even as Agricola readies himself to take on the last of Britain's tribes, Domitian leaves Rome for Gaul. Ostensibly he is on some official business, but the fact that while he is there he orders a campaign against the Chatti in Germany suggests that this had always been his plan. In Gaul, the new emperor prepares for the campaign that will give him military credibility. To do so, he requires an army, and while he has legions on the German border, there is evidence to suggest that vexillations were taken from Britain in support of the new army.

Thus while Domitian prepares for his German odyssey, Agricola finds himself stripped of troops. Perhaps this is why the campaign in Britain begins slowly, as the governor reorganises the manpower available and runs a recruitment drive. We have no evidence of this, of course (but then so much of Agricola's life is conjecture anyway), though since Agricola had been given the task of levying new troops at the start of the Flavian dynasty, he certainly had the relevant experience.

Tacitus opens the year with: 'In the summer in which he entered on the sixth year of his office, his operations embraced the states beyond Bodotria, and, as he dreaded a general movement among the remoter tribes, as well as the perils which would beset an invading army, he explored the harbours with a fleet, which, at first employed by him as an integral part of his force, continued to accompany him.'[1]

The Bodotria was the Forth. It is still reasonable to assume that the Gask Ridge was manned at this point as far as Bertha, and the Tay, the ridge, and the land of the Venicones are all already beyond Bodotria. That first sentence of Tacitus then only makes sense if taken in a specific way. The line of the Forth/Clyde barrier that would eventually become the Antonine Wall neatly cuts through the middle of the territory of the Damnonii. Realistically, if Agricola is intent on advancing, he no longer needs that narrow barrier across the isthmus and it would be better to move it forward, embracing the rest of the Damnonii and sealing off the Highlands instead. Also, there is a possible explanation for the states embraced that lies with the tribe of the Maetae (a name that brings a smile to my face whether pronounced 'Mai Tai' or 'Meaty'). Cassius Dio refers to the tribe, and they are around in the time of Septimius

Severus, during which they occupy lands 'between the wall and the Caledonii'. If this wall referred to the Antonine Wall, rather than that of Hadrian, then that would put the Maetae in the same territory as the Damnonii, between the Forth and the Highlands. The Maetae are often assumed to have come about through the merging of tribes in the late second century, but the possibility of their being extant when Agricola encompasses that land, contemporaneous with the Caledonii, remains.

This, then, is what we might understand by him 'embracing states' beyond the Forth. Once again, the archaeological evidence of sites in Roman Scotland makes it extremely difficult to pin down a date, even within decades, let alone to a specific year. Without such tools as dendrochronology (and hopefully such sites will see more and more of these modern dating techniques in future), we can often only say with reasonable satisfaction that a site is Flavian. But that gives us a date range of nearly thirty years, and so we can only use literary sources and logic to narrow the field.

As such, we know that a line of forts along the edge of the Highlands came into existence at some time in the late Flavian era. They are often assumed to date to the end of Agricola's tenure or even to that of his his successor, but there is a certain logic to dating them to this particular year.

Cast your mind back to Agricola's first time on the island, traipsing around the soggy hills of Wales as a tribune on the staff of Suetonius Paulinus. Remember how he would have seen first-hand the work of the great general Ostorius Scapula, and how he perhaps gained a personal respect for, and even modelled himself upon, the man. How Scapula had built a line of fortifications along the border of Wales, effectively sealing off all the valleys and approaches to the good arable land from the hill-dwelling Welsh tribes I mentioned earlier it was important and that we'd come back to the notion of the 'Glen-blocker' forts.

Here we are at last. A line of forts has been identified in much the same manner as those Welsh ones around the periphery of the Scottish Highlands, doing precisely the same thing, guarding each approach into the highland massif. Five of these forts occupy the line from the western coast to the north-eastern end of the Gask Ridge system, the limit of advance at the end of 81. Of these, construction and occupation of the western three would effectively embrace the northern Damnonii and advance the line of Roman control to the edge of the Highlands. The three forts of Drumquhassle, Malling and Bochastle would then create a new temporary frontier that ran from the extant fort of Old Kilpatrick and connected to the Gask Ridge at Ardoch (see map 13). This effectively answers the question of what 'states' north of Bodotria Agricola could have annexed: the northern Damnonii, and the Maetae if they existed at this time. The remaining two Glen-blocker forts at Dalginross and Fendoch may well not have been part of this initial plan, since they more deeply intrude into the hills and would not be required to surround the Damnonii.

It is worth noting here the importance of two pieces of archaeological evidence in dating Roman sites. The first is the 'Stracathro-type gate', a distinctive form of camp gateway that adds an oblique earthwork to the normal clavicular gate, creating an impressive narrow killing zone. The second is the 'parrot's beak', a method of constructing external defences that joins two ditches at the ends outside the gates, forming the causeways into a funnel shape, rather than a straight crossing. Both of these designs are considered Flavian and are used to date camps to this era, and the Stracathro gate, given that it is almost uniquely found in this region of campaigning, is associated specifically with Agricola. While it is good to be able to date forts that are found with these two forms, we must remember that we cannot discount any site that does *not* use them. They may, after all, be the work of different units with different preferences. At Hadrian's Wall, the work of three different legions has produced very individual styles, and the same might be true here. The parrot's beak might be preferred by one legion, the Stracathro gate by another, and neither by a third. As always, sadly, uncertainty is the name of the game.

For the record, of those five forts mentioned above, each have Parrot's Beak ditches, while at both Bochastle and Dalginross adjacent temporary camps also have Stracathro gates. Of course, all this tells us is that they almost certainly date to this series of campaigns (within less than a decade.) It in no way helps us to pin down annual sequences of events.

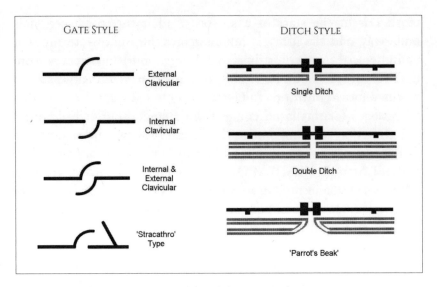

Comparison of varying systems of fort defences. (Author)

If we feel the need to account for Tacitus's pluralisation of 'state' in reference to Agricola's activities in the spring, then it is also possible that at the beginning of this season the forts of Cargill, Cardean, Inverquharity and Stracathro were also manned, which would effectively seal off the Vacomagi in addition to the Damnonii. I have already postulated that Cargill and Cardean may have already been built in the time of Frontinus in some form or other, and it is possible that Agricola now reoccupied them and extended the line with two more forts. This would give him, as map 13 shows, a continual line of garrisons from the west coast at the Clyde, around the southern edge of the Caledonian highlands, to the east coast past Stracathro, encompassing the Venicones, the Damnonii and the Vacomagi.

Given the vague dates we have for the various sites, it is also more than possible that the great new legionary fortress of Inchtuthil (possibly the Roman *Pinnata Castra*) was begun at this point, slotting in rather neatly with that fortified line and giving Agricola a new legion base at the northern edge of occupied lands, precisely where he would need it for the control and settlement of the north once he had achieved conquest.

All this at the start of a season. And if this construction is underway and the army is not marching into enemy territory it would give the governor time to call in support in numbers from the sites further south, bolstering an army that had been weakened by the removal of troops to Gaul.

Evidence for this latter comes from a single source. Inscription ILS 1025 that was found near Tivoli, east of Rome, belongs to one L. Roscius Aelianus and tells us he was 'TRIB MIL LEG IX HISP VEXILLARIOR EIUSDEM IN EXPEDITIONE GERMANICA' (a military tribune in the Ninth Hispana, a vexillation of which was involved in the German expedition). This has been taken to be Domitian's Chatti war, and certainly that makes the most sense. This suggests that part of the Ninth Legion was withdrawn to fight in Germany in early 82. Of course, that doesn't mean such removed vexillations were unique to the Ninth and that the other legions hadn't done the same, and it is more than possible that at least a cohort had been stripped from each of the four British legions to bolster the emperor's army.

Agricola would have to make do.

The alarmist and rather un-Agricolan phrasing of 'he dreaded a general movement among the remoter tribes' in Church and Brodribb requires examination. We also find this translated as 'Fearing a general rising of the northern nations',[2] and 'Because there were fears that all the peoples on the further side might rise'.[3] The general sense we are left with from the three is that Agricola at least suspected that the tribes of Caledonia were gathering against him.

Though we might refer repeatedly to Agricola's foe as the Caledonii or the tribes of Caledonia, Roman geographers have supplied us with the names and rough locations of a number of other tribes cut off in the northern half of the Scottish Highlands (the Creones, Carnonacae, Caereni, Cornavii, Smertae, Lugi and Decantae). When the 'tribes' are mentioned, any gathering may have involved a number of these groups in addition to a more southern Caledonii.

A fear that the tribes to the north might be mustering to oppose Rome would be a very realistic and sensible notion. At this point it had been almost three years since Agricola last advanced north, and he had contented himself with consolidation in the meantime. What, though, had the northern tribes done with their time? After all, they cannot possibly have been ignorant as to what was coming. They had watched their southern and eastern neighbours being systematically conquered, hemmed in with forts and Romanised now for years. No one could possibly be so naïve as to think that Rome had stopped its inexorable advance. It seems likely that what had been a rather loose confederation of tribes in the north had held councils of war and forged an army. Agricola probably had good reason to worry about what he faced in the north. It may even be at this time that many distinct tribes of the north formed into the uber-tribe that Roman authors call the Caledonii and we have thus far been applying the term retrospectively. It is therefore no surprise what we are told that Agricola used his fleet to scout north. The fleet was probably now based on both coasts, in Ayrshire or Galloway in the west and at the Tay and the Forth in the east. It seems likely that both the army and the navy were weighted towards the east, given the terrain, the tribes and the theatres of war thus far. The Classis Britannica had been used primarily for transport to this point, and it is here intimated that for the first time it took on a more active military role.

It is conceivable that Agricola had more sense of the value of the navy than most governors. He had been raised in Frejus and Marseilles, both busy ports, and at the time of his birth at least, Frejus had been the main naval base of the Roman fleet before it moved to Misenum. His early days would have seen him surrounded by naval activity.

Sadly we have even less archaeological evidence for the activity of the Roman fleet than we have for the army. To this date no sign of a port from the era has been found, though there are intriguing possibilities. I have already mentioned potential harbours at Cramond and Carpow, but the camp at Dun, near Montrose, remains a possibility as a more northerly temporary base. Dun stands on the Montrose Basin formed from the River Esk before it empties into the sea, a mere 6 miles from Stracathro, the most northerly Roman fort. Its strategic efficacy cannot be overemphasised, and while now the Montrose Basin is a wide and shallow area of silt, at the time of Agricola it would almost certainly have been a wide, deep basin; a natural harbour. Perhaps one day excavation in the locale will unearth evidence of the fleet.

Why, when the navy had been used thus far largely for transport, was it now given orders to scout ahead up the coast? For the answer to that we should look at the sea power of the natives of the island, or rather the lack thereof. Barry Cunliffe suggests that the same types of seagoing vessels favoured by the Gauls on the Bay of Biscay may have been in use by the British tribes: 'archaeological evidence for iron age sea-going ships is at present wanting except for the iron anchor found with a hoard of metalwork at Bulbury, Dorset, but in all probability robust vessels of Venetic type were widely in use in the waters around Britain.'[4] While there is every likelihood of this being the case, matters would be very different between the Gallic-influenced tribes of southern England and the remoter peoples of Scotland. Around the south, trade with the continent would make such ships a necessity, while the vastness of the seas surrounding Scotland would strip the local Iron Age tribes of the value of seagoing vessels. Indeed, the overwhelming evidence of water travel among these tribes comes in the form of logboats, which could not have withstood the open sea and would certainly have been laughable if pitted against a trireme.

Consequently, the Romans in northern and western Britain had almost certainly never felt the need to pit a navy against any force, for there would be no recognisable seaborne opposition. Thus Agricola's fleet would be at liberty to sail up and down the coast with impunity, and so while Agricola, at the start of his season, concentrates on moving his border to the edge of the Highlands as he reorganises his army for the coming campaign, he sends his fleet north to check out the lands ahead.

Tacitus goes on to say 'The spectacle of war thus pushed on at once by sea and land was imposing; while often infantry, cavalry, and marines, mingled in the same encampment and joyously sharing the same meals, would dwell on their own achievements and adventures, comparing, with a soldier's boastfulness, at one time the deep recesses of the forest and the mountain with the dangers of waves and storms, or, at another, battles by land with victories over the ocean. The Britons, too, as we learnt from the prisoners, were confounded by the sight of a fleet, as if, now that their inmost seas were penetrated, the conquered had their last refuge closed to them.'

The very fact that we are now told the fleet advanced alongside the army, sharing camps, can only mean that the forces began to move at last, and did so in a north-easterly direction, continuing up the flat lands of Angus and Aberdeenshire towards the Moray coast. The army must have kept within reach of the coast for a joint operation, and it is possible that this gives us Agricola annexing the northern lands of the Vacomagi and perhaps even the Taexali, finally taking all the flat arable lands of the east. Temporary camps have been found as far as the land near Elgin, and it is quite conceivable that the army reached further than this. Suspected or rumoured sites of Roman camps that are as yet unconfirmed reach up beyond the Moray Firth.

The army is described as being in extremely good spirits, and this is clearly not merely a process of annexation, given the phrase 'spectacle of war' and the avowed taking of prisoners. The tribes who were so shocked by the Roman fleet must be the ones that had not yet come into contact with the ships of Rome, yet who were close enough to the sea to be so shocked. This suggests the Taexali of northern Aberdeenshire and Moray once again.

An interesting possibility is opened up with the activities of the fleet. According to the above Church & Brodribb translation 'their inmost seas were penetrated.' Mattingly and Handford offer 'the secret places of their sea were opened up,' with Birley being almost identical. What secret inmost places of their sea were opened up then? Given that we can conjecture naval forays at least as far as the Spey on the Moray coast, might we not suggest that the fleet went further? It is the thinnest of evidence, but in the nineteenth century one, or possibly two, small fortifications that were believed to be Roman were identified at the head of Loch Ness, close to the river that leads out to the Moray Firth. Unfortunately, we will never learn anything more about them, for work on the Caledonian Canal obliterated the site. It does, however, introduce the tantalising notion that the inmost sea the Roman fleet reached was Loch Ness. This would undoubtedly put the wind up the native tribes, for the loch all but cuts northern Scotland in half, and if the Romans could secure the eastern end of it, the tribes of the far north would be largely isolated from the rest.

Once more this is all conjecture, but then the application of geography and archaeology to the text of Tacitus is what this is all about. What we can perhaps glean from this is that having advanced his line, encompassed all the tribes within reasonable reach, reorganised his forces and scouted the coastal region to the north, Agricola's force advances north through the eastern flat lands, perhaps as far as the furthest extant camp identified with any level of confidence (Fochabers on the bank of the River Spey near the coast). They conquer the northern Vacomagi and the Taexali of the flat lands, and survey as far as the Moray Firth with a combination of land and sea power.

That something roused the northern tribes is made clear as Tacitus continues: 'The tribes inhabiting Caledonia flew to arms, and with great preparations, made greater by the rumours which always exaggerate the unknown, themselves advanced to attack our fortresses, and thus challenging a conflict, inspired us with alarm. To retreat south of the Bodotria, and to retire rather than to be driven out, was the advice of timid pretenders to prudence, when Agricola learnt that the enemy's attack would be made with more than one army. Fearing that their superior numbers and their knowledge of the country might enable them to hem him in, he too distributed his forces into three divisions, and so advanced.'

Once more we are at the mercy of textual interpretation. This Church & Brodribb translation suggests that the tribes rose and surged south with the intent of attacking Roman fortresses. Did they merely threaten, or did they reach the Roman lines? 'They went so far as to attack some of our forts,' according to Mattingly and Handford, and Birley says 'by attacking some forts'. The difference between the meanings is enormous, but the Latin favours the idea that the tribes assaulted Roman fortifications. Opinion is divided upon the details of this part of the campaign. What seems most likely to be the case is that the angered natives, now a sizeable force, moved with speed along highland glens they knew well and fell upon a number of Roman forts, not up in the lands of the Taexali or the north-east, but at the heart of Roman control, back down near the Gask Ridge at the centre of the line.

For it to create such alarm among the Roman forces and to even have officers among them calling for a complete retreat to the Forth/Clyde line, this cannot have been peripheral camps in the north, but something the Romans thought safe. Grant points out that if the tribes had gathered at the native settlement at Dunkeld,[5] they would be within easy striking distance of Roman installations right at the heart of the Roman lines, including Strageath, already postulated as the command centre for the system.

Somewhat confusingly we are then told that Agricola learns that the enemy are about to attack in three columns, though we have postulated that the Roman force is now in the north-east, while the enemy assault likely happens some way to the south. For there to be time for alarm and suggestions of withdrawal among the Romans suggests that the attacks on the forts were small preliminary assaults, probably carried out by local Caledonii, and that there was likely sufficient time for Agricola to pull his forces back to that same area at the heart of Roman control and support the battered garrisons there. It is reasonable to assume that upon learning of the attacks, Agricola would move his forces to the endangered zone immediately. That he could reach the site of the attacks before the mass of northern tribes should be no surprise. The Roman legions' speed of march is legendary, and they would be supported by naval ships that could convey men down the coast at speed. Even allowing for the force having to skirt the Grampians, a journey of some 80–100 miles would take a legion moving at urgent pace only three or four days, which is a speed of which the Highland tribes moving through mountainous terrain could only dream.

If this sequence of events is to be accepted, Agricola arrives back at the heart of his line of forts with his army some time in the early summer. Word comes thereafter that the mass of the Caledonian tribes has split into three forces and they are advancing to war.

How Agricola received word of the advance is a question as yet unanswered. It may be a simple case of rumour, or word of mouth from disaffected tribesmen or allied groups outside the region of Roman control, or it may have been scouts or outposts deliberately put in place by Agricola following the attacks on the forts. The watchtower of Sma' Glen that serves the fort of Fendoch gives an excellent field of vision along two different valleys, and this may be indicative of something Agricola now had in place, especially if he was already expecting trouble. Unless further sites are identified we will never be able to confirm the truth of this, but there are other ways that Agricola could have learned of the tripartite approach of the Caledonian army in any case.

Despite having clearly campaigned along the northerly coastal route, Agricola is now back at the heart of matters and in a position to deal with an enemy advance. In response to a three-pronged tribal attack, the governor splits his own force into three groups to meet the enemy. It seems logical that Agricola would divide his three legions among those forces, one to each advance, supported by auxilia. Caesar often divided his army during the Gallic Wars, handing over command of large vexillations to trusted lieutenants such as Brutus, Cicero and Labienus. Indeed, Cerialis seems to have done the very same thing with Agricola in the conquest of the Brigantes. We know the names of none of Agricola's senior officers, which is a shame, as we cannot even make a guess as to who led the legions in this campaign, some of whom may have gone on to become illustrious commanders in their own right. We do know from what Tacitus tells us next that Agricola was not in the advance with the Ninth Legion, but that he must have been close by.

It has often been assumed that this action took place to the north, way beyond the Roman fortifications, but given that the enemy's heartlands are in the hills, and that it seems only logical that their previous attacks had been against permanent forts at the heart of the defended line, we can deduce that Agricola's three-pronged response in fact heads east, into the edge of the Highlands. If his force was once more based around the Gask Ridge area, the route towards the enemy would take them into the glens.

Grant suggests a line of advance for the three forces along the rivers Tay and Almond and into Strathearn.[6] She postulates a connection between the Ninth Legion and the Strathearn locale, based upon potential connections between that unit and the forts of Strageath and Ardoch. As such we can accept the strong possibility of an advance of the Ninth Legion out of Strageath fort and along the line of the River Earn, the southernmost of the three routes. The largest of the three rivers is the Tay, to the north. It would not be navigable for the Roman fleet beyond Bertha but might be useable for shallow boat transport, and a tenuous connection might then be made to link the Second Adiutrix to the Tay, advancing from Cargill. This would leave the Twentieth Legion moving from Bertha along the River Almond as the central prong. That Agricola would personally command the Twentieth, a legion with whom he has a long history, would seem only logical. Moreover, this would place him at the centre of the entire Roman advance, the perfect position for an overseeing general.

Unfortunately, Agricola is not the only one getting advanced warning.

'This becoming known to the enemy, they suddenly changed their plan, and with their whole force attacked by night the ninth Legion, as being the weakest, and cutting down the sentries, who were asleep or panic-stricken, they broke into the camp. And now the battle was raging within the camp itself, when Agricola, who had learnt from his scouts the enemy's line of march and had kept close on his track, ordered the most active soldiers of his cavalry and infantry to attack the rear of the assailants, while the entire army were shortly to raise a shout. Soon his standards glittered in the light of daybreak. A double peril thus alarmed the Britons, while the courage of the Romans revived; and feeling sure of their safety, they now fought for glory. In their turn they rushed to the attack, and there was a furious conflict within the narrow passages of the gates till the enemy were routed. Both armies did their utmost; the one for the honour of having given aid, the other for that of not having needed support. Had not the flying enemy been sheltered by morasses and forests, this victory would have ended the war.'[7]

It is hardly surprising that the tribes might know of what was happening within the glens of their own territory. While the Romans would rely upon scouts and signalling systems, these lands were the ancient home of their enemy. It is quite easy to imagine that the Ninth Legion managed to advance slightly faster than the other two prongs, and came to the enemy's attention first. Regardless of any perceived weakness, if the Ninth were ahead, they would make a natural target. If the enemy moved fast enough they could conceivably cut off this attack and annihilate them in detail before any other Roman force could come to their aid. Whatever the thinking behind it, Tacitus tells us that the tribes learn of Agricola's similar three-way split, and in response they swiftly combine their own army back into one and fall upon the advancing Ninth. That the tribes could with relative ease split and recombine forces with speed and without Roman anticipation can once more be explained by their familiarity with the terrain, compared with the comparative ignorance of the Roman invaders.

We are told that the Ninth is the numerically weakest of the three prongs, and that this was why the tribes fell upon it. As noted earlier, epigraphic evidence places a subunit of the Ninth in Germany for Domitian's war, and while we can postulate that the same is true for the other legions, this certainly would explain the weakness. In addition, of the three legions present, the Ninth occupied the most northerly fortress. Based at York now, they would have the responsibility for maintaining control over the north of England, Brigantian lands that had only been brought under control a decade earlier and which were possibly still restive. So it is quite possible that the Ninth were required to leave a larger garrison at their home fortress than the Twentieth or the Second.

If we are of a mind to write off Tacitus as a source of trustworthy evidence, then we might suspect that in seeking a unit for his story he selected a legion that had already suffered a similar catastrophe during the revolt of Boudicca. Certainly the Ninth seem to be an unlucky legion. Since, however, there is no evidence to be raised against these events as recorded, then we have no reason to doubt that the Ninth were the weaker target.

Given Grant's postulated routes of the Roman advance, the geography of the area explains how events might unfold as Tacitus relates them. The Twentieth, advancing up Glenalmond, make camp for the night, possibly somewhere in the area of Fendoch. Ahead of them, the Ninth are advancing along the Earn and throw up the defences of the known temporary camp at Dalginross. The Second, at this point, are some way off to the north (see map 14).

The camp of Dalginross has long been associated with the Ninth and with this event by historians and enthusiasts. The camp has been dated to the Flavian era by the Stracathro-type gates, and

Carving of an eagle, the symbol of the legions, from the Ninth's fortress of Eboracum. (Image from author's collection by permission of the Yorkshire Museum)

covers an area of roughly 22 acres. A calculation was made in the nineteenth century, based upon military requirements of the day, which put the number of legionaries that could camp in an acre at 280. This figure and the calculation upon which it is based are still considered viable by historians, and using this, we can see Dalginross camp as adequately sized for roughly 6,000 men – to put it another way, the right size for a single under-strength legion and several supporting auxiliary cohorts. I earlier postulated this year for the construction of forts along the edge of the highlands but not those of Dalginross and Fendoch. If the signal tower at Sma' Glen existed in time to warn Agricola of the attacks, then it is likely that the nearby fort of Fendoch did not. A strong case for Dalginross fort not having been constructed by this time is the temporary camp mentioned above, that may have housed the Ninth. What of the attack on the Ninth? One might expect the site of such a fight to turn up plenty of archaeological evidence, and it is notable that no signs have been unearthed around Dalginross. However, only one small scale investigation has taken place in the mid-20th century, based around the ditches, and there is evidence that those ditches were re-cut at a later date, suggesting that the camp was reused, perhaps in the Antonine period. Since the location was occupied by the garrison fort in between it is unlikely that the remnants of battle would be left to rot within reach of the fort, and the site would have been cleared by a subsequent occupier. Without further excavation at Dalginross, we can neither confirm nor discount this.

In the cinematic mind's eye, we can picture the Ninth and their support, having dug the ditch and raised the rampart of this large camp, placed a fence of stakes around the top, set out sentries and pitched their tents, relaxing into camp. Evening gives way to night and the camp is asleep. We can pick out the massive army of the Caledonian tribes swarming along the valleys to the north and the west as quiet as they can be under the cover of darkness. Rome does not do night attacks any more than she campaigns in the winter. The Scottish tribes are less fussy.

The Caledonii emerge emerge from the valleys, bellowing their war cries as they surge in a shapeless mass towards the encamped and startled Ninth Legion. Sentries shout a warning, but there is little time. The defenders hurry to the ramparts and prepare to fight off the tribes, knowing immediately that they are drastically outnumbered. The legion is an excellent, well-trained and veteran unit, but the odds are so heavily stacked against them numerically that the failure of the defences is only a question of time, and before long the enemy are in the camp, butchering with impunity.

The Second Legion, along the Tay, are too far north to be of any help, and the Ninth is in a desperate situation. If, however, the Twentieth under Agricola had advanced along the Almond to the Fendoch area, they would be in a position to respond. With something like 10 miles separating them the distance is no object. Moreover, at Fendoch the valley diverges and a wide, flat approach leads in a south-westerly direction towards Dalginross. That Agricola would have advance scouts out ahead of his force is quite logical and normal practice. It is conceivable that his pickets set out some distance from his camp are already aware of the position of the Ninth. The unfolding disaster at Dalginross must have created a terrific commotion and, at night, amplified by travelling along a valley, it is quite feasible that advance units from the Twentieth could pick up faint signs of trouble. A second possibility, of course, would be that riders from the Ninth, as soon as the alarm went out, raced for help. It is worth considering the possibility that just as Agricola could know that the Ninth were ahead of him, the Ninth might be aware of the proximity of the Twentieth in their wake.

It is not fantastical then that word of the attack reaches the ears of the governor. Agricola's response is swift. He dispatches the fastest troops, which would include all of his cavalry units, and possibly swift-moving light infantry among the auxilia, to race to the aid of the Ninth, while the rest, the heavy infantry, fall in and head west on the tail of their fellows. Likely the Twentieth discard all their equipment except their fighting kit and hurry off at double pace. At a distance of 10 miles it would take the cavalry less than an hour to come to the aid of the Ninth, with the infantry perhaps an hour after that.

The cavalry reach the camp to find the Ninth completely surrounded, the ramparts breached in places and fighting going on inside the camp itself. Without delay, they attack the rear of the enemy lines. This is perfectly believable and in line with Roman cavalry tactics. Unlike the heavy Norman knights, the Romans rarely employed a cavalry charge until the advent of heavily armoured Clibanarii horsemen. Cavalry of this era were light troops, used for skirmishes and for harrying an enemy's flanks. Being able to use open ground to sweep in in waves and pick off the edges of the tribal force would be their natural tactic. This they do and one can only imagine how the morale of the attacking tribes dips at being attacked from behind during the fight. Still, though, the numbers are on the side of the Caledonii and they are within the defences. Despite the arrival of the cavalry victory is still in sight.

As the strains of dawn begin to thread through the sky, with the war calls of buccinae and cornua and the roar of angry legionaries, Agricola's Twentieth emerge from the valley to the north-east, sunlight glinting off armour and standards and pilum tips. The sight must have sent a surge of dismay through the tribes. Still, the fighting goes on, like the last round of a boxing match when both fighters are desperate to land the killer punch. The enemy must have been pushed back out of the camp by the reinvigorated Ninth, for we are specifically told that they are now fighting in the narrow gates. Finally, someone of import among the Caledonii decides that time is up. They tried, but relief came too soon for the Romans, and now the numbers are much more evenly matched. With the ease of men born to the terrain, the tribal army scatters, possibly before the relief actually hit them.

The natives melt away into woods and marshes, abandoning their attack, and the Ninth is saved. If we are led to wonder why Agricola made no effort to halt the flight of the natives and bring the entire war to an early conclusion, as Tacitus regretfully notes might have happened, simple logic provides the explanation. The tribes were familiar with the terrain. They woould have had with them men from the area who would know every track and way through the woods and hills. Given that this is still just past dawn, it would have been foolhardy indeed to try and pursue the natives into their own territory. Moreover, even though two legions had now combined, they would still have been outnumbered. Seventy years earlier three legions had been massacred by German tribes in an unfamiliar forest. Agricola would have no desire to be the general who led his army to Teutoburg 2.

What can we say of the historicity of Tacitus here? Is this account, as has been suggested, simply Tacitus reusing Caesar's tale of the besieging of Cicero's camp in 54 BC? There are two pieces of evidence in support of Tacitus. First is his description of the last stage in the battle. We are told in specific terms of the 'narrow passages of the gates' of the Ninth's camp. Given that the majority of camps would have a standard clavicular or titular gateway, it would seem odd to draw specific attention to the narrowness of the gate, unless those gates are in fact Stracathro type, and therefore more constrictive than the other forms. Dalginross camp, of course, sports those very Stracathro gates. It is easy to marry the description up to the evidence on this point.

The other defence is what happens when the siege breaks. The enemy melt away into 'morasses and forests'. Anyone acqainted with the Highlands of Scotland will be very familiar with this description. It certainly adequately describes the terrain to the west and north of Dalginross. If Tacitus had indeed served in Britain with his father-in-law, it had been for only a few years at the start of his northward push, and the writer would not have personally seen the Highlands or their landscape. That this description so neatly matches the terrain gives some credence to the notion that this is a story Tacitus heard straight from the horse's mouth. Equally possible on this last point is Birley's suggestion in his notes on Agricola 26 that Tacitus may have lifted the entire incident from Agricola's own campaign report to the emperor, which would undoubtedly have remained on record in Rome. One might question why Agricola would admit to such a near disaster, but the simple fact that he personally took an imminent defeat and turned it around into a victory would do his reputation no harm. He may have been using the fact that he had so nearly managed to bring the tribal confederation to defeat to request a further year's extension on his tenure from the emperor. He had met the tribes in the field and defeated them thus but been prevented from finishing it by the landscape, so if he could do the same again but in more favourable terrain, he would be close to full conquest.

For the record Forder considers a number of possible sites for the attack other than Dalginross, from the widely accepted to the extremely unlikely, such as the camp of Marcus.[8] That camp, which is defended by less constrictive, non-Stracathro-type gates, lies towards the north-east in the flat lands of Angus and not close enough to any forest or morass for the enemy to melt into. Dalginross fits the bill as much as any camp and better than most.

The Ninth Legion, then, having scraped through disaster against Boudicca and been reinforced in the aftermath, once more almost met with oblivion at the hands of the Caledonian tribes in 82 somewhere in Scotland. Yet thanks to the timely arrival of the relief under Agricola's command, they hang on by the skin of their teeth. So much for the disappearance of the Ninth.

What is more, just to hammer the nail into the coffin of that particularly persistent legend, the Ninth are attested by both a tile stamp and the inscription LEG HISP IX on the rear of a phalera found at Nijmegen in the Netherlands and dated between AD 121 and 130.[9] Indeed, a tribune of the Ninth, Lucius Aemilius Karus, cannot have served before AD 122,[10] confirming that the Ninth remained an active legion after having left Britain and during the reign of Hadrian.

Before we leave the tale of the Ninth's peril, we might once again recall Tacitus's ardent stand that 'no fort on a site of [Agricola's] choosing was ever taken by storm.' Barring semantic argument, the events of 82 rather fly in the face of Tacitus's statement. For the sake of convenience let us come down on the side of semantics and note that while the fort was breached, it was not truly taken, and move on.

Little remains to be said of the rest of the campaigning year of 82. The legions were apparently filled with enthusiasm for the war, and the earlier doubters found renewed faith and purpose, as Tacitus tells us. 'Knowing this, and elated by their glory, our army exclaimed that nothing could resist their valour – that they must penetrate the recesses of Caledonia, and at length after an unbroken succession of battles, discover the furthest limits of Britain. Those who but now were cautious and prudent, became after the event eager and boastful. It is the singularly unfair peculiarity of war that the credit of success is claimed by all, while a disaster is attributed to one alone. But the Britons thinking themselves baffled, not so much by our valour as by our general's skilful use of an opportunity, abated nothing of their arrogant demeanour, arming their youth, removing their wives and children to a place of safety, and assembling together to ratify, with sacred rites, a confederacy of all their states. Thus, with angry feelings on both sides, the combatants parted.'[11]

The 'recesses of Caledonia'. Birley phrases his translation 'deep into Caledonia'. Either way, we are told that the army desires to press on into enemy lands until they reach the furthest coast of the island. We are told nothing more of the campaign of 82 after the attack on the Ninth, and since Tacitus equally unhelpfully skips the majority of the following year in his zeal to get to the grand finale, we have nothing really to go on for the best part of a year.

Tacitus tells us that the Caledonian tribes, having been close to a victory, now sent away the non-combatants and held a council of war, gathering a confederacy of all the northern tribes. Such tidings might well leak back to the Roman forces. This is another reflection of part of Caesar's Gallic Wars. If Tacitus did indeed adapt Caesar's great work for his own, then this is his retelling of the rise of Vercingetorix, chief of the Arverni, who managed to pull together a similar confederacy of Gaulish tribes, culminating in the siege of Alesia.

From the phrasing of Tacitus's next line, we can assume that all this had happened by midsummer. What did the Romans do during the rest of the season while the Scottish tribes gathered? We might presume that the meeting of native peoples, if it happened, occurred somewhere deep in the Highlands, far from the Romans and closer to the more remote peoples. Agricola would be looking at the last few months of his campaigning time and doubting he would be able to bring the enemy to battle before he is recalled. Possibly he is waiting, tense, for word from Domitian, who is close, across the Channel in Gaul, as to whether he will get another year.

We have been told that after the battle with the Ninth, the entire campaign might have been concluded had the enemy not fled into forests and marshes. So it would undoubtedly be preying on Agricola's mind how he could draw the enemy confederacy out into the open where he could defeat them decisively. One thing that is certain is that pressing deeper into the shadowed valleys of the Highlands was not going to gain him any better ground for a fight. Anywhere in the mountains the enemy would be just as liable to flit away from a defeat and regroup. He would logically have to stay in the open flat lands and somehow draw the enemy to him.

Thus the most likely turn of events for the rest of 82, while the enemy gather for an almighty punch-up, is that Agricola founds more forts along the Glen-blocker line (Dalginross and Fendoch seem likely candidates now, and those of Cardean and Inverquharity if not already complete) and has them heavily garrisoned, prepared for a fight, sealing off the agricultural low lands from the hard hills and valleys and preventing the seasonal movement of transhumant stock. Closing the agricultural stranglehold on the northern tribes, he could then squeeze. There has already been a hint that lack of grain had been at the root of the Ordovices launching a desperate attack on a cavalry base. Could Agricola be trying to recreate the situation in the north now? To squeeze the tribes until they had no choice but to come for him?

It is likely that many of the temporary camps throughout Angus, Aberdeenshire and Moray were part of Agricola's activity over the autumn, winter and spring of 82/83. As his fortifications protect the low agricultural lands from the Highland tribes, and work continues on the legionary fortress of Inchtuthil as a campaign base, he is free to move north once more, imposing control over what remains to this day Scotland's richest arable farmland.

Temporary camps such as Raedykes, Ythan Wells and Logie Durno suggest the presence of a large army, with those three alone capable of housing 27,000, 30,000, and 40,000 men respectively. Sadly, we cannot confirm the dates of these camps, as usual, and it is possible that any of them date to the later Severan campaigns, though it is just as possible that they were part of Agricola's push north. For the army, then, we can discern no more proof of activity in 82. One story we have cause to revisit takes place this year, though. In one of his more interesting asides, Tacitus tells us a story: 'The same summer a Usipian cohort, which had been levied in Germany and transported into Britain, ventured on a great and memorable exploit. Having killed a centurion and some soldiers, who, to impart military discipline, had been incorporated with their ranks and were employed at once to instruct and command them, they embarked on board three swift galleys with pilots pressed into their service. Under the direction of one of them – for two of the three they suspected and consequently put to death – they sailed past the coast in the strangest way before any rumour about them was in circulation. After a while, dispersing in search of water and provisions, they encountered many of the Britons, who sought to defend their property. Often victorious, though now and then beaten, they were at last reduced to such an extremity of want as to be compelled to eat, at first the feeblest of their number, and then victims selected by lot. Having sailed around Britain and lost their vessels from not knowing how to manage them, they were looked upon as pirates and were intercepted, first by the Suevi and then by the Frisii. Some who were sold as slaves in the way of trade and were brought through the process of barter as far as our side of the Rhine, gained notoriety by the disclosure of this extraordinary adventure.'[12]

This tale of derring-do, of murder and mutiny, of theft and seaborne flight, of desperate cannibalism, piracy, capture and slavery, seems to have absolutely no bearing on the events to either side. It has nothing to do with the man Tacitus is eulogising. It feels very much shoehorned into the narrative and far-fetched, though nowhere near as far-fetched as Cassius Dio's version mentioned earlier. There are two feasible explanations for its inclusion in Tacitus. Firstly, the writer may be taking the opportunity to have a stab at Domitian. There is no doubt that he repeatedly damns Domitian in favour of Nerva and Trajan in his works, and the opportunity to use an exciting and memorable story to condemn the man further might have been too tempting. Domitian is busy launching a war against the Chatti, a German neighbour of the Usipi. If Domitian's decision to prosecute a war is having the effect of making German auxiliaries rebel against Rome, then his campaign might be seen in a more negative light. The German tribes supplied a sizeable number of regiments to the Roman army, after all. The second potential reason is that this event with renegade Usipi is recalled later in the text by the Caledonian chief, and it is possible that as a writer Tacitus is at this point working in a foil to use later in his build-up to the main event.

Of course, there is a much simpler explanation available, that Tacitus heard this story, thought it too juicy to ignore, and simply added it for colour, as a sort of palate cleanser between big battles.

I would be inclined to dismiss the passage as fiction, were it not for a couple of points. Firstly, as I just mentioned, the fact that the neighbouring lands of the Chatti were now under threat might well lead to Usipi units reneging on their oaths and trying to get home to protect their families. It is certainly far from impossible. Furthermore, a general suspicion levied at the German tribes at this time might hint at such events, and we find in Martial, written during Domitian's reign, the line 'So may the inconstant race of the yellow-haired Germans flourish, and whoever loves not the rule of Rome!'[13]

The season of 82 ends, then, with Rome in control of all the flat eastern lands as far as the Moray Firth, probably a line of forts keeping the hill tribes from reaching good farmland, the northern tribes forming a great army, and likely Agricola receiving grudging confirmation from Domitian that he has another year, on the understanding that this will be the last one, and the conquest will be completed.

14

MONS GRAUPIUS

The main event of Tacitus's tale unfolds with a personal aside: 'Early in the summer Agricola sustained a domestic affliction in the loss of a son born a year before, a calamity which he endured, neither with the ostentatious fortitude displayed by many brave men, nor, on the other hand, with womanish tears and grief. In his sorrow he found one source of relief in war.'[1]

Domitia Decidiana had been with her husband when he had governed Asia, and here we have the confirmation that she had equally accompanied him him in his governorship of Britain. More than this, though, everything we have seen over the preceding seasons has suggested that Agricola remained on campaign in the north, overseeing the ongoing war, probably spending the winter with the troops also. There is certainly no indication in Tacitus that he returned to the south for the winter during the Scottish campaigns. In his first years we can assume he did so because Tacitus told us of his civic endeavours. Now there is no mention of such activity, and the suggestion is that Agricola remained in Scotland, probably with the iuridicus in London as his deputy dealing with his ongoing building projects. After all, we know from his record now that he is not a man afraid of action late in the season or beyond and, given his apparent personal involvement in the siting of fortifications, he may well have wished to oversee the construction of his various installations during winter. One tempting suggestion is to look at the Carlisle tablet mentioned earlier and see the presence of Agricola's bodyguard there as indicative of him using Carlisle as his winter quarters, though it seems more likely that that would be during earlier times, and that quarters somewhere north of the Forth/Clyde line would be more reasonable for campaigns in the Highlands.

This leads us to the question of where his wife resided while he was on campaign. One would assume she was left in the safety of a good civic locale, such as London, far from danger and the unknown. However, since travelling from Aberdeenshire to London to visit his wife would mean a journey of more than 500 miles, taking some two and a half weeks by horse or a week by sea, *if* the Roman sailors felt brave enough to tackle the North Sea in the winter season, it may be that Domitia travelled with her husband in the north.

Agricola's second son (third child) had been born in 82, whether as a result of winter visits or constant proximity. If Domitia had remained in the south, then news had to travel to reach Agricola. He had begun his campaign by the early summer, so the tidings would have arrived while he was at war. Thus there is little chance that he broke off the campaign and went south to be with his wife. If she was with him in the north, he would be able to continue the campaign even as he dealt with his personal disaster. Whatever the case, Agricola followed one of the age-old platitudes of grief: 'you've got to keep yourself busy.' In his case, the business in hand was war, and so he poured all his frustration and anguish into the campaign. Though Tacitus expounds on Agricola's virtues here by making sure we know how manly he is, still the reaction is a natural one, and again it seems unlikely that such a thread in the tale is invention, for Tacitus's wife at least would know the truth, if not other readers.

Irritatingly, with Tacitus's usual lack of fine detail we are told nothing of the campaign that took place between the death of Agricola's son and the final conflict, and the temptation is to see the war as moving swiftly from personal tragedy to a final cataclysmic battle. There are a number of clues in the text, though, that point to a lengthy campaign. Firstly, we were told that he found relief in war. The phrase just does not suggest a swift and conclusive fight, being more indicative of a drawn-out and brutal campaign. Moreover, after the coming battle, Tacitus tells us plainly that 'summer was now over', and that suggests that the campaigning season was already almost finished when the battle took place. September seems to be the likeliest time. So what actually happened in the intervening summer months?

In the speech Tacitus relates where Agricola addresses his troops before the final battle, interesting phrases are included. 'Often on the march, when morasses, mountains, and rivers were wearing out your strength, did I hear our bravest men exclaim, "When shall we have the enemy before us? – when shall we fight?" He is now here, driven from his lair.' Assuming this is not a generalisation of the entire war and that the general is referring to the seasonal campaign that has brought them to this point, then some of the action took them into the Highlands once more. We have already contemplated the likelihood that Agricola's plan was to strangle the enemy, cut off their access to food sources and force them to come down and fight in open ground. This theory is supported by the fact that we are told of his army demanding to know when they would get to fight the enemy. The suggestion is clearly that the army has been engaged upon a strategy of aggravating the natives and pushing them into coming out for a fight. We are also told in that speech that they 'have accomplished so great a march, to have traversed forests and to have crossed estuaries', which points to extensive movement, and while some of it seems to have been in the Highlands, some must therefore have been coastal. The reference to estuaries crossed brings to mind such locations as the Ythan and Findhorn estuaries, the former north of Aberdeen in Taexali lands, the latter on the Moray coastline, roughly halfway between the northernmost confirmed Roman camp and the mouth of the River Ness.

'Having sent on a fleet, which by its ravages at various points might cause a vague and wide-spread alarm, he advanced with a lightly equipped force, including in its ranks some Britons of remarkable bravery, whose fidelity had been tried through years of peace, as far as the Grampian mountains, which the enemy had already occupied.'[2]

This further information comes from a purported speech that is very likely Tacitus's own invention, but it does still support the notion that Agricola was goading the enemy into open war. If the fleet had been set to harrying the tribes along the coast in order to spread alarm, that fits perfectly with the army engaged in similar pursuits in the hills. If the army is crossing estuaries and the fleet is working along the coast, this echoes the combined operations of the preceding year.

It seems beyond doubt, then, that attempting to goad the natives into coming out onto the plain is precisely what Agricola's army and fleet were doing over that summer. Roman temporary camps have been confirmed scattered around the flat lands of eastern Scotland all the way from the Tay to the Spey, and it seems likely that a number of these were in use during this campaign, even if they had been constructed before and may have been manned again later. It is extremely difficult to be certain of any of them, barring perhaps the camps displaying Stracathro-type gates. Only two military campaigns by Roman commanders are confirmed to have taken place north of the Tay – those of Agricola and of Septimius Severus in the early third century. Thus camps in this region have to have belonged to one or the other, and in places camps overlie one another or are in too close proximity to be contemporary. The most northerly camp at Auchinove, though, sports Stracathro gates, and so we can say with confidence that the campaign reached at least this point.

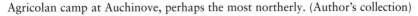

Agricolan camp at Auchinove, perhaps the most northerly. (Author's collection)

I do not intend to divert into an in-depth discussion over which camps might be of what date, and why camps of a certain size may be linked to Agricola. For closer studies into this matter, I would refer you to Grant's *Roman Military Objectives in Britain Under the Flavian Emperors* pp.104-105 and to Simon Forder's detailed investigation in *The Romans in Scotland and The Battle of Mons Graupius*. Our purpose is not to delve into such matters beyond their application to Agricola's life story. The simple fact is that some of these camps must be attributed to Agricola, and they are strongly indicative of campaigns around the region at this time.

In our ongoing story, then, we can see Agricola fighting down his anguish over the loss of a son, sending his fleet off to destroy any coastal settlements and to generally harry and panic the natives, very likely all the way up to the north coast and perhaps even to the Orkneys. While they do that, he uses his land forces to similar effect, continuing to cut off the free tribes from the better farmland, damaging them in any way he can and continually goading them into coming out to fight. Soldiers cross estuaries, which places them in coastal regions; build camps in the flat eastern lands, confirming their presence there; and we are told they also cross mountains and forests, suggesting that they operated at least within the edge of the Highlands. This puts Agricola's army over more or less the entirety of Aberdeenshire and the Grampians in that season, which suggests that the army was split into several forces, despite the trouble to which similar decisions had led the previous year. This notion is somewhat backed up by the fact that we have been told 'he advanced with a lightly equipped force'.

Caesar once wrote that he moved 'with four legions marching light',[3] giving us a precise make-up of his army, but we cannot be certain of the details of the army Agricola commanded on this occasion. The fact that Tacitus specifically draws our attention to the lightly equipped nature of this force implies that it is far from his full army. Later, we are told that in the battle Agricola fields 8,000 auxiliary infantry and 3,000 cavalry as well as 'legions'. This pluralisation need not refer to all three legions at his command, and may only refer to two. A third may have been active elsewhere, after all. It is tempting to suggest that the Second Adiutrix might be engaged around the coast in conjunction with the fleet. That would leave Agricola with only the Ninth and the Twentieth as the core of his force, and the Ninth, having taken a serious battering the previous year, may well be a long way below their nominal strength. It is not unreasonable to suggest that despite having at least two legions at this point, in terms of manpower they could number less than one full legion's worth. A quick glance at the table of units that we can comfortably place in Britain in the late Flavian era (Appendix 2) shows a strength on paper of more than 12,000 infantry and more than 5,500 cavalry. Although we have to remember that many units would be in garrisons across the island, the numbers given in the table are a conservative estimate, and the table only covers *known* units. There were undoubtedly other auxiliary units in Britain at the time of whom we know nothing, and thus Tacitus's numbers do not seem unrealistic.

None of the units attested in that table are of British origin, while we are told by Tacitus specifically that Britons were among his force. It was not common practice for Romans to raise auxiliary units and set them to serve in their own province, for the sake of security, and traditionally they were posted abroad. That Agricola has them in his army suggests that he was short of manpower and was forced to draft in locals to make up the numbers.

Birley notes the raising of units in Britain in the 80s among the tribes of the Belgae, the Dobunni and the Coritani (aka Corieltavi),[4] and so it seems quite possible that it was these peoples fighting for Agricola this year. While this would pit British tribes against one another, it is worth remembering that those three tribes occupy Romanised south/central England, while the Caledonii are in the far north of Scotland. The tribes from which the auxilia were drawn were geographically closer to Germany than to the Caledonii, and may never even have heard of this northern people, so we can safely cast aside any notion of feelings of doubt over fighting fellow Britons.

In the lead-up to our grand finale, the famous Battle of Mons Graupius, it is important to note the etymology of the battle. In the earlier extract from Tacitus, Church and Brodribb translated the text as the Grampian Mountains, and they were not the first to do so. The *Montem Graupium* of Tacitus is now inextricably linked with the range of the Grampian Mountains in north-east Scotland, but this may be misleading. The location of the battle has never been confirmed, and it is thanks to an earlier translation of Tacitus in 1476 when it was misprinted as Grampius, applied in 1520 to this range of hills, that the Grampian Mountains take their name. It is not an ancient corruption of a Roman name, but the words of Tacitus being applied to geography in the sixteenth century that links the range to the battle.

Thus, when Tacitus tells us that his lightly armed force approached the Graupian Mountains, we cannot for certain say even in which part of Scotland this was. There is still a strong case for the Grampians, however, especially given where we know the Romans were campaigning.

What this seems to tell us, then, is that Agricola's strategy had worked. By strangling the tribes, he drew the massed confederacy out from the Highlands to the very edge, somewhere on the slopes of the Grampians, and prepared to face them with the force he had available at the time.

The location of Mons Graupius is debated repeatedly by historians and enthusiasts, with propositions ranging from the highly possible to the wildly improbable. Once again, the detail is important to this text only in so far as geography may help determine the veracity of Tacitus's account. As such, I will examine just four of the proposed sites of the battle. If Tacitus is giving us accurate information, then we are looking for a location that could accommodate 30,000 natives including cavalry and, at a conservative estimate of 50 per cent effective manpower, 7,500 legionaries, 8,000 auxiliary infantry and 3,000 cavalry, totalling 18,500 Romans. The natives deploy on high ground with hilltops, the Romans in an entrenched camp, with space on the plain in between to field chariots. Nearby are woodlands enough to shelter large numbers.

In his investigations Forder examines a number of sites, and I was interested to find an unusual choice among them, suggesting that the campaigns of 82 may have continued to take place in the more southerly reaches, just north of the Tay. This is based partially upon a theory that Tacitus telling us of the army and the marines sharing camps would limit the operations to such feasible sites, which are all around the Tay region. The Roman camp at Carey (Abernethy) near Perth, south of the Tay, would be the site of Agricola's force, and the hill of Moncrieff the 'Mons Graupius' of the natives.

Geographically, the hill would certainly support a force of 30,000, and at 116 acres the camp could house roughly the same number, certainly enough for Agricola's force. The plain between the camp and the hill would provide adequate space for the manoeuvring of chariots and cavalry. In Moncrieff's favour, there is a native hill fort atop it, and there is certainly enough etymological similarity to see how Mons Graupius could be corrupted over time to Moncrieff. The camp of Carey is aligned to the River Earn that lies between the two sites. The crossing of that river, though, here in excess of 100 feet wide, would surely be notable enough to make it into Tacitus's account. Also, following the battle, while he notes that the region would have been marshier before drainage systems were put in place, the survivors would be stuck on a peninsula, without forests and adequate escape routes, and it seems likely that Rome would have little difficulty trapping and disarming the losing side. As such, I find this one of the weaker choices.

Secondly, Maitland, Stuart, Crawford and Surenne proposed the site of Kempstone Hill near Stonehaven. This hill, at perhaps half a mile across, is considerably smaller than Moncrieff and, in fact, smaller than the nearby Roman camp of Raedykes, which at 93 acres could accommodate an army of around 26,000. This would be adequate for Agricola's force, but at a smaller size than the camp, Kempstone Hill would be rather inadequate for the natives. In fact, it is a rather unimpressive hill, and with only a few standing stones connected to the ancient world there is no reason to picture it as a stronghold for the natives. Moreover, there is a poor line of sight and a considerable distance between the two, the terrain could hardly be described as a plain, and in fact, Raedykes is actually higher than Kempstone Hill.

Lastly, Kempstone lies between Raedykes camp and the sea, and is a long way east of the Highlands, and was almost certainly within the area already controlled by Agricola. As such, the location seems unlikely, and is far from reminiscent of Tacitus's description.

Continuing northwards, our third site is the one most often agreed upon by historians: the hill of Bennachie. Logie Durno temporary camp nearby is one of the largest in Scotland, at in excess of 140 acres, allowing it to accommodate around 40,000. Even if Agricola had three legions at full strength, numbering some 15,500 men, added to his auxiliaries and cavalry, that totals 26,500. Logie Durno, then, seems excessive in size for Agricola's army, though the extra space might be accounting for artillery, support units and more. Certainly Bennachie seems favourite as a choice for the native position, especially if Campbell is correct that the Latin name has been corrupted over time to become Graupius, and that the real *Mons Cripius* would suggest a ridged hill, reminiscent of a comb. Bennachie would fit such a description. Once again there is adequate space on the low ground in between for the activity of horse and chariots.

One source I read writes off Bennachie as being too steep for any kind of action, though I am inclined to accept it regardless. In researching Caesar's wars, I walked from the small Roman camp up the slope towards the Gaulish oppidum of Gergovia and Bennachie offers no more terrain difficulty than that. The watercourses that lie between Durno camp and the hill are negligible and would not present a real obstacle. Importantly, Bennachie plays host to an ancient fortification and could even be seen as something of an eastern outpost of the Grampian Range. Forests abound, and survivors would not find it difficult to flee into the Highlands.

The last of our four, and the northernmost, was favoured by Burn, but also by the stalwarts in Agricola study Ogilvie and Richmond. The Pass of Grange is enigmatic in that it is linked with the northernmost Roman sites in the world. Strategic arguments aside, little recommends Knock Hill and the Pass of Grange. The nearest Roman camps are Auchinove and Muiryfold, but the former is too small, holding only 7,500 men, while the latter, though large enough, is commonly dated to the Severan campaigns. Knock Hill is some distance away. Having visited several of these sites, I would have loved the Pass of Knock to be feasible as Mons

Graupius, but there are simply too many negatives to favourably compare it to Bennachie.

Of course, the actual attempts to identify the site are problematical at best. Tacitus was not in Britain at the time of Mons Graupius, and any information he acquired for his account, whether it be from his father-in-law or other witnesses, was gathered in subsequent years. That details may have been lost or changed between the event and its recall seems a given. We therefore encounter once again an uncertainty over Tacitus's veracity. We have no other source against which to compare, and so Tacitus is our only information. All we can safely be certain of is that the Roman force would have been based in a camp, and the appellation 'Mons' tells us that a big hill faced it. The simple answer, then, is that despite the favouring of various sites, in truth just about any hill within sight of a Roman camp could be considered.

In a recent social media conversation in a Roman history group, one participant avidly insisted that Mons Graupius was a complete fiction and that the battle never happened. This seems more blind to possibility than a claim that Tacitus was 100 per cent accurate would be. No matter Tacitus's audience and his purpose, Mons Graupius was simply too important and high profile to have been entirely created by Tacitus. There will have been people at court at the time of publication who were involved in one way or another, and plenty of people around who knew the story to some extent. That it never happened at all seems simply too fantastical. To have minor details omitted or added, however, is almost certain. Thus it is exceedingly difficult to apply Tacitus's description to any place in Scotland. If Tacitus's source in his excitement of relating the tale forgot to mention crossing a small river, or overemphasised the numbers at all, then all our criteria for trying to identify the site are worthless. Such is the study of Agricola. The only real confirmation we will ever have is if a lucky individual stumbles across archaeological evidence of a large battle somewhere that fits the bill.

What we have to realistically assume is that the bones of Tacitus's account of Mons Graupius are true to life, but that we have to take all details with a pinch of salt, as we shall most certainly see. Of these four more famous choices of site, the one which upon visiting made me shiver with possibility was Bennachie. Even the photographic evidence in the colour plates gives something of the atmosphere of the site. It most closely fits Tacitus. It makes sense in the narrative.

For the sake of our tale, then, I shall take Bennachie as my battle site. After a summer of the navy harrying the coast and the army making life unbearable for the hill tribes, Agricola brings a column that clearly does not constitute his entire force to the edge of the Grampians, where word has it that the Caledonian alliance has now gathered. He locates them at Bennachie and finds good ground – we have been told how excellent he is at this – siting the camp now known as Logie Durno.

In his scene setting for this, Tacitus tells us 'For the Britons [...] by embassies and treaties, summoned forth the whole strength of all their states. More than 30,000 armed men.'[5] In this description, he also uses the words 'old age was still fresh and green,' Tacitus's borrowing of Virgil's line 'He look'd in years; yet in his years were seen a youthful vigor and autumnal green.'[6]

Do you have a block of salt handy? You'll need it by the pinch for the next step in our narrative. Tacitus has the Roman force drawn up before their camp's ditches, facing the Caledonii on their hill, where they have massed, and here we drop from an account of the campaign into traditional heroic oratory. It is seemingly impossible for a Roman audience to contemplate reading of a battle without a speech from each commander. While we can assume that with witnesses to the events still around, Tacitus did his best to conform to the truth of the campaigns and battles as he heard it, it is highly unlikely that he could have much of a notion of what the commanders said to their men. At best he would have had Agricola recounting years later that he made a stirring speech, but clearly no one who could have witnessed the speech of the enemy commander would have a way to pass it on to Tacitus. At least the Caledonian speech is therefore certainly complete fabrication, and Agricola's speech is almost certainly as much, too.

The speeches from the Church and Brodribb translation have been added as Appendix 6, but here we will deal only with small portions of the speeches for the purpose of what they tell us about Tacitus, Agricola and the events of the campaign. The first speech we are given is that of the Caledonian leader, a man named Calgacus, otherwise attested nowhere in history, and therefore almost certainly Tacitus's personal creation. Tacitus has created Calgacus to be the perfect foil, to be the 'noble savage', to draw attention to the wickedness of Rome in the age of Domitian, and to be in many ways the 'Anti-Agricola'. Pugh[7] convincingly links Calgacus's name to the Celtic Calgacos, which would translate as 'The Swordsman', and the Irish Calgach, translating as 'Possessor of a sword'. The ironic comparison with 'Agricola' (The Farmer) is hard to miss, and the very name makes the Caledonian leader the iconic warrior-king. Moreover, Calgacus's speech is impassioned and powerful, cutting deep into the heart of the invasion, while Agricola's is shorter and more military, appealing to the soldierly nature of his men. We might remember that even though this is Tacitus manufacturing the native's words, they still have value for they show what Rome believed the contemporary Scottish tribes to be feeling. Their leader would have a difficult time keeping numerous usually conflicting tribes working as a single army, and that, then, is the purpose of this speech.

Calgacus delivering his speech from the *Pictorial History of Scotland* by James Taylor, 1859. (Public domain)

Calgacus appeals to the tribes in a very traditional and expected manner, citing their endangered liberty, that they are the last of the free peoples, and that all Rome offers is slavery. One might here find an echo of Tacitus's description of Agricola's civic policy in his early days as governor, when he encourages the Romanisation of the conquered tribes, and the natives 'called it civilization, although it was a part of their enslavement'.[8] Tacitus does not only recall his own words in this speech, though, but takes the highlights from other great speeches by endangered noble savages and reworks them for Calgacus. The Caledonian leader calls the Romans 'Robbers of the world, having by their universal plunder exhausted the land', echoing the words of Mithridates in Sallust 'the plunderers of all the nations'.[9] He rises to a crescendo with the now famous line 'they make a desert and call it "peace"' which somewhat neatly reworks Pliny's 'the arms of Rome that made the country a desert'.

He goes on in chapter 31 to rail against conscription of Britons to serve in other provinces, against the dangers of rape, of slavery, of taxation and overlordship, citing once more their status as the last of the free peoples (apparently ignoring Ireland). One of the few obvious mistakes in Tacitus appears in this part of Calgacus's speech where he has the Brigantes under a woman's leadership burning a colony, which we can be reasonably confident should be the Iceni. Whether this is Tacitus making a genuine mistake or a mistake in later copying of the text, we will likely never know. Interestingly, in this speech we could have further confirmation of the past year of Agricola's campaign and the theory that he had squeezed the tribes and forced them to a fight. '[We] are marked out for destruction. We have neither fruitful plains, nor mines, nor harbours,' says Calgacus, which would certainly be the case if for more than a year the Roman army had prevented them from reaching the 'fruitful' flat lands of the east, while the navy had been battering their coast.

The third chapter of his speech brings his harangue to a close, suggesting that Rome's army is made up of peoples from many nations, most of whom would hate one another were it not for a mutual service to Rome. His suggestion, recalling the revolt of the Usipi cohort, is that if the Romans are beaten, the bond that holds their army together will come undone and Britain will be saved. Clearly this is once more Tacitus's own interpretation of the position of the Caledonii, for there is little chance of the leader of an only recently encountered northern tribe having the detail of the Roman world Calgacus displays. The speech is serving to make the enemy a little more impressive, and the situation that little bit more critical, so that Agricola's victory is all the more glorious.

By comparison, Agricola's speech over the next two chapters simply exhorts his men to victory, reminding them of the great efforts they have put in over the past years and pointing out that this is not so much a grand army gathered against them, as the last of the natives pushed into a corner (in a moment reminiscent of the trapping of the Welsh tribes on Anglesey). He lauds their fifty years' service, which almost certainly is a copying mistake somewhere down the centuries, as AD 83 marks precisely forty years since the initial conquest of Britain. Over the centuries some copyist has likely missed an X from the L. 'It's almost over, men,' he is saying. 'One last push.' Unsurprisingly his men roar with approval and are champing at the bit. This speech, as opposed to that of Calgacus, is not only down-to-earth and very realistic, it is very much in line with similar speeches noted by Roman generals from the days of the early republic down to the empire, and indeed throughout the rest of history to the present day.

As Birley points out, in the days long before the invention of the PA system, Agricola would have tremendous difficulty addressing even a fraction of an army this size, let alone Calgacus exhorting his 30,000 people. Monty Python's *Life of Brian* and the sermon on the mount.

'You hear that? Blessed are the Greek.'

'The Greek?'

'Mmm. Well, apparently, he's going to inherit the earth.'

'Did anyone catch his name?'

The scene is set. As expected by his audience, Tacitus has had both leaders make speeches, telling us what is at stake. All that is left now is the action.

15

PUGNARE

Tacitus's account of his father-in-law's greatest battle opens with a useful strategic explanation, setting the battle scene for us.

'He arrayed his eager and impetuous troops in such a manner that the auxiliary infantry, 8,000 in number, strengthened his centre, while 3,000 cavalry were posted on his wings. The legions were drawn up in front of the entrenched camp; his victory would be vastly more glorious if won without the loss of Roman blood, and he would have a reserve in case of repulse.'[1]

It may seem odd to the modern reader with preconceived notions of Roman warfare that Agricola chose to field the auxiliaries as his main fighting force, keeping the legions in reserve. Tacitus ascribes this to a desire to preserve Roman blood, but that realistically must be the author applying his own motives to the general. The legions had been recruited from places like Spain and Gaul for many years, and their blood would have been in principle no more Roman than that of at least some of the auxiliary units. Tacitus is perhaps using the citizen status of the legions against the non-citizen of the auxilia to make an audience in Rome think more highly of the general. I doubt it would work.

The simple fact is that there are many reasons why Agricola might choose such a formation, and a study of Roman deployment for battle from the late republic to the Flavian era shows a huge variation in strategies. Indeed, had not Ostorius Scapula (Agricola's role model?) defeated the Iceni with a purely auxiliary force, and Bolanus later use a force mainly of auxiliaries to rescue Cartimandua? Agricola is doing nothing new or surprising here. Besides, in earlier text we were told that the army Agricola had brought to the site was 'a lightly equipped force' and at no point does he tell us how many legions are present, nor their strengths. We are given specific numbers for the auxilia and the cavalry, but just the vague plural of 'legions'. It is therefore entirely possible that the number of legionary soldiers Agricola is capable of fielding at Mons Graupius was considerably fewer than his 8,000 auxilia.

More sense can be made when we look back upon other events. Agricola had taken German units with him to Mona because he knew he would be able to use them to great effect. He deployed the navy in a more offensive manner than his predecessors, probably because he was more familiar with their capabilities than other governors. Agricola was a man, so we have come to learn, who knew what his men could do and utilised them to the best of their ability. It is therefore more than possible that Agricola looked across the plain with all its difficulties, and to the slope atop which the enemy waited, and decided that his legions were the least suited to stomping across and up at the Caledonii. Conversely, he had Britons, Germans and Spaniards in his auxilia, and certainly with the former, there is a good chance that they were more suited to the advance. The cavalry being deployed upon the wings is a standard practice, although since some of the German auxiliary units were mixed cohorts of infantry and cavalry, we cannot be certain whether their cavalry contingents had been moved to the flanks with the rest of the horse, or remained as pockets of riders within the ranks. The cohorts would be trained to work in concert, so splitting them may not have been considered, though as we shall see when the battle unfolds there is good reason to presume the horse contingents *had* been moved to the flanks alongside the other cavalry units. Tacitus describes the enemy in the same passage: 'The enemy [...] had posted himself on high ground; his van was on the plain, while the rest of his army rose in an arch-like form up the slope of a hill. The plain between resounded with the noise and with the rapid movements of chariots and horses.'

This is fairly straightforward. If the enemy formed like a rainbow on the slopes of the hill, the suggestion is that they intended to surround Agricola's army, flanking them on both sides. Given the difference in numbers, it might have been possible, and it is not unlikely that the tribal leaders settled on such a plan. Perhaps their cavalry and chariots racing about were goading the Romans, trying to draw them into the trap. Tacitus goes on to explain why they failed: 'Agricola, fearing that from the enemy's superiority of force he would be simultaneously attacked in front and on the flanks, widened his ranks, and though his line was likely to be too extended, and several officers advised him to bring up the legions, yet, so sanguine was he, so resolute in meeting danger, he sent away his horse and took his stand on foot before the colours.'

So Agricola thins his lines out somewhat dangerously, perhaps to prevent being flanked, but also perhaps in response to the dangers of the chariots. Chariots were already an antiquated machine for war, and Roman tactics against them had proved successful more than once, generally revolving around pulling back or opening up ranks to let them past where they could be dealt with by lines of sharpened stakes or the like.

That he might stand with his troops (almost certainly behind the front rankers, for he was no fool) recalls a the actions of Julius Caesar at the battle of the Sabis in 57 BC. The ambush of the encamped legions by the Nervii was so sudden and brutal that Caesar spent the height of the battle rushing from one legion to the next, personally throwing out orders and boosting the morale of the beleaguered men. Agricola is probably positioned at the rear of his auxiliaries but before the ranks of the legions, where he can direct from the heart of the action, able to directly command his army as Caesar had done, rather than from some high observation point via tribunes on horses. Rome, then, is ready. Battle can commence.

'The battle opened with fighting at long range: the Britons not only stood firm but displayed skill in parrying the javelins of our men with their massive swords or catching them on their short shields, while hurling a great rain of spears themselves. Then Agricola exhorted the four Batavian and two Tungrian cohorts to fight hand to hand at sword's point.'[2]

Agricola had launched the first attack, which involved the hurling of missiles as a standard Roman tactic. Tacitus has told us that the space between the armies was wide enough for chariots and horses to race about, and as the enemy were arrayed in an arc, the only place they might be close to the Roman force is at the wings, where the cavalry is stationed. Given that the maximum effective range of the Roman pilum is around 30–35 metres, give or take, the chariots must now have vanished and the lines closed for such an exchange of missiles to take place. More of this shortly.

We are told that the natives managed to parry the missiles with small bucklers and large swords, and then responded with a shower of spears, though not what effect this had on the Roman force. The mention of large swords is perfectly in line with the known nature of Celtic weapons, though the small shields or bucklers is an interesting addition not seen in other sources. It is reminiscent of the later medieval *targes* of the Scottish Highlanders and perhaps illustrates one difference between these Highland tribes and the more southerly tribes of Britain. It is a detail we might consider as proof of Tacitus having an eyewitness account to work from, as the shields of the Celtic tribes with which most Romans would be familiar are much larger, oval body shields. If Tacitus was simply manufacturing this account, it seems likely he would have used shield types with which he would be familiar.

Comparison of shield types. The Chertsey and Battersea Shields dated c. 400-50 BC, and a Yetholm-type shield from Wales c. 1200-900 BC, British Museum. All three were seemingly made for offerings or decorative purposes, but their form and size would mirror contemporary combat examples. (Author's collection)

An exchange of missiles complete, Agricola gives the order to close for combat. Notably he focuses on six German cohorts, and they must clearly be his favourite and most familiar auxiliary units after the various engagements in which they have fought. These six cohorts, which would probably number just over 3,000 men according to our calculated table of units, formed the front lines, more than a third of the auxiliary contingent. In our next part of that same passage, it becomes clear why Agricola has chosen these men for the fight.

'This was what they [the Tungrians and Batavians] had been trained for in their long service, whereas it was awkward for the enemy with their small shields and enormous swords – for the swords of the Britons, having no points, were unsuited for a cut-and-thrust struggle and close-quarters battle. So the Batavians rained blows indiscriminately, struck with their shield-bosses, and stabbed in the face. When they had cut down those posted on the plain, they started to push their battle-line up the hillsides. The other cohorts, in eager competition, pressed forward to attack, and cut down the nearest of the enemy. In the haste of victory a good many were left half-dead or untouched.' In truth, given that the success of this engagement is ascribed to the usability of the Roman gladius in close combat compared with the long, chopping swords of the natives, this does not entirely explain the selection of auxiliaries over the legions, who would have enjoyed the same advantage.

Given the initial deployments, it is but a single line that explains rather poorly why the auxiliaries engage in battle across the hillsides without seemingly having to push through the chariots we know to have been racing about on the plain. Yet again, Tacitus supplies us with irritatingly meagre information. 'Meanwhile – for the charioteers had fled – the cavalry squadrons joined in the infantry battle.'

So with their departure, Agricola sends cavalry in to join the German infantry in the melee. What happened to the chariots? We will never know. It seems likely that they were for mere show and fled the scene before any engagement. Caesar had noted on his first visit to the island more than a century earlier the tactics of the natives: 'Their mode of fighting with their chariots is this: firstly, they drive about in all directions and throw their weapons and generally break the ranks of the enemy with the very dread of their horses and the noise of their wheels; and when they have worked themselves in between the troops of horse, leap from their chariots and engage on foot. The charioteers in the mean time withdraw some little distance from the battle, and so place themselves with the chariots that, if their masters are overpowered by the number of the enemy, they may have a ready retreat to their own troops.'[3]

Various explanations for the failure of the Caledonian chariots have been put forward, including poor terrain and Roman infantry spacing, and they may have merit, but given Caesar's earlier words, it seems highly likely that the chariots were there to make a lot of noise and to panic the Romans, then they dropped off their loads, noble warriors all, before racing away out of danger. Like horses, chariots would be of little large-scale military use in much of the Highlands, and so it seems likely they were more status symbols and personal transport than weapons of war. we can connect these chariots to the ones noted by Silius Italicus as used by the tribes in the Shetlands: 'the woad-stained native of Thule drives his chariot armed with scythes round the close-packed ranks in battle.'[4] Certainly Shetland and the absolute north-eastern tip of the mainland are gentle enough terrain to accommodate chariot warfare. However, it is entirely likely that Silius's inclusion of this aside on the natives of Thule is either entirely fictional or hearsay from some unknown source, as the poet has no known connection to Britain. We can perhaps brush aside this and consider the chariots at Mons Graupius as there for dramatic effect to impress the Romans and perhaps to convey the nobles into the fray.

In the time of Trajan, perhaps two decades later, several of the Germanic units that must have been at Mons Graupius (at least II Tungrorum and II, VIII and IX Batavorum) are equitata units, formed of mixed horse and foot, and that was almost certainly already the case in 83. However, since the cavalry would use the longer spatha rather than the shorter gladius, and the description by Tacitus of the initial engagement specifically illustrates only gladius-wielding infantry advancing, it is highly likely that the cavalry contingents of the Batavians and Tungrians have been positioned on the flanks thus far and are now ordered into the press alongside two alae of cavalry from the wings. In Arrian's treatise on the battle formation of the Roman forces against the Alani, he goes into some detail on the centre of the Roman force, noting entirely infantry units, then says 'The entire cavalry arrayed together in eight wings and squadrons must stand next to the infantrymen on both flanks,'[5] suggesting that standard Roman tactics in battle would be to deploy the cavalry section of mixed units alongside the alae on the wings.

This would effectively put perhaps 1,500 cavalry into the battle, while keeping 2,000 on the wings in reserve. The Germans would be used to fighting alongside their infantry partners and so the mixed units could merrily slaughter their way up the hillsides. What happened in that press concludes '[the cavalry] began to stick fast in the solid ranks of the enemy and the uneven ground. The battle bore little resemblance to a cavalry action: our men could hardly keep their footing and were at the same time jostled by the horses' flanks. Often, too, runaway chariots or terrified, riderless horses with nothing but fear to direct them careered into the ranks from the side or head on.'

What Tacitus gives us now is confusion. No grand image of Roman strategy, but the chaos of battle. As such, this strikes me as one of the most authentic moments to be found in Tacitus. One can almost see a world-weary, ageing Agricola by a fire, talking to his son-in-law over a glass of Falernian wine and describing the tumult of the battle. Here is captured an astonishingly lifelike glimpse of battle: men losing their footing, empty chariots rattling around, horses bumping into men in the press. It is not the image of a well-oiled Roman army machine, and probably better describes the horrors of the scene than any carefully crafted description of manoeuvres.

For the record the variation in translation of the Agricola has led to some confusion over the cavalry activity at Mons Graupius. Some historians will place Caledonian cavalry down on the plain with the chariots, seeing *covinnarius eques* in the text as meaning 'chariots and cavalry', though it is at least equally possible that this is referring to the chariots and the horses pulling them. If this is the case then there is no description of British cavalry at the battle. Certainly the terrain of the Highlands is not suitable for cavalry and so it seems likely that while the tribes had horses, they had at no time developed cavalry warfare, and that barring a few nobles and the chariots, the Caledonian army was basically an infantry force.

So the melee has erupted into chaos, though the Batavians and Tungrians are clearly getting the best of it, since they are pushing up the hill among the enemy. Agricola has thus far committed six cohorts of his Germans and two alae of cavalry to the fray, and so some 3,000 foot and half that number of horse are pushing their way up into the enemy ranks. That leaves 5,000 auxiliaries in the centre, 2,000 cavalry on the wings, and the unknown number of legionaries in reserve.

We cannot know how many of the Caledonii were now committed, though it would appear that the number was but a part of the forces available. 'Those of the Britons who, having as yet taken no part in the engagement, occupied the hill-tops, and who without fear for themselves sat idly disdaining the smallness of our numbers, had begun gradually to descend and to hem in the rear of the victorious army, when Agricola, who feared this very moment, opposed their advance with four squadrons of cavalry held in reserve by him for any sudden emergencies of battle. Their repulse and rout was as severe as their onset had been furious. Thus the enemy's design recoiled on himself, and the cavalry which by the general's order had wheeled round from the van of the contending armies, attacked his rear.'

Seeing the mess now on the plain and the lower slopes, and perhaps that a thousand cavalry had been committed from the flanks, the Caledonian tribes make their one great play. They descend from the hilltops in a wide arc, spreading out like bull horns to encircle the Romans. If they can flank Agricola's force, then with what are almost certainly still superior numbers, they will be able to carry the day despite the advance of the Roman front lines.

Agricola had committed part of his army, but of his horse, he had kept two-thirds in reserve. Four squadrons (alae) each of 480 riders, sat on his wings, likely evenly split. Bennachie's lower slopes across the entire western face are gentle enough to allow for effective cavalry action. As previously noted, there is every reason to believe that the Caledonians were not proponents of mounted warfare, and the only battle we have seen them involved in thus far was the night attack on the Ninth, when it was the arrival of Roman cavalry that turned the tide. The natives, if they are not familiar with the capabilities of large-scale horse warfare, could not have known how to counter 4,000 cavalry slicing away at their edges, and panic would set in surprisingly easily.

This is the turning point of Mons Graupius. The auxiliary cohorts are carving their way up the slope at the heart of the Caledonian army, and the tribes respond by trying to surround them, only to find the two pincers descending the hills hit head-on by the nightmare of Roman cavalry. The moment those two native advances panic and break, the battle is effectively over. The fact that Tacitus tells us their 'repulse and rout was as severe as their onset had been furious' tells us everything we need to know. The Roman cavalry were brutal. They continued on past the panicked pincer movement and fell on the rear of the enemy force in the traditional Roman cavalry tactic of achieving the maximum kills possible among a panicked and broken enemy. By this time, the Caledonii had descended far enough down the hill to allow the cavalry full access.

Panic spread throughout the native army.

'Then, indeed, the open plain presented an awful and hideous spectacle. Our men pursued, wounded, made prisoners of the fugitives only to slaughter them when others fell in their way. And now the enemy, as prompted by their various dispositions, fled in whole battalions with arms in their hands before a few pursuers, while some, who were unarmed, actually rushed to the front and gave themselves up to death. Everywhere there lay scattered arms, corpses, and mangled limbs, and the earth reeked with blood.'

This description resounds strongly with me. Tacitus is writing to shock his audience with the brutality of it all. The description carries echoes of other great Roman writers with their tales of battlefields, such as Sallust with 'Then there was a fearful sight in the open plains – pursuing, fleeing, killing, capturing, horses and men dashed to the ground, many of the wounded unable either to flee or to remain quiet, now making an effort to rise and at once collapsing; in short, wherever the eye could reach, the ground was soaked in blood and strewn with weapons, arms, and corpses.'[6] But this is not a *heroic* scene. Despite the purpose of this text being to eulogise the great general, Rome is not painted here as a

Roman cavalry riding down barbarians, detail from an Antonine dedication slab now in the National Museum of Scotland. (Author's collection)

glorious victor and Agricola not as a careful and noble commander, for clemency was considered a virtue in a general. Julius Caesar achieved half his great success through the careful application of mercy. Even after the battle of Pharsalus he simply released many of his strongest opponents with a light admonishment. There is no clemency shown by Agricola and his army in the closing stages of Mons Graupius. We are told that the Roman force took prisoners and then slaughtered them when they found more to capture. While many of the beaten tribesmen flee individually, seeking any place of safety, some turn, dropping their weapons and submit to the pursuers. Tacitus suggests that in despair they were committing suicide though the likelihood, especially after the description of the prisoners' fate, is that they were attempting to surrender and were simply cut down out of hand by the rampaging and victorious Roman force.

The grisly description of the field leaves a lasting image in the mind's eye, and despite the notorious bloodthirstiness of the Roman psyche, one wonders whether even Tacitus's audience would be unstinting in their approval. After all, these were not criminals pitted against one another in the arena for the crowd's entertainment, but enemy warriors bested in battle. Rome liked to win, but literary evidence suggests that they liked to know that their opponents were worthy. The Caledonian tribes have already been painted by Tacitus as the noble savage, a creature for which the audience is supposed to show sympathy. How, then, does such wanton butchery of the noble savage sit with the audience?

'Even the conquered now and then felt a touch of fury and of courage. On approaching the woods, they rallied, and as they knew the ground, they were able to pounce on the foremost and least cautious of the pursuers. Had not Agricola, who was present everywhere, ordered a force of strong and lightly equipped cohorts, with some dismounted troopers for the denser parts of the forest, and a detachment of cavalry where it was not so thick, to scour the woods like a party of huntsmen, serious loss would have been sustained through the excessive confidence of our troops.'

That Agricola is shown as being omnipresent (again echoing Caesar against the Nervii) can only mean that he approved of the utterly savage manner of the pursuit of the fleeing Caledonii. We are not told that he attempted to restrain his men as Caesar was wont to do. Agricola merely allows his soldiers the violence of the victory. He is often shown to be wily and authoritative, brave and supportive, but at no point here does he show mercy. Additionally, Roman military minds reading this story would have shaken their heads at Agricola's willingness to let loose his men in pursuit of the fleeing enemy, for more than once in Roman history such a decision had led to the pursuing Romans being flanked or ambushed and slaughtered, as would have happened here had Agricola not prepared a reserve force just in case. A wise general kept a tight rein on his victorious forces.

An unwritten explanation for all this might still be discerned. This is the last stand of the last tribes, and Agricola's only chance to complete the conquest of the island. The emperor is now engaging his German foe and is unlikely to give Agricola another extension on his governorship to finish the job. However, before now the Iceni had been beaten yet rose again to burn cities. The Brigantes had been beaten more than once. The Silures rose from their own subjugation to cause further trouble, and the Ordovices were suppressed, and yet appeared once more to massacre Roman cavalry. Agricola has to be *sure* of his victory. He needs Mons Graupius to be such a total victory that it will be years, if ever, before the natives manage to gather sufficient strength to make a stand. He needs them beaten thoroughly enough and for long enough to Romanise them and subject them to that luxurious slavery of which we have been told. So it is not enough to win the battle and let the enemy flee in force. He has to tear chunks from them all the way home to stop them wanting to do this again.

Agricola narrowly averts this last disaster when the Caledonii, fleeing the field, try to rally, only to meet more Roman troops sent by the general into the woods. Once more, it is interesting to think that if the legions had been the force sent out here, they would have been considerably less use than the more flexible auxiliary forces, some of whom were almost certainly used as scouting and foraging parties and could perfectly 'scour the woods like a party of huntsmen'.

'When, however, the enemy saw that we again pursued them in firm and compact array, they fled no longer in masses as before, each looking for his comrade; but dispersing and avoiding one another, they sought the shelter of distant and pathless wilds. Night and weariness of bloodshed put an end to the pursuit. About 10,000 of the enemy were slain; on our side there fell 360 men, and among them Aulus Atticus, the commander of the cohort, whose youthful impetuosity and mettlesome steed had borne him into the midst of the enemy.'

Agricola, then, has regrouped his men from the melee and set them to marching after the force that had formed of their survivors, who can only avoid the pursuit by splitting up and fleeing by gulleys and woodland tracks. The survivors are hunted till nightfall, and only then does Agricola rein in his men. That the enemy are no longer thinking in terms of a combined force, but are instead fleeing, each man alone and for his life, suggests that Agricola has achieved his aim. The Caledonii have been beaten on a sufficient scale to claim total victory over the island at last and to be confident that it will be a long time before the enemy can rise again.

Agricola can only have heaved a deep sigh of relief as he looked across the battlefield on a cold September evening, knowing that the dispatch he had to write in his tent would race off to the emperor on the morrow with the best of all possible tidings.

He had done it.

We are told with clear and typical Roman exaggeration that the casualty rate was roughly 28:1. With the best will in the world the notion that for every Roman on that field who died, twenty eight natives joined him in the afterlife is laughable. The downplaying of losses is traditional, however, and not something for which we should unfairly judge Tacitus. In the battle of Pharsalus, Caesar claimed to have lost fewer than 200 men, while Pompey lost 15,000. By Caesar's example Tacitus is being unusually restrained with his figures. We cannot guess at how many Agricola truly lost in the fighting, although I suspect it is safe to say that there were more than the 360 Tacitus notes. That the Caledonian tribes might have lost 10,000 is perhaps not too far beyond probability. That would account for roughly a third of their force, and suggests that some 20,000 natives survived the battle. Needless to say, we can assume that a sizeable proportion of those survivors wound up in chains being led south, but the numbers are still not too obviously inflated.

In his diaries, Caesar occasionally mentions a lesser officer who does something of note, such as Centurion Baculus who, despite being ill and wounded in the medical tent, realises the legion is in trouble and hauls himself out of bed, grabs a shield and staggers out to the front line to take command. Sometimes such men are only mentioned because of the manner of which they meet their end. Since the legions are not deployed at Mons Graupius, then the Aulus Atticus named by Tacitus must have been the prefect of an auxiliary cohort, and given the stages of the battle, it is quite possible that he was the commander of one of the Batavian or Tungrian cohorts. While we cannot say for certain who this man was, the fact that he was named by Tacitus suggests that the audience would be familiar enough with him to groan at the mention of his death. Syme put forward an interesting theory. Cast your mind back to the very beginning, and to the father Agricola never met, Julius Graecinus. Columella, in his book on agriculture, lauds Graecinus's work on viticulture, and names him a student of Julius Atticus, also a writer on vines. It is more than plausible, given what we know of how Roman political and military appointments were made, that the Aulus Atticus who died commanding a cohort at Mons Graupius was a scion of the same family to whom Agricola's father had been a pupil. A neat little web, and a feasible explanation as to why Tacitus feels the man's name worth mentioning specifically.

Incidentally, Birley suggests another named officer present at Mons Graupius. An inscription found at Cyrene mentions 'C. IVLIO C.F. VO[L.] KARO EX PROVINCIA NARBONENSI, [...] PRAEF. COH. II ASTYRUM EQU. DONATO BELLO BRITANNICO',[7] which strongly suggests that this Julius Karus was the prefect of a unit we can comfortably connect with Mons Graupius, and even tells us that he won awards during a war in Britain. That this is our battle in Scotland seems very likely. Thus, while Agricola heaves a massive sigh of relief, and soldiers carry the remains of Prefect Aulus Atticus away for cremation, one of the men present who would go on to great things was Prefect Julius Karus of Cohors II Asturum, a man who, quite possibly, would be among Tacitus's audience upon publication.

One last name worthy of attention comes to us in Juvenal's Satires, where we are told 'Some King will be thy captive; or Arviragus will be hurled from his British chariot. The brute is foreign-born.'[8] Juvenal would have been a young or middle-aged man at the time of Mons Graupius, and his writings were published at similar times to those of Tacitus, and so it seems quite possible that Juvenal was writing of the same events. Is it possible that Arviragus was another tribal leader at Mons Graupius whose name had become known in Rome, yet who Tacitus omitted in favour of his Calgacus? Or perhaps it might be that Calgacus (the Swordsman) and King Arviragus were one and the same.

The sun sets, then, on the slopes of Bennachie, casting darkness over a field of blood and bodies, but heralding the final conquest of Britannia. Agricola returns to his headquarters and sits in his tent, penning the letter that will be the high point of his career and for what he remains famous to this day.

Gn Iulius Agricola to Titus Flavius Caesar Domitianus Augustus, greetings.
I have the honour to bear the very best of news...

16

WINTER OF CONTENT

In the aftermath of the battle, we are told of the victorious army only that 'Elated by their victory and their booty, the conquerors passed a night of merriment,'[1] which seems entirely likely. Of the vanquished tribes, however, Tacitus has a great deal to say, despite the fact that it is all his own invention, for there clearly could have been no Roman eyes or ears among the survivors of the Caledonian tribes that night. Tacitus describes them in chaos, which is quite reasonable, but has them taking out their anguish and frustration upon each other, their wives and children, and even their homes, setting fire to them. Perhaps he is extrapolating from what the Romans present could see the next day and reported, yet still this is a literary invention and we must reach for that block of salt once more.

What we are told next is interesting in light of Tacitus's abilities as a writer more than the story itself: 'The following day showed more fully the extent of the calamity, for the silence of desolation reigned everywhere: the hills were forsaken, houses were smoking in the distance, and no one was seen by the scouts.'

It is quite reasonable to picture barren and lifeless hills, smoking houses in the distance, perhaps more likely the work of Roman scouts during the pursuit the previous evening than of their owners, and a complete absence of any sign of the natives. This could be said to be the expected aftermath of Mons Graupius. But this brings Tacitus's tale of the battle full circle. Calgacus's fears have been realised, his words before the conflict have become truth. 'They make a desert, and call it "peace"' the Caledonian leader had said of the Romans. Witness the 'silence of desolation' the Romans have wrought.

Agricola's victory has been sufficient that we are told that the enemy have no chance to rally, and that it is now too late in the season for such a thing to happen anyway. Scotland has been bested. Britain is conquered and ripe now for settlement and Romanisation, and so 'Agricola led back his army into the territory of the Boresti.'

This is one of those nuggets in Tacitus that jars historians. To this point the Boresti have never been mentioned, and historians argue over the details. Through the possibility of medieval translation and copying errors, some see the Boresti as the Cornavii, who occupied the very north of Scotland, while others suggest that this is a sub-tribe and part of the Vacomagi. Given that the Caledonii are more a cooperative of tribes rather than a tribe in itself, it may be that the Boresti were a part of that group not individually important enough to have been previously mentioned. Wolfson presents an elegant solution to this mysterious people by making them not a tribe at all, but a mistranslation, offering for *in fines Borestorum exercitum deducit* instead *in fines boreos totum exercitum deducit*,[2] which would translate as something along the lines of 'Agricola led back his army into the lands of the far north.'

Despite this fascinating aside, the question is moot in our case, for the fact remains that we are told Agricola led back his troops to occupied lands, and that is all we need to know. Now would begin the massive task of securing control over the newly conquered territories, and while Agricola can initiate such a thing, he must have been aware that this would be his last winter in command of Britain. He had already gone some way beyond ordinary tenures, and had achieved what he had set out to do two emperors earlier.

If the great legionary fortress of Inchtuthil was not already under construction in the preceding seasons, then this must have begun that winter at the latest. The plan would be to impose a grid of roads and forts across the new lands in the same way as Agricola had done over North Wales in the aftermath of war with the Ordovices, and under Cerialis in Brigantian lands. There were already permanent installations as far north as Stracathro, and impinging on the edge of the Highlands. What were now required were forts to control the Great Glen, and roads and garrisons in the various accesses to it.

'Agricola himself, leading his infantry and cavalry by slow marches, so as to overawe the newly-conquered tribes by the very tardiness of his progress, brought them into winter quarters.' This suggests a southerly march through Taexali lands, the winter quarters being anywhere from the north of England up to the Tay. The presence of the Twentieth is attested in Carlisle in this year, and so perhaps that is part of the winter troop disposition. Newstead also seems a likely candidate.

One thing Agricola does, though, before he heads south, is to initiate one last project that seems to have been received with as much awe as his victory at Mons Graupius. '[He] ordered the commander of the fleet to sail round Britain. A force for this purpose was given him, which great panic everywhere preceded.'

This might have been a decision on a whim, influenced by the crazy tale of German deserters more than a year ago doing something similar, or it may have been a deliberate show of Roman power, circling the lands of the newly conquered so that they could see that Rome was everywhere. It may have been Agricola symbolically conquering the ocean for Rome, as Caligula is said to have done in his own time. It may have been simply for the achievement itself. Whatever the case, this was no small decision. Remember that this is at the earliest mid-September, and such a voyage would take a fleet around the perilous north coast of Scotland, past Cape Wrath, around the craggy western islands and down through the choppy Irish sea, out around the tip of Cornwall and up into the channel. This would not be a journey for the faint of heart aboard a trireme in autumn. Cassius Dio tells the same tale, though, with 'Thereupon Agricola sent others to attempt the voyage around Britain, and learned from them, too, that it was an island.'[3]

What the terrifying force that had been given to him was we can only guess. Perhaps it refers to the fleet itself, or to the marines, or perhaps even the Second Adiutrix, who were still only fourteen years a legion since they themselves had been sailors. That they might create panic wherever they went was probably as much the effect of word of mouth spreading what had already happened as the force itself.

We can assume that the fleet had been somewhere close to the battle site, and good money would be on somewhere along the Moray coastline. The circumnavigation would therefore have to begin there, though it may not have ended there, despite the notion that they sailed completely around the island. Given that the fleet's base had been at Richborough in Kent, and the navy had been operating up the east coast as far as Moray for years, this North Sea stretch may have been assumed already covered, and the voyage would therefore have to go only around the north and west and circle back to their base. Ogilvie and Richmond put this at a distance of 1,500 miles and suggest that it could be done within a month.

Tacitus goes on to tell us that 'the fleet, with a favourable wind and reputation behind it, occupied the Trucculensian harbour, from which it had set out to coast along the adjacent shore of Britain, and to which it had now returned intact.'[4]

As with the Boresti above, this sentence has had scholars twisting and turning in attempts to identify a site. The commonly held belief is that this is once again a copying or translation error somewhere along the line, and that Trucculensem is a corruption of Rutupiensem, being Richborough. Grant favours the possibility that the Trucculensian harbour is somewhere around Southampton. Another equally viable possibility is that Trucculum is a harbour in Scotland of which we remain entirely ignorant, and that the fleet did indeed completely circle the island. There is, as I have previously stated, little evidence for Roman anchorages this far north, but the basin at Dun we have considered, as well as Bertha and Carpow, and even Cramond, and an anchor found at Camelon provides another hint.

Once again, Wolfson provides a neat possibility that ignores these identification problems. He sees *tempeste ac fama Trucculensem Portum* as a corruption, the original being *tempeste ac fama trux Tulensem Portum*, which would instead translate as 'made ruthless by fame and storms, reached the port of Thule'.⁵ Given how Thule continually crops up in connection to Agricola and the fleet, this is a far from far-fetched possibility, and suggests that the fleet landed in Shetland after their circumnavigation. That Tacitus claims this is also where they set out from could be argued away.

If the Boresti are to be associated with the Cornavii, then they are the closest point on the mainland to the Shetlands. If after the battle, Agricola took his army up into the far north, around Wick, and took slaves among the Boresti/Cornavii, then he could easily have sent the fleet to Thule/Shetland from there and the fleet circumnavigate out of Thule. The fact that there is enough familiarity with Thule that Silius Italicus can describe their inhabitants means that the Shetlands were not as remote as one might think.

The survival of the entire fleet in the conditions they would have faced would be nothing short of remarkable, and might explain something of why Tacitus and other Roman writers place such weight on this event. Of course, this extra achievement by Agricola, shoehorned in at the end of his governorship, might be suggested as fictional. Tacitus might have made the entire thing up, and we cannot consider Dio as confirmation, since his words would have been based upon Tacitus anyway. However, two extra sources give us enough support that we can perhaps accept this great achievement and Tacitus's relating of it at face value.

Firstly we have a line from Plutarch, another contemporary of Tacitus. The great biographer was in Athens in 84 for the Pythean Games where he met one Demetrius who was, as he states very specifically in his work on the Obsolescence of Oracles, 'journeying homeward from Britain to Tarsus'.⁶ This is the year following Mons Graupius and the fleet's circumnavigation. Demetrius tells Plutarch that 'among the islands lying near Britain were many isolated, having few or no inhabitants, some of which bore the names of divinities or heroes. He himself, by the emperor's order, had made a voyage for inquiry and observation to the nearest of these islands which had only a few inhabitants, holy men who were all held inviolate by the Britons.'⁷

The 'emperor's order' would come via the mouth of the governor, of course. More than any words of Tacitus, this seems to provide independent verification that prior to 84 Demetrius had travelled among the islands of Britain in a voyage of observation. His descriptions seem rather apt of some of the more remote islands of Western Scotland.

If we seek more evidence, then it might be found in exhibits now in the Yorkshire museum. Two bronze plaques with text hammered into them are on display, found outside the military area of Eboracum in an excavation in the Colonia, close to where a bath house was discovered that has been suggested as part of a governor's palace. These two artefacts bear the following legends in Greek:

ΘΕΟΙΣ
ΤΟΙΣ ΤΟΥ ΗΓΕ
ΜΟΝΙΚΟΥ ΠΡΑΙ
ΤΩΡΙΟΥ ΣΚΡΙΒ
ΔΗΜΗΤΡΙΟΣ

Which translates as: 'To the gods of the legate's residence Scribonius Demetrius (set this up)', linking Demetrius with the governor.

And

ΩΚΕΑΝΩΙ
ΚΑΙ ΤΗΘΥΙ
ΔΗΜΗΤΡΙ[.]

Giving us 'To Ocean and Tethys Demetrius (set this up)', which links Demetrius with the sea.[8] One Scribonius Demetrius seems to have been involved in the circumnavigation in 83, may have been present in the governor's residence in York, and then described his voyage to Plutarch in Athens. While we have no direct confirmation that Agricola resided in York, it was the most northerly completed legionary fortress, and very likely Cerialis and his successors had a residence of some sort there. It seems highly unlikely that over the years of his governorship Agricola did not spend time in York, and it is quite possible that York was a temporary halt on the journey south after Mons Graupius.

Bronze tablets of Demetrius in the Yorkshire Museum. (Author's collection by permission of the Yorkshire Museum)

Given the words of Plutarch and of Tacitus and the finds in York, there is no reason to dispute the text of the Agricola on this, and so we can say with reasonable confidence that no matter what deeds of Agricola can be debated, his being the first man to see Britain circumnavigated is a reasonable claim.

Agricola, knowing this was his last winter, would have returned with his wife to the south, to the comfortable and Romanised region of the province. Perhaps York was a lengthy stopover, but he likely spent the heart of the winter and the start of the following year in London. Here he could oversee any ongoing works and could put his affairs in order ready for his successor. He would expect to be replaced in the spring as was the norm. Following the noteworthy activity of the fleet we are told nothing of Agricola's last winter in Britain, for Tacitus now focuses on the wider empire, ready for Agricola's departure.

'Of this series of events, though not exaggerated in the despatches of Agricola by any boastfulness of language, Domitian heard, as was his wont, with joy in his face but anxiety in his heart. He felt conscious that all men laughed at his late mock triumph over Germany [...]. It was, he thought, a very alarming thing for him that the name of a subject should be raised above that of the Emperor; [...] he decided that it was best for the present to suspend his hatred until the freshness of Agricola's renown and his popularity with the army should begin to pass away.'[9]

The opening line here is of some importance with respect to the veracity of Tacitus's account. He tells us that the events of 83 are 'not exaggerated in the despatches of Agricola by any boastfulness of language', which strongly suggests that Tacitus had read the despatches personally. It would likely be a matter of record, but Agricola may have kept diaries or notes on his campaigns in a similar manner to Caesar from which Tacitus could work.

It seems to be the case that a governor kept ledgers during his tenure, given that in the trial of the infamous Verres, Cicero quoted from just such an account. That these ledgers are termed *commentarii*, which also happens to be the term used for Caesar's account of his Gallic Wars, suggests that this is not limited to the sort of civic accounting that helped bring Verres down, but also included accounts of military campaigns. If this is the case, then

Tacitus would have access not only to Agricola's reminiscences in person, but to a written contemporary account that, if Caesar is anything to go by, contained detailed strategic documentation on each season of his tenure. Indeed, from the principate, the governor's staff seems to have included one or more commentaries, which suggests that more than one type of record was kept.

If anything speaks of Tacitus's veracity, then it has to be this. So what does he go on to say?

In short, Tacitus tells us that Domitian was currently horribly insecure over his German triumph, that he was secretly filled with fear and resentment of Agricola, but that Agricola was riding a high enough wave of popularity that he dare not do anything rash, and was thus biding his time. For reference, the only sources we have on Domitian's triumph are Suetonius and Tacitus, who claims that 'slaves had been purchased in the market, who could, with suitable clothing and their hair treated, be made to look like prisoners of war.'[10] This seems to be too blatant a ruse for a man as devious as Domitian is made out to be, and would surely have swiftly become public knowledge. Our only other source on the triumph, Suetonius, tells us 'He began an expedition against Gaul and the Germanies, which was uncalled for and from which his father's friends dissuaded him, merely that he might make himself equal to his brother in power and rank.'[11] In truth, this was no more uncalled for than the vast majority of Rome's campaigns across its borders, and in trying to make himself Titus's military equal, he was following a well-worn path.

What of this wicked emperor then?

One of my own projects has been a series of fictionalised biographies of the damned emperors, thus far rewriting the horror stories that are Caligula and Commodus. When the biased propaganda of their successors and enemies is removed from accounts, along with anything clearly farcical, and archaeological evidence and common sense are factored in, entirely different pictures of these emperors begin to arise. Domitian is no different. He may not have been a saint, by any stretch of the imagination, but given his popularity with the common people and the army right to the time of his death, his legal and administrative care and reforms, his strengthening of Rome's economy and the like, it is playing into the hands of his detractors to assume that all stories are true and that there are no redeeming qualities to be found.

Domitian's successes in his German campaign have been constantly reassessed in more recent years, and evidence is growing of a real achievement that has been ignored by history. It is therefore not impossible that Domitian's German campaign was actually an important and successful one and that whatever we are told, his triumph was perfectly acceptable and deserved. We are reliant for our accounts on those who defame him, after all. Tacitus seems to have been perfectly content to be one of Domitian's clients during the emperor's life, owing the latter portions of his career advancement to the man, yet is filled with nothing but bile after the emperor's death and writing during the reign of a successor who needs to distance himself from Domitian. Tacitus's bias is clear and he makes no apology for it.

As such, we might want to consider just how much faith we put in what Domitian's private thoughts were as related by Tacitus. In truth, Domitian had his own military success, and he could only increase it vicariously through Agricola's achievement. The general was an ageing provincial with no noted influence in the court. He should not, realistically, be a threat to the emperor, and having been a loyal servant of the Flavians throughout, Domitian should have no reason to suspect him. Agricola has, at this time, never stood against the family, nor spoken out against Domitian.

Coin of Domitian showing the emperor on horseback riding down a German, commemorating his victorious Germanic campaign, British Museum. (Author's collection)

Recall from Britain would be natural and expected, and in no way ignominious. So why would Domitian fear Agricola?

Simply, Domitian probably felt none of these things Tacitus tells us. If he did, and he feared Agricola as a potential rival, then one might argue that there could be a reason. Had not Domitian's own father been a provincial with a strong military reputation and the support of an army who managed to secure the throne, just as Agricola now might? The difference in the situations is striking, though. This is only two years into Domitian's reign and he is not a pariah as Nero had become by the time usurpers rose up against him. Still, whether Domitian feared the worst or not, there was a neat way around the problem: bribery. Our last days on the island are given by Tacitus: 'For Agricola was still the governor of Britain. Accordingly the Emperor ordered that the usual triumphal decorations, the honour of a laurelled statue, and all that is commonly given in place of the triumphal procession, with the addition of many laudatory expressions, should be decreed in the senate, together with a hint to the effect that Agricola was to have the province of Syria, [...] generally reserved for men of distinction. It was believed by many persons that one of the freedmen employed on confidential services was sent to Agricola, bearing a despatch in which Syria was offered him, and [...] that this freedman in crossing the straights met Agricola and without even saluting him made his way back to Domitian. Meanwhile Agricola had handed over his province in peace and safety to his successor.'[12]

Since the days of Augustus successful generals had not been the recipient of the traditional triumphal procession through the city of Rome. This was now reserved for the emperor and his immediate family. But recognition of a general's outstanding achievement was still forthcoming in the form of 'triumphal honours'. Agricola, then, received such a thing from the emperor. He would be granted awards and honours, a statue raised in the forum and all the talk of Rome would be about him.

Thus would the military aspect of Agricola surely be appeased, to be recognised and lauded by the emperor and the people. He deserved the triumph, after all, for the minimum enemy fatalities required for a triumph was 5,000, and if Tacitus is to be believed, then Agricola doubled that number. Slaves would have been filling the markets of Rome, which would create something of a boom in the economy.

Moreover, Agricola has his future secured here. The emperor suggests that Agricola would next take on the governorship of Syria, which was one of the most prestigious positions in the empire. If Agricola *had* been of a mind to usurp, then this might just be enough to buy him off. Syria came with four legions, just as Britain had done, but from Agricola's point of view, Syria was more prestigious and lucrative. From the emperor's point of view, Agricola had no ties of loyalty to the Syrian legions, while the British ones might well cleave to him even above an emperor. All neatly tied up.

Thus a paranoid emperor could hope to avoid trouble with the successful and popular general. Of course, if we were to decide that Domitian was not half as paranoid as we are led to believe and that Tacitus is painting a deliberately biased picture, still these two offers make sense, the grateful emperor offering high position and honours to the man who had just added Britain to the empire. Either way we have no reason to doubt the events, just the motives behind them.

That Domitian might decide to offer Syria to Agricola, send a message to that effect with an important freedman, and said freedman to treat Agricola with a 'cold shoulder' makes little sense. The messenger mentioned in the text is not an unreliable and menial palace functionary. We are told he is one of the emperor's own freedmen, and the Latin *secretioribus ministeriis* makes this man a private minister, while the word *codicillos* states that this letter was in the emperor's own hand. The phrase 'It was believed by many persons', of course, tells us that this was rumour that Tacitus is reporting, but in its own way that provides veracity, for by extension, anything else where he does not lay his facts at the feet of public belief might be said to be gleaned from a trustworthy source. We are told that the courier 'in crossing the straights met Agricola and without even saluting him made his way back to Domitian'. Indeed, in the other translations, Birley says the freedman 'met Agricola actually in the Channel crossing and, without even speaking to him, returned to Domitian', and

Mattingly and Handford say that he 'met Agricola's ship in the Channel, and without even seeking an interview with him returned to Domitian'. One might note the remote possibility of ships meeting mid-channel, let alone two bearing a messenger and its intended recipient. Even if we were to credit the tale with any truth, it seems unlikely that such a meeting, happening aboard ships mid-crossing off Britain, would become common rumour in Rome. It also seems unlikely that Domitian would send such an offer and order his freedman to be so insulting with it. And if it were the freedman defying his emperor's wishes by insulting the man, hot pokers and sharp blades would await him beneath the Palatine, and the last thing he would do would be turn around and run home to the emperor.

What we are likely dealing with here, then, is simple rumour. That in a letter to Agricola informing him that he was to receive triumphal honours, possibly the same letter confirming his replacement and recall, the emperor might hint at Syria as a possibility is more than possible. After all, Vespasian had done exactly the same while Agricola was leaving Aquitania, dangling the governorship of Britain before him. It would be a natural progression.

That there was any expected trouble between Agricola and the emperor seems unlikely, especially given how Agricola ends his tenure. We are told that he hands the province over to his successor 'in peace and safety'. Agricola has conquered the whole of Britain and now leaves the task of creating the infrastructure of control to his replacement, though he has made a strong start, and with the foundation of Inchtuthil created a focus for new legionary control in Scotland.

Before we move on to Agricola in Rome once more, it is important to look briefly at Britain following his removal. The governor must have left in the spring of 84, while ships were sailing once more after the winter. We do not know the name of his successor, though a strong candidate is one Sallustius Lucullus, who definitely governed Britain at some point after Agricola in 84 and before Domitian's death in 96. What his remit was we can only guess. He will not have been given military objectives, though, for the only campaign awaiting Rome in Britain was the conquest of Ireland, and it was too soon to contemplate such a thing. Domitian had troubles on the Danube, where the Dacians were causing difficulties, and he would require the focus of the military to shift there. Presumably Lucullus was told to consolidate the gains of his predecessor and begin the Romanisation of the newly conquered north.

The dating of any work to Lucullus is as difficult as it has been with his predecessors. It is reasonable to assume at least a three-year tenure for the man, with no difficulties requiring his removal and no reason for extension, and so we can perhaps place Lucullus in Britain from 84 to 87. During his time, then, the last Flavian work is carried out in Scotland. It would appear that during his command the Glen-Blocker forts were occupied and strengthened (or possibly even built if they were not already extant), the fortress of Inchtuthil nears completion, and various other installations remain occupied. One notable thing, though, is that nothing is done with the territory for which Agricola had fought. The most northerly garrisoned fort remains Stracathro, and no effort seems to have been made to impose control north of there. No roads are driven into the Highlands. What we are perhaps seeing, then, is Domitian's order to consolidate what they already had, without expansion, and Lucullus doing precisely that.

It is in 87 that everything changes. Lucullus is likely recalled to Rome then and some unknown successor takes his place. In 87, under this replacement, work on Inchtuthil is halted and the fortress is systematically dismantled, the army pulling back from this site. Other locations seem to have been abandoned at this time, and the Second Adiutrix is removed from Britain to the Dacian frontier on the Danube where a new war is in the offing. Coin dating evidence suggests a large-scale abandonment of sites in Scotland, with a few key installations continuing to be manned until the time of Trajan, when these sites too are abandoned.

Scotland had been won.

Scotland would now be lost.

17

A PRIVATE CITIZEN

Do you still have that block of salt handy? Grab it now, because you're going to need it by the handful henceforth, for in Tacitus's closing chapters while the facts may bear out, the spin the author puts on everything will have you clinging to your seat and begging to be let off the ride. Tacitus here departs from biography and begins an uncomfortable combination of history, name-calling, political statement and eulogy.

'And not to make his entrance into Rome conspicuous by the concourse of welcoming throngs, he avoided the attentions of his friends by entering the city at night, and at night too, according to orders, proceeded to the palace, where, having been received with a hurried embrace and without a word being spoken, he mingled in the crowd of courtiers.'[1]

This event jars the reader. It does not sit well with the image of Agricola that Tacitus has built so lovingly throughout. It is not without precedent, admittedly, but the adventus (the arrival in Rome of a governor returning from his term or also of an emperor) was a major event, especially when that governor had been granted triumphal honours. Cicero described his own adventus thus: 'I returned to my country, and saw the senate which had come forth to meet me, and the whole Roman people; while Rome itself, torn, if I may so say, from its foundations, seemed to come forward to embrace her saviour. Rome, which received me in such a manner that not only all men and all

The Adventus of Marcus Aurelius, reused in the Arch of Constantine. (Image by David Castor)

women of all classes, and ages, and orders of society, of every fortune and every rank, but that even the walls and houses of the city and temples appeared to be exulting.'[2] He goes on to compare this with the entry into Rome of Lucius Calpurnius Piso Caesoninus. Cicero had been attacking Piso in the senate, and the somewhat disgraced governor returned to Rome under cover of night: 'Having lost your army, you have brought nothing safe back with you except that pristine countenance and impudence of yours. And who is there who knows where you first came to with those laurelled lictors of yours? What meanders, what turnings and windings did you thread, while seeking for the most solitary possible places? What municipal town saw you? What friend invited you? What entertainer beheld you? Did you not make night take the place of day? solitude of society?'

This is remarkably similar to Agricola's return in Tacitus, but Piso was in disgrace. In the Annals, Tacitus tells us of another Piso's triumphant return to Rome in which he rather ostentatiously 'added to the exasperation of the populace by bringing his vessel to shore at the mausoleum of the Caesars. It was a busy part of the day and of the river-side; yet he with a marching column of retainers, and Plancina with her escort of women, proceeded beaming on their way. There were other irritants also; among them, festal decorations upon his mansion looming above the forum; guests and a dinner; and, in that crowded quarter, full publicity for everything.'³ This Piso was almost immediately called to trial, during which he committed suicide before the inevitable verdict. But once again, this Piso was in trouble, and had come to Rome rather incautiously and suffered as a result.

Why, then, would Agricola arrive quietly at night? In these other examples, Cicero had done nothing wrong, expected no trouble, and so came home to rapturous applause. Piso 1 knew he was in trouble, so snuck into the city, and Piso 2 arrived with flamboyance and paid the price because he was being targeted. Agricola, though, had no reason to sneak. To this point Agricola has neither acted nor spoken against Domitian, and there has not been a single hint of such a thing from the emperor against Agricola. Their relationship seems to have been unmarred. Even though Tacitus goes on to describe a jealous, dangerous emperor who sees Agricola as a potential enemy, even if this were true, there is no reason why Agricola should suspect it at this point. Quite simply this does not fit with the facts. That Agricola might eschew the grandest return and enjoy a modest adventus would be appropriate, ignoring all that pomp that Cicero enjoyed, but to come alone at night seems to be a case of Tacitus greatly exaggerating.

It would be nice to think that Tacitus was mistaken, rather than lying, but what we cannot accuse him of here is being uninformed, for he would have been in Rome at the time of Agricola's return and would remain so until AD 90. Given that Tacitus was also tied to Domitian's patronage and was on the cursus honorum at the time, he may well have been at court. Tacitus should have first-hand knowledge of what goes on, and therefore anything that does not seem to fit can only be the deliberate decision of the writer. He would have access to Agricola himself, but probably also to the lion's share of the men who had lived through the events he described. What we have here would appear to be Tacitus starting us on a slippery slope for the rest of the text, twisting and exaggerating the facts to put Domitian in the worst possible light. Although the description of his return that we are given describes it as Agricola's decision, we are left with the impression that the emperor had it in for the general, that Agricola was playing a safe game, and that the cold, brief greeting at court shows the emperor's displeasure. This impression he is creating only increases as he goes on: 'Anxious henceforth to temper the military renown, which annoys men of peace, with other merits, he studiously cultivated retirement and leisure, simple in dress, courteous in conversation, and never accompanied but by one or two friends, so that the many who commonly judge of great men by their external grandeur, after having seen and attentively surveyed him, asked the secret of a greatness which but few could explain.'

Here, Tacitus is recalling moments from earlier in his tale, pulling in threads he placed carefully like the clever author he is. Under the dangerous reign of Nero we were told of Agricola's 'consistent quietude' and the way that had kept him from the disasters that befell many, which we are told he employs once more. We see him once again cloaking his military nature and wearing a mantle of peace, as we saw him do when governing Aquitania. Here, Agricola is using all the skills of survival he has learned doen the years. He even keeps the number of friends he socialises with limited. Why? Because in an oppressive regime, gatherings could be dangerous, even in the reign of Trajan as he once explained to Pliny in a letter: 'You are of opinion it would be proper to establish a company of firemen in Nicomedia, agreeably to what has been practised in several other cities. But it is to be remembered that societies of this sort have greatly disturbed the peace of the province in general, and of those cities in particular. Whatever name we give them, and for whatever purposes them may be founded, they will not fail to form themselves into factious assemblies, however short their meetings may be.'[4] Tacitus is telling us that Agricola does not want to be accused of plotting with gatherings of men. Once again, though, all of this behaviour only fits if Agricola is expecting Domitian's ire, which we have no reason to suspect. If the emperor and Agricola were on reasonable terms, or even if Agricola was unaware of any ire, then this behaviour is unreasonably paranoid. Quite simply, Tacitus is once again building the persona of the wicked emperor by exaggeration. A reread of the paragraph while forcing a neutral opinion of Domitian instead suggests that Agricola merely retired and enjoyed a quiet leisurely life. That he was simple in dress suggests that he did not bother with the triumphal regalia he had been voted, but from what we now know of Agricola and his unpretentious ways, that would hardly be out of character.

So Agricola returned to Rome quietly, had a low-key meeting with the emperor, and thereafter retired to a quiet life. He had been told that he would be given the province of Asia, but he could not expect it straight away anyway. There would be at least the traditional two-year gap between governorships. Agricola, then, was undoubtedly simply taking a well-earned rest after a long and arduous campaign in Britain, socialising with a few friends, and regaling Tacitus with endless tales of his exploits.

'During this time he was frequently accused before Domitian in his absence, and in his absence acquitted. The cause of his danger lay not in any crime [...] but in a ruler who was the foe of virtue.'[5]

Tacitus attempts to make us despise Domitian. He ascribes to the emperor repeated attempts to bring Agricola to trial, and we are left with that impression, though what we are actually told is that *other people* approached the emperor with accusations, which were uniformly thrown out without Agricola even being present. This suggests that the fault would be on the part of others, and that Domitian is, in fact, instrumental in Agricola's acquittal. What these accusations might be we are not told, but at times in Rome such an atmosphere of accusation was commonplace. This compares with the situation under Tiberius and Sejanus, where senators were selling one another out for the emperor's favour and for mere financial gain, and where Sejanus had created a network of spies and informers he used to remove anyone he perceived to be a threat. For an account of these times, see Cassius Dio's Roman History 58.4. These accusers, then, are probably the less blessed in the court, attempting to curry favour with the emperor and to bring down a man they see as an opponent. Agricola has a successful record, has enjoyed imperial favour, and has now been promised the most lucrative and important province in the empire. That jealous men might take against him should come as no surprise. That Domitian perhaps was the man who protected him should also be no surprise, were it not for Tacitus's constant bile towards the emperor.

Tacitus continues with 'And then followed such days for the commonwealth as would not suffer Agricola to be forgotten; days when so many of our armies were lost in Moesia, Dacia, Germany, and Pannonia, through the rashness or cowardice of our generals. [...] And so when disaster followed upon disaster, and the entire year was marked by destruction and slaughter, the voice of the people called Agricola to the command [...]. And so at once, by his own excellences and by the faults of others, Agricola was hurried headlong to a perilous elevation.'

This gives us a good opportunity to date events. Tacitus may apply dizzying spin to his account, but there is evidence that the wider *events* he recalls are accurate. In 85 an army from Dacia (modern Romania) crossed the Danube and struck deep into the Roman province of Moesia. The attack was so huge that the governor, Gaius Oppius Sabinus, was killed leading his troops in defence. The province was ravaged, forts and towns destroyed, and there must have been enough damage and enough shock and feeling among the people of Rome that this led to Domitian's Dacian war in reprisal. Sadly, as yet no archaeological evidence of the Dacian invasion or the battles it led to has turned up in modern Bulgaria, so we have to turn to literary evidence to support Tacitus. The events of the invasion are related by Cassius Dio in his History (67.7-8). He may have used Tacitus as a source, but they are also corroborated by Suetonius (Life of Domitian 6), who lived through the time. Both describe the Dacian disaster, yet neither mentions Agricola or the public pushing for his reinstatement.

Tacitus gives us an image of the public calling for Agricola to lead against the Dacian menace, and it is easy to picture Agricola, aware of the danger of being so popular, stepping back into the shadows with a finger pressed to his lips, hushing the crowd. Once again, though, we have Tacitus to thank for this, and almost certainly not the truth of events. We are picturing Agricola trying not to be the next Corbulo, a general so successful that the emperor ordered him to commit suicide. The difference here, though, is that Nero had displayed great fear of his successful generals (and rightly so, given how he ended), which is why he had Corbulo fall on his sword. Despite Tacitus's painting of Domitian, however, there is no evidence of him following suit. Dorey notes the cases of numerous very successful generals who flourished under Domitian (Frontinus, Tettius Julianus, Verginius Rufus, and even the future emperor Trajan).[6]

Tacitus is guilty of omission here. He tells us of the Dacian trouble, and of the public feeling for Agricola, but what he does not mention is that this is the sequence of events that causes the Second Adiutrix to be recalled from Britain, almost certainly along with a substantial number of auxiliary units, heralding the end of Roman occupation in the north, for it is highly likely the removal of these troops from the less important theatre of war makes the abandonment of Scottish gains inevitable. Given the importance Tacitus places upon Agricola's success in Scotland, it might seem odd that he misses such an opportunity to point the finger. The answer might lie in the fact that the blame for this would have to lie with the Dacian invaders and with unsuccessful governors in the east who failed to contain the disaster, and Tacitus is now only interested in blaming Domitian for everything, thus he omits mention of it, concentrating all our anger on the emperor.

The truth, then, is probably that there is nothing untoward in any of this. Domitian cannot be held accountable for the withdrawal from Scotland, nor from failing to head up an appropriate response to Dacia. Agricola is still enjoying quiet retirement and has no great urge to be thrown straight back into a war zone. Domitian, if he follows his father in any way, would likely seek to appoint the most appropriate man for the job in Moesia, and Agricola, weary and with experience only in the north, would not be the man to send to Dacia. As such, he chooses first Cornelius Fuscus to command the army, a man serving as prefect of the Praetorian Guard, but who had experience also in Greek-speaking Illyricum, close to the war zone, and then Tettius Julianus, who had previously commanded the Seventh Claudia in the beleaguered province itself. That Agricola was not chosen over men who knew the region and had their own proven track record should not be taken as a sign of ill favour, and the abandonment of

Scotland would be the inevitable consequence of having to transfer troops to the Danube to limit the damage there.

As Tacitus moves on, since Agricola has no part in this war, we have a little more trouble applying a specific date: 'The year had now arrived in which the proconsulate of Asia or Africa was to fall to him by lot, and, as Civica had been lately murdered, Agricola did not want a warning, or Domitian a precedent.'[7]

The time has come of the promised appointment to govern Asia, along with Africa one of only two prestigious provinces that had to be governed by a senator. At the earliest, this would be 87, since Agricola would not have returned until the summer of 84, and there would be at least two years to wait. Dorey and others favour the idea that Civica's revolution that had caused his downfall was involvement in the revolt of Saturninus in 89, which would therefore make this year 89/90, and there is no reason to doubt that. Civica's downfall is an event recorded and corroborated by Suetonius (Life of Domitian 10) who would have been a grown man at this time and therefore not reliant upon Tacitus. So Civica dies for having risen against the legitimate emperor, and the lot of Asia falls to Agricola. Tacitus tells us: 'Persons well acquainted with the Emperor's feelings came to ask Agricola, as if on their own account, whether he would go. First they hinted their purpose by praises of tranquillity and leisure; then offered their services in procuring acceptance for his excuses; and at last, throwing off all disguise, brought him by entreaties and threats to Domitian. The Emperor, armed beforehand with hypocrisy, and assuming a haughty demeanour, listened to his prayer that he might be excused, and having granted his request allowed himself to be formally thanked, nor blushed to grant so sinister a favour. But the salary usually granted to a pro-consul, and which he had himself given to some governors, he did not bestow on Agricola, either because he was offended at its not having been asked, or was warned by his conscience that he might be thought to have purchased the refusal which he had commanded.'

Agricola is told to turn down the appointment? Odd, but we are told that this is precisely what Agricola does. To the reader this seems almost unbelievable. Not only does he turn down Asia, but he also does not apply for the proconsular salary that could be granted in exchange. In rather blasé terms, Tacitus tells us that Agricola was well enough off that he did not need to. This whole episode reads highly suspiciously. Again, only if Domitian really did have it in for Agricola would this make sense, and yet once again we have no evidence of this other than Tacitus describing the emperor's private emotions, which is clearly an invention or at least an extrapolation of suspicions. Agricola should have no reason to fear the emperor, and the emperor has no reason not to appoint him.

Dorey provides an unusual and somewhat seductive explanation for this turn of events, as well as for the general's lack of activity during the time since his return from Britain. Dorey put forward the theory that Agricola and Domitian in fact enjoyed a reasonably close relationship, and that after forty-four years of very active life, some sort of illness or fatigue overtook Agricola upon his return to Rome. Dorey puts it down to the governor having more or less worn himself out, but certainly any number of slow, gradually debilitating illnesses might possibly have slowed down the man without a horrifying outward sign that would be of note. Following Dorey's postulated version of events, Tacitus's description might have the actual events presented accurately, but once more coloured by his own bias. In Dorey's version, Agricola's name comes up for the governorship of Asia in the wake of Civica's death, and with his usual devotion to duty, even though he is physically failing, Agricola goes forth to accept it, while his friends, and even men sent by Domitian, try to persuade him to turn it down for the good of his health.[8] Ogilvie and Richmond staunchly reject this idea, which is no surprise given how closely they cleave to Tacitus, but it goes a long way to explaining some otherwise very ill-fitting events.

On the subject of Agricola turning down Asia, it is interesting to note that the same inscription that names Salvius Liberalis the iuridicus of Britain under Agricola also has him turning down the governorship of Asia, just as Agricola as done, some time in the following years:

Surviving section of the Liberalis inscription in the wall of the Palazzo
Communale of Urbisaglia. (Author's collection)

'Gaius Salvius Liberalis Nonius Bassus, consul, proconsul
of the province of Macedonia, imperial judicial legate of
Britain, legate of the Fifth Macedonica legion, member
of the Arval Brethren, enrolled by the deified Vespasian
and the deified Titus among the ex-tribunes, and by the
same emperors enrolled among the ex-praetors, four times
member of the council of four with censorial powers,
patron of the colony. When selected as proconsul of Asia he
declined the office.'⁹

In a further interesting connection, Pliny records being joint
prosecutor alongside Tacitus in the case against a governor of
Africa, in which Salvius Liberalis spoke for the accused, showing
once again how the web of connections in Rome is both widespread
and convoluted (Pliny, Letters 2.11).

Tacitus continues by telling us that 'the Emperor [...] was
softened by the moderation and prudence of Agricola [...]. Let
it be known to those whose habit it is to admire the disregard of
authority, that there may be great men even under bad emperors,
and that obedience and submission, when joined to activity
and vigour, may attain a glory which most men reach only by
a perilous career, utterly useless to the state, and closed by an
ostentatious death.'

The intimation here is that the entire episode had been Domitian attempting to get Agricola to Asia, where he could then engineer a case against him and bring him to trial, perhaps in the way Civica had already fallen. The temptations for embezzlement and treason when in charge of one of Rome's most critical provinces had led to plenty of trouble there in the past. But Agricola's attitude and his actions robbed the emperor of his ire and his purpose, and so all was well for the time being. Not only is Tacitus once more attempting to make his father-in-law appear the greater man even as he bends to the will of a wicked emperor, this is clearly a tacit excuse for the writer's own behaviour during Domitian's reign. Tacitus and numerous other nobles had prospered under that regime by playing the willing tool of the emperor, and at the time of writing Domitian has been damned, so distancing oneself from him and providing excuses would be paramount in Tacitus's mind.

Of the last few years of Agricola in Rome we are told nothing. Domitian and the state had plenty of their own business to attend to, in the aftermath of the revolt of Saturninus, and fresh trouble with the Chatti on the Rhine. Presumably, Agricola simply continued to live the quiet, retired, and possibly convalescent, life of a Roman nobleman, while the world moved on.

The next event, indeed the final one, comes in 93: 'The end of his life, a deplorable calamity to us and a grief to his friends, was regarded with concern even by strangers and those who knew him not. [...] Men's sympathy was increased by a prevalent rumour that he was destroyed by poison. For myself, I have nothing which I should venture to state for fact.'[10]

The first thing to note now is that Tacitus has been absent from Rome since 90, almost certainly commanding a legion in one of the provinces, and so from this moment he was no longer a witness to events, and this has all come down second-hand at least. This is one of those rare moments where we can be almost certain that Tacitus is reporting events without spin, because he plainly states that he has no way to be sure of the truth of this. He is reporting hearsay and is content to tell us this, though of course the power of suggestion lets the idea that Agricola was poisoned seep into our consciousness anyway, so in a way Tacitus is twisting our perceptions even as he tells us that this is just rumour. That he does so gives us a veiled suggestion that the information he has related elsewhere is by extension *not* subject to uncertainty, though once again Tacitus is subtle enough that this may even have been his plan.

In his work on the Arval Brethren, Syme notes a grouping of premature deaths between 89 and 93, which may have been one of the seemingly endless epidemics that sweep through Rome from time to time, and which are at their worst in the summer when the dust and dung fill the air and no breeze blows the germs away and no chill kills them off. It was during the summer that Agricola died. Continuing Dorey's notion, it would be quite reasonable to suggest that if Agricola had been suffering from some long-term malady, then his constitution might have been weakened, which would put him at risk of infection from such a plague. It certainly seems a very believable course of events. Other than Tacitus's manufactured enmity between Domitian and Agricola, we have no reason to suspect foul play, after all, and death comes often and easy at times in Rome.

As is often the case with the portrayal of damned emperors in the ancient sources, events that are related in order to shock the reader sometimes do not add up when closely examined. Domitian had brought to trial and executed men, such as Civica, and in the years to come his persecutions and proscriptions excelled, but poison seems a somewhat outlandish notion when the man Tacitus describes would hardly blink at simply engineering an imagined crime and ordering an execution. Given that even Tacitus tells us that he cannot confirm this rumour, we can reasonably push aside the notion that the emperor had Agricola poisoned, and lay the blame at the foot of simple anti-Domitianic feeling. Cassius Dio tells us 'Finally, he was murdered by Domitian for no other reason than this [being too good a general],'[11] but given Domitian's record with successful generals and that Cassius Dio was writing over a century later and reliant upon sources who were already damning Domitian, it would be safer to put aside this reference also. Indeed, Tacitus himself seems to deny it as he continues: 'Certainly during the whole of his illness the Emperor's chief freedmen and confidential physicians came more frequently than is usual with a court which pays its visits by means of messengers. This was, perhaps, solicitude, perhaps espionage. [...] Yet in his manner and countenance the Emperor displayed some signs of sorrow, for he could now forget his enmity, and it was easier to conceal his joy than his fear. It was well known that on reading the will, in which he was named co-heir with Agricola's excellent wife and most dutiful daughter, he expressed delight, as if it had been a complimentary choice.'

The phrasing here seems to support not only the notion that Agricola died of an illness, but also to some extent Dorey's notion of a long-term malady. The 'whole of his illness' has been translated by Mattingly and Handford as 'throughout his illness' and by Birley as 'all through his last illness', each of which carries the suggestion of a long-standing condition or series of conditions. There are clearly some actions of the emperor which even Tacitus has trouble making wicked. We are told that Domitian sends his own court physicians and a slew of freedmen throughout Agricola's illness. Admittedly, Tacitus slips in the sly suggestion that they were perhaps spies, but by now that salt bag must be nearly empty. Domitian's actions here do not match those of a man with a long enmity. Indeed, they speak of a mutual respect between the emperor and his faithful general.

The splitting of a will between a man's next of kin and the emperor had become common practice at this time, and so nothing should be read into this decision in either a positive or a negative light. Even some thirty years earlier and half a world away, we saw a brutal revolt crushed because a procurator would not honour the will of an Iceni chieftain who left his possessions split between his wife and the emperor Nero.

In an age when great men would die in battle or on the tip of their own sword, it would appear that Agricola was one of those rare cases of a man who died of natural causes, surrounded by his loved ones, under no cloud of suspicion, and with his reputation intact.

'Agricola [...] died in his fifty-fourth year, on the tenth day before the Kalends of September.'[12]

The great man died, therefore, on 23 August AD 93. From here, the chapter moves into the form of a traditional consolation and eulogy, telling us once more of Agricola's physical description and many virtues, none of which I intend to relate here, for there is nothing remarkable in there that we have not already come across in fifty-four years of the man's life.

In our penultimate extract, Tacitus cannot let slide the opportunity to have a jab at Domitian again: 'As his daughter and his wife survived him, it may be thought that he was even fortunate – fortunate, in that while his honours had suffered no eclipse, while his fame was at its height, while his kindred and his friends still prospered, he escaped from the evil to come. For, though to survive until the dawn of this most happy age and to see a Trajan on the throne was what he would speculate upon in previsions and wishes confided to my ears, yet he had this mighty compensation for his premature death, that he was spared those later years during which Domitian, leaving now no interval or breathing space of time, but, as it were, with one continuous blow, drained the life-blood of the Commonwealth.'

The infamous purges that characterise the last days of Domitian's reign were to begin hot on the heels of Agricola's own death, and Tacitus is unrepentant in labelling his father-in-law lucky to have died when he did and miss what followed. Of course, Tacitus was a man who survived the purges by being one of Domitian's favoured, no matter how avidly he might denounce the man to his successors, and we can be realistically content that Agricola was similarly tied to Domitian as he had been to the other Flavians. Perhaps Agricola would have coasted through the troubled times just as Tacitus did. Still, there can be no denying that in a world where life was cheap, the manner of Agricola's passing was one to be cherished.

The notion that Agricola had from time to time, even in private, advocated the possibility of Trajan on the throne seems highly unlikely. Trajan may have been a successful military and political figure at the time, but he was as far removed from any potential imperial succession as Agricola was, and it would be unlikely that until the regime had changed anyone would even think of Trajan in such terms. It seems unlikely that Agricola and Trajan were well acquainted. While Agricola was in Britain, Trajan was in Syria and Germany, and while Agricola was back in Rome, Trajan was a legionary legate in Spain. By the time Trajan was making waves in Rome, Agricola would have been dying. At this point the world was still a Flavian one. After all, even if Domitian died, there were other members of the Flavian family around. Vespasian's brother Sabinus seems to have had sons and grandsons, one of whom was consul in 95 and while they might not have outlasted Domitian, they were still hale and powerful at this time. Looking to lesser-known provincials at this point seems unlikely. If this happened at all, and is not just Tacitus shoehorning in a glowing connection between Agricola and the emperor who would read the published work, then it can only have been the result of a drunken night of speculating who might be fun to have in charge.

We have come, then, to the end of Agricola's journey, for the remaining two chapters of Tacitus's work devolve into simple and unremitting vilification of Domitian. We have watched the young and thoughtful philosopher learn the ropes in Asia and then in Aquitania; learn the way of the soldier in Britain as a junior and a senior officer, campaigning against some of history's most notable Celtic figures; we have seen him rise and complete a conquest that he would not live to see abandoned; and we have watched him fade from prominence and pass away quietly and peacefully. Of his funeral we know only that Tacitus gave the oration, and of his burial we know nothing. Perhaps he was buried in Rome in that same mausoleum where his uncle had buried his father, interred by Tacitus and the great man's daughter, or perhaps he was taken back to Liguria to be buried close to his mother. With luck, one day, excavations in Rome or northern Italy/southern France will turn up a tombstone. For now, we can only speculate as we appreciate the man we mourn.

To end our examination of Agricola's life, I can do no better than to provide Tacitus's own final judgement: 'Whatever we loved, whatever we admired in Agricola, survives, and will survive in the hearts of men, in the succession of the ages, in the fame that waits on noble deeds. Over many indeed, of those who have gone before, as over the inglorious and ignoble, the waves of oblivion will roll; Agricola, made known to posterity by history and tradition, will live for ever.'

CONCLUSION

Tacitus's Agricola remains the go-to source for the great man's life and will likely ever be so. Barring the possibility that one of the many lost works of the Roman writers (Pliny's continuation of Bassus's 'History', for example) might come to light with further mention, this is as far as we can go, cross-checking Tacitus with archaeology and contemporary written sources.

There can be no denying a bias to Tacitus's work, and at certain points in the Agricola that bias shines like an irritating firefly, portraying Agricola in the best possible light while vilifying Domitian in favour of his successors. Moreover, being a political statement and a eulogy as well as a biography, the direct relating of events is not Tacitus's prime concern in the work, which goes a long way to explaining how little detail he sometimes provides for truly important events, while going to some trouble to detail things that seem to the historian of less value.

Because of this, and because of the potential that for this, his first work, Tacitus lifted wholesale from earlier writers, including Julius Caesar, opinion among scholars remains divided over the veracity of the Agricola. Some come down staunchly on the side of Tacitus, such as Ogilvie and Richmond, while others, like Hoffman, prefer to treat Tacitus with extreme suspicion, believing him to be a purveyor of fiction at least as much as fact. Many, like myself, find comfort in the middle ground.

That Tacitus had all the information he required to hand is seemingly undeniable, and so we should allow for the fact that his narrative of events ought to be credible. It is how he presents those events, and the spin he puts on them that devalues this as a work of historical record, a factor that is nowhere more visible than in the closing chapter of his work.

As Wells notes, Tacitus called on the works of Pliny, Cluvius Rufus, Fabius Rusticus and Domitius Corbulo, and even the memoirs of Nero's mother, Agrippina. He goes on to say 'Tacitus also used biographies, funeral orations and other speeches. He consulted the minutes of the Senate (Annals xv.74), the official gazette (acta publica), the emperor's archives (comentarii principis), and drew information from inscriptions and from pamphlets.'[1] He goes on to say 'If we have to treat Tacitus's account of events with caution, it is not because he gets his facts wrong, but because of the interpretation he puts upon them and the things he leaves out.'

The best analogy then, might be to see the Agricola as a river. It flows through the landscape of ancient Rome, taking the most direct and natural course as it follows the great man's life, and we can sail along it and appreciate the view as we pass, but we must always keep our eyes out for the rapids, rocks and submerged branches of bias and navigate around them carefully. If we do so, then the Agricola still holds immense value as a source.

Indeed, Woodhead states 'The understanding and appreciation of the reader for Agricola is gradually and subtly built up as the narrative proceeds, rather than forcibly provoked by a statement of his virtues. Agricola is not overdrawn or exaggerated: he is throughout a completely credible person, able and competent and with sound common sense.'

In the age-old argument of nature vs nurture, we can see both at work throughout Agricola's life, in Tacitus's writings, and suggested by what little other evidence we can glean. Agricola is well prepared for the trials of his life by his own personality from childhood, taught and guided by a sensible mother and the tutors of a renowned city. His personal skills shine out many times, in his ability to judge military ground, in his moderation in governance, in his treatment of natives and his dealing with contemporaries. His ties to the Flavian dynasty never seem to have wavered, despite Tacitus's best efforts to drive a wedge between him and Domitian.

Nurture can take great credit. Agricola's time served in Asia gave him a dislike of corruption that clearly stayed with him, his time in Aquitania taught him the value of understanding the people in his care. Observing the works of Ostorius Scapula seems to have lodged certain ideas in his mind that reappear throughout his time in Britain, and indeed that form the backbone of Scotland's Roman remains to this day. His training under both Paulinus and Cerialis prepared him for Scotland in teaching him the nature of divide and conquer, and the value of a network of control. Moreover, his youth in the home of the Roman fleet and then a great port city influenced his understanding of the untapped value of the navy, and his experience with Germanic cavalry units gave him the ability to select just the right men for the job in all sorts of circumstances. Throughout Agricola's life we are shown that he learns from what goes before and then puts it all into practice himself.

One of the two main accusations levelled at Agricola in modern scholarship is that the great decisions that resulted in the conquest of Britain and the Romanisation of its people, and even the circumnavigation of the island, come not from Agricola but from the emperor.

While it is true that a governor in this era is more an extension of the emperor's hand than a de facto ruler, and policy would certainly come down from the emperor himself, we must assume that that policy was somewhat general and that much of the actual decision-making occurred at governor level. Ulpian states that 'there is in a province nothing which may not be admitted to process by his [the proconsul's] order.'[2] To make Agricola out to be little more than a mouthpiece and a puppet of the emperor's is to diminish the value of a provincial governor, a role that was sought after and prized, and allowed a man to have more authority in the province than anyone other than the emperor. And just because a decision has come down from the top level does not tell us how detailed that policy was. That Vespasian might give Agricola the command 'conquer Britain' does not mean that he told the governor how to do it, and so the glory for achieving it must go to the man who did the work, and not the man who gave the order to have it done.

The second such accusation is that Agricola's achievements can now be seen to be largely the work of others. Between re-examinations of accounts such as Statius and Silius Italicus, and the archaeological evidence now arising from Scottish and northern English Roman sites, it is becoming hard to deny that earlier governors at least campaigned in Scotland before Agricola. I have seen it written that Agricola's conquest in Wales was little more than a tidying-up operation and that the great work had already been done. To such notions I stick out my tongue, for on that basis, my own work here is not mine but the credit instead belongs to all those scholars whose work I have perused, evaluated and used in drawing my own conclusions. No matter how many sites in England and Scotland might be proved to be pre-Agricolan, that he achieved the conquest of Wales and Scotland is unchallenged. That he had his fleet circumnavigate the island is unchallenged. That he laid out, perhaps initially as an officer under other governors, the network of forts and roads that would characterise the north of Britain for the next three and a half centuries is unchallenged.

Was Agricola the architect of Roman Britain? Despite all the troubles of Tacitus and the uncertainty of modern archaeology, can we still see Agricola as the conqueror of Britain, and the man who made the province what it remained thereafter?

Evidence seems to point to a rise and fall of Roman conquest in Britain. Governors from Plautius onward gradually expand the horizon north and west and slowly incorporate the controlled lands into a fully Romanised province. At the peak of this, at the turning point, we find Agricola, though on further examination, we can also spot him as a driving force for the preceding two-and-a-half decades alongside other great men. Indeed, until his recall, since Rome had first trodden British soil in 43, Agricola had been involved in the island's destiny for more than half that time. That his achievements were to come to naught is not the fault of the achiever, nor in retrospect do they appear to be the fault of anyone in particular. That a crisis arose on another border and required troops to be pulled away from Britain, forcing the abandonment of fresh-won territory, cannot be blamed on Agricola or Domitian.

Though Tacitus is swift to blame Domitian, this is not an isolated case: German lands abandoned after Teutoburg under Augustus, Parthia and half of Dacia let go by Hadrian, indeed, the inter-wall area of Britain gained by Antoninus Pius and then abandoned mere decades later. Land won was lost. That was the way of Roman border policy. That it happened diminishes Agricola's victory in no way, and not just the victory in Scotland.

The world lays the achievements of the Boudiccan campaign and the suppression of the druids at the feet of Suetonius Paulinus, but we might remember that Agricola was on his staff throughout. History makes Petilius Cerialis the conqueror of the Brigantes, but it is clear that Agricola commanded half the forces during the campaign. And while Bolanus or Frontinus likely carried out the first foray into Scotland, and set up some of the fortifications there, the main campaign that took Rome further than ever, and which broke the back of the Scottish tribes, was Agricola's. The evidence shows major work in the province, linking him to the monumental forum of St Albans and the mysterious elliptical building in Chester.

Quite simply, despite everything, Agricola remains the man credited with completing the Roman conquest of Britain. It is often said that all his achievements came to naught in the end, with Tacitus saying darkly that 'perdomita Britannia et statim omissa' or that Britain was conquered and then immediately abandoned. Yet to say that is to ignore the long-lasting effects of his involvement: the civic advances, the infrastructure, and even if they were subsequently abandoned, Roman sites as far north as the Moray Firth, which continue to fascinate both scholars and the casual observer.

In researching this book, I stood on the site of Logie Durno camp and gazed at the slopes of Bennachiepicturing the Caledonii massing. I stood in the churchyard at Stracathro and knew I was in the northernmost Roman fort in the empire. I stood in a museum looking down at artefacts discovered in the Brigantian stronghold of Stanwick Camp. I stood on Maiden Castle fortlet in the Stainmore Pass looking down on a world below me. I stood by the Menai Strait and peered across at Anglesey. I looked in awe at 2,000-year-old water pipes bearing Agricola's name, and at the reconstructed inscription from the forum of St Albans. I looked at artefacts and sites, I walked roads that he almost certainly began, and all the time the importance of that brief life affected me.

Was Agricola the only man who influenced the destiny of Roman Britain? No. But before him the island had never reached such heights and after him it would never again come so close to being a new Roman world, and so I feel comfortable bowing to Agricola as the architect of Roman Britain.

Appendix 1

CHRONOLOGY OF EVENTS

58 BC		Caesar appointed proconsul of Cisalpine Gaul
50BC		Conquest of Gaul complete
49 BC	6 Sept	Siege and annexation of Massilia
49 BC		Founding of Forum Julii
27 BC	16 Jan	Augustus becomes emperor
14	18 Sept	Tiberius becomes emperor
37	18 Mar	Gaius Caligula becomes emperor
40		Praetorship of Graecinus, Vespasian & Suetonius Paulinus
c. 40		Death of Graecinus
40	13 Jun	Agricola born
40		Agricola and family leave Rome for Forum Julii
41	25 Jan	Claudius becomes emperor
43		Invasion of Britain by Aulus Plautius
43		Legion XX Valeria Victrix moves to Colchester
c. 45		Legion IX Hispana moves to Longthorpe & Newton on Trent
c. 45		Legion XIV Gemina moves to Leicester
47		Agricola sent to Massilia for education
47		Ostorius Scapula appointed as governor of Britain
48		Legion XX Valeria Victrix moves to Kingsholm
48		Ostorius Scapula defeats the Iceni with auxiliaries

48		Ostorius Scapula campaigns against the Deceangli
48		Ostorius Scapula puts down rising of the Brigantes
49		Founding of St Albans (Verulamium)
49		Legion II Augusta moves to Dorchester
50		Ostorius Scapula campaigns against the Silures
51		Defeat of the Silures & capture of Caratacus
52		Ostorius Scapula dies in office, Scapulan frontier in place
52		Defeat of Legion XX under Manlius Valens by the Silures
52		Didius Gallus appointed as governor of Britain
54	13 Oct	Nero becomes emperor
54		Corbulo campaigns in the east
c. 54		Civil war among the Brigantes. Gallus intervenes
55		Legion IX Hispana moves to Lincoln
55		Legion XIV Gemina moves to Wroxeter
55		Legion II Augusta moves to Exeter
c. 56		Tacitus born
57		Quintus Veranius appointed as governor of Britain
57		Legion XX Valeria Victrix moves to Usk
57		Quintus Veranius campaigns against the Silures
58		Quintus Veranius dies in office
58		Suetonius Paulinus appointed as governor of Britain
58	13 June	Agricola assigned as senior tribune of Legion II Augusta
58		Corbulo campaigns in Armenia
59		Corbulo captures Tigranocerta in Armenia
59		Paulinus & Agricola campaign in Wales
60		Invasion of Mona & suppression of druids by Paulinus
60		Revolt of the Iceni. Destruction of Colchester, London & St Albans
60		Boudicca defeats Legion IX Hispana under Petilius Cerialis
60		Battle of Watling Street, defeat of Boudicca by Suetonius Paulinus

60		Titus, as a tribune, brings troops to Britain from Gaul
61		Julius Classicianus appointed as procurator of Britain
61		Paulinus withdrawn. Turpilianus assigned as governor of Britain
63		Agricola marries Domitia Decidiana
63		Birth of Agricola's first son
63		Marcus Trebellius Maximus appointed as governor of Britain
63	Summer	Salvius Otho Titianus appointed as governor of Asia
63	13 June	Agricola appointed as Quaestor of Asia
63		Birth of Agricola's daughter Julia
64	19 July	Great fire of Rome
65	19 Apr	Pisonian Conspiracy against Nero uncovered
65		Ostorius Scapula younger dies. Agricola in retirement in Liguria?
66	Jan	Agricola appointed as Tribune of the Plebs
66		Trial of Publius Clodius Thrasea
66		Legion XIV Gemina withdrawn from Britain
66		Legion XX Valeria Victrix moves to Wroxeter
67		Nero orders Corbulo's suicide
68	8 Jun	Galba becomes emperor
68	13 Jun	Agricola appointed as Praetor
68	After Jun	Agricola appointed to investigate corruption in temples
69	15 Jan	Otho becomes emperor
69	Spring	Vitellius moves against Otho, withdrawing 8,000 men from Britain
69	Early Mar	Otho's fleet deploys on Ligurian coast
69		Mutiny of the legions in Britain under Roscius Coelius
69		Vettius Bolanus appointed as governor of Britain
69		Bolanus brings Legion XIV back with him
69	Mar	Clashes between Othonian & Vitellian forces
69	Mar	Death of Agricola's mother in Liguria
69	14 Apr	First Battle of Bedriacum. Otho defeated

69	After Apr	Agricola in Liguria for family duties
69	17 Apr	Vitellius becomes emperor
69	1 Jun	Vespasian proclaimed emperor in Alexandria
69	After 1 Jun	Agricola in Liguria sides with Vespasian
69	24 Oct	Second battle of Bedriacum
69	Late	Agricola assigned to levy troops by Mucianus
69		Bolanus leads a campaign to rescue Cartimandua of the Brigantes
70	Spring	Agricola appointed as Legate of Legion XX Valeria Victrix
70		Bolanus campaigns in northern Britain, possibly establishing Newstead
70		Legion XIV sent to Germany
71	Spring	Petilius Cerialis finishes putting down the Civilis revolt in Germany
71	Spring	Petilius Cerialis appointed as governor of Britain
71	Spring	Legion II Adiutrix arrives in Britain, probably based at Lincoln
71	Spring	Legion XX possibly moved to Chester for war with Brigantes
71	Spring	Foundation of York by Legion IX Hispana
72	Spring	Cerialis and Agricola campaign against the Brigantes
72	Summer	Carlisle founded by Agricola
72	Summer	Foundation of Corbridge Red House fort?
72	Summer	Agricola marches SE from Carlisle, founding Stainmore Pass system
72	Autumn	Cerialis and Agricola defeat Brigantes at or near Stanwick Camp
72	Winter	Foundation of forts to keep the Brigantes in line
73		Campaigns north of Stanegate & defeat of Venutius near Newstead?
73		Cerialis and Agricola both recalled from Britsain
73		Frontinus appointed as governor or Britain
73		Frontinus begins to campaign against the Silures
74		Agricola sent to govern Aquitania
74		Legion II Augusta moves to Gloucester

75		Caerleon founded by Legion II Augusta
76	Summer	Agricola called back to Rome
76		Frontinus advances into Scotland?
76		First foundations on Forth/Clyde & Gask Ridge
76	Nov	Agricola made suffect consul
76		Tacitus and Agricola's daughter betrothed
77		Tacitus and Agricola's daughter marry
c. 77		Tacitus appointed as military tribune
77		Ordovices massacre cavalry unit in North Wales
77	Summer	Agricola made Governor of Britain
77		Conquest of the Ordovices
77		Conquest of Mona (Anglesey)
77		Foundation of North Wales forts
77	Winter	Reorganisation of Grain distribution in Britain
78		Legion II Adiutrix moves to Chester
78	Summer	Conquest of the Selgovae, creation of forts and roads north
78		Work begins on the Stanegate and Dere Street
78	Winter	Dedication of St Albans forum
78	Winter	?
79	Spring	Advance north to the Tay
79	24 Jun	Death of Vespasian. Titus becomes emperor
79	Summer	Storms ravage Britain
79	Summer	Agricola begins fortification on the Gask Ridge line
79	Winter	Construction of elliptical building in Chester underway
79	Winter	Richborough Arch and Arthur's O'on finished and dedicated
79	Winter	Colosseum inaugurated with games including a Caledonian boar
80	Summer	Forth/Clyde line is fortified and garrisoned
81	Summer	Conquest of the Novantae. Agricola considers conquest of Ireland
81	14 Sept	Death of Titus. Domitian becomes emperor
82	Spring	Vexillations recalled from Britain for Domitian's German wars

82	Spring	Agricola advances to encompass the northern Damnonii
82	Summer	Campaigning in Angus and Aberdeenshire by land and sea combined
82	Summer	Caledonian attacks on Roman forts
82	Summer	News of Caledonian three-prong advance, Agricola responds
82	Late summer	Night attack on the camp of the Ninth Legion (at Dalginross?)
82	Autumn	Creation of the Glen Blocker fort system
82	Autumn	Construction begins on Inchtuthil legionary fortress?
82	Autumn	Flight and debacle of the Usipii cohort
83	Summer	Ravaging of lands to the Moray Firth and naval harassment of the coast
83	September	Battle of Mons Graupius
83	Autumn	Circumnavigation of Britain by Agricola's navy. Landing in Shetland
84	Spring	Agricola recalled, Sallustius Lucullus assigned to Britain?
87		Inchtuthil demolished and abandoned. Large-scale withdrawal south
87		Legion II Adiutrix withdrawn from Britain
88		Legion XX Valeria Victrix moves to Chester
96	18 Sept	Nerva becomes emperor
97	1 Jan	Tacitus becomes consul
98	28 Jan	Trajan becomes emperor
98		Tacitus's 'Agricola' is published

Appendix 2

ROMAN UNITS PROBABLY SERVING IN BRITAIN IN AD 83

Legio II Adiutrix	Legion	5,200	Roman	Repeatedly attested
Legio VIIII Hispana	Legion	5,200	Roman	Repeatedly attested
Legio XX Valeria Victrix	Legion	5,200	Roman	Repeatedly attested
Cohors II Asturum	Mixed	600	Hispanic	Suggested by diploma CIL XVI 51
Cohors I Baetasiorum	Infantry	480	Germanic	Suggested by diploma CIL XVI 48
Cohors III Braca Augustanorum	Infantry	480	Hispanic	Suggested by diploma CIL XVI 48
Cohors I Celtiberorum	Mixed	600	Hispanic	Suggested by diploma CIL XVI 51
Cohors I Cugernorum	Infantry	480	Germanic	Suggested by diploma CIL XVI 48
Cohors IIII Delmatarum	Mixed	600	Dalmatian	Suggested by diploma CIL XVI 48
Cohors II Delmatarum	Mixed	600	Dalmatian	Suggested by diploma CIL XVI 51
Cohors I Frisiavonum	Infantry	480	Germanic	Suggested by diploma CIL XVI 51
Cohors I Hispanorum	Mixed	600	Hispanic	Suggested by Ardoch burial RIB 2213 and diploma CIL XVI 43

Cohors I Lingonum	Mixed	600	Belgic	Suggested by diploma CIL XVI 51
Cohors II Lingonum	Mixed	600	Belgic	Suggested by diploma CIL XVI 43
Cohors III Lingonum	Mixed	600	Belgic	Suggested by diploma CIL XVI 48
Cohors I Morinorum	Infantry	480	Belgic	Suggested by diploma CIL XVI 48
Cohors I Nerviorum	Mixed	600	Belgic	Suggested by diploma CIL XVI 51
Cohors II Nerviorum	Infantry	480	Belgic	Suggested by diploma CIL XVI 43
Cohors II Pannoniorum	Infantry	480	Pannonian	Suggested by diploma CIL XVI 51
Cohors I Tungrorum	Infantry	480	Germanic	Suggested by diploma CIL XVI 48
Cohors II Tungrorum	Mixed	600	Germanic	Dates uncertain. Attested in Britain on many inscriptions.
Cohors I Vangionum	Mixed	600	Germanic	Suggested by diploma CIL XVI 48
Cohors I Fida Vardullorum	Mixed	600	Germanic	Suggested by diploma CIL XVI 43
Cohors II Vasconum	Infantry	480	Hispanic	Suggested by diploma CIL XVI 51
Cohors I Batavorum	Infantry	480	Germanic	Attested by inscription as the first garrison of Carvoran, moved during the second century to Camboglanna
Cohors III Batavorum	Mixed	480	Germanic	Attested on Vindolanda tablets II 263 & 311
Cohors II Thracum	Mixed	600	Thracian	Suggested by diploma CIL XVI 48
Cohors VIII Batavorum	Mixed	600	Germanic	Attested on Vindolanda tablets II 263 & 242 and various others

Cohors IX Batavorum	Mixed	600	Germanic	Mentioned on numerous Vindolanda tablets of the Flavian era
Ala I Hispanorum Asturum	Cavalry	480	Hispanic	Suggested by diploma CIL XVI 43
Ala I Thracum	Cavalry	480	Thracian	Suggested by diploma CIL XVI 48
Ala I Tungrorum	Cavalry	480	Germanic	Suggested by diploma CIL XVI 43
Ala Classiana	Cavalry	480	Gaulish & Thracian	Suggested by diploma CIL XVI 51
Ala Petriana	Cavalry	480	Gaulish	Suggested by tombstone RIB 1172 and diploma CIL XVI 43
Ala Tampiana	Cavalry	480	Pannonian	Suggested by diploma CIL XVI 48
Ala Vettonum	Cavalry	480	Hispanic	Suggested by diploma CIL XVI 48
Ala Sebosiana	Cavalry	480	Gaulish	Attested Carlisle in Flavian era and suggested by diploma CIL XVI 48

All numbers have been given at the smaller unit size (quingenary) as a conservative estimate. Many of these units are also attested later as milliary units that would be double strength, and this change came into effect over the Flavian era, but we cannot be certain that this happened before or after Agricola's time.

Appendix 3

MAP OF AGRICOLA'S CAMPAIGNS

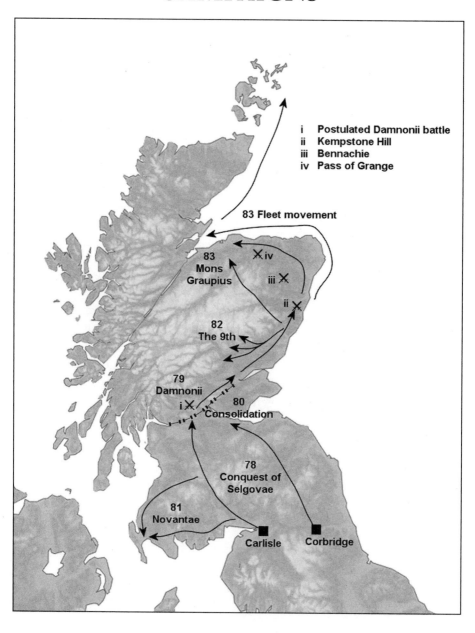

i Postulated Damnonii battle
ii Kempstone Hill
iii Bennachie
iv Pass of Grange

83 Fleet movement

83
Mons
Graupius

×iv

iii ×

ii ×

82
The 9th

79
Damnonii

i ×

80
Consolidation

78
Conquest of
Selgovae

81
Novantae

Carlisle

Corbridge

Appendix 4

MAP OF THE DISPOSITION
OF BRITAIN'S LEGIONS

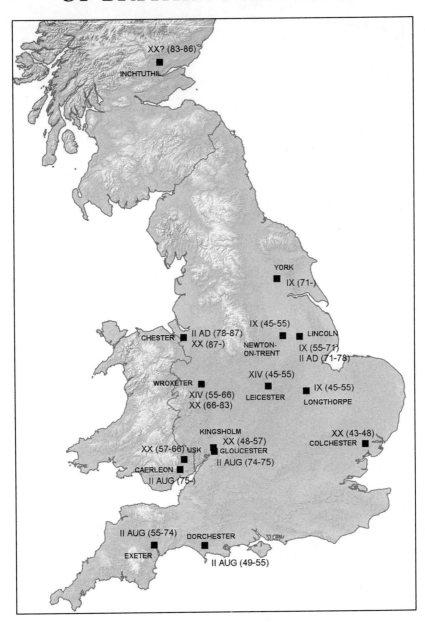

XX? (83-86)
INCHTUTHIL

YORK
IX (71-)

IX (45-55)
II AD (78-87)
XX (87-)
CHESTER
NEWTON-ON-TRENT
LINCOLN
IX (55-71)
II AD (71-78)

XIV (45-55)
WROXETER
XIV (55-66)
XX (66-83)
LEICESTER
IX (45-55)
LONGTHORPE

KINGSHOLM
XX (48-57)
XX (57-66) USK
GLOUCESTER
CAERLEON
II AUG (74-75)
II AUG (75-)
XX (43-48)
COLCHESTER

II AUG (55-74)
DORCHESTER
EXETER
II AUG (49-55)

Appendix 5

ADDITIONAL MAPS

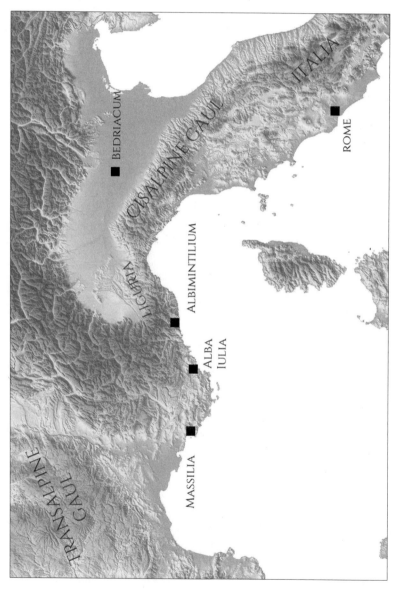

Map 1. Liguria.

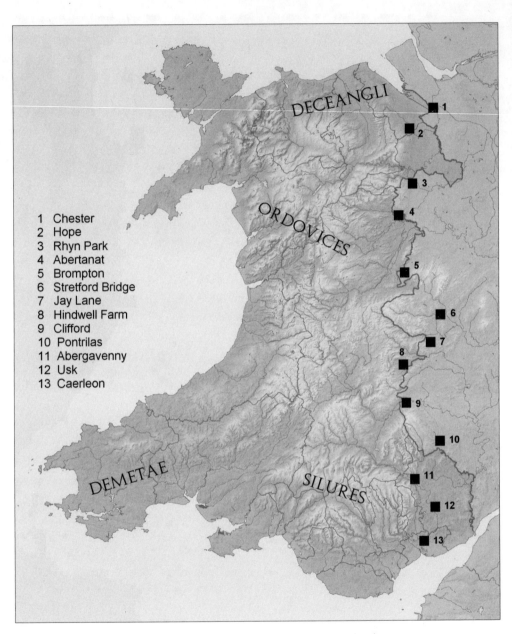

1 Chester
2 Hope
3 Rhyn Park
4 Abertanat
5 Brompton
6 Stretford Bridge
7 Jay Lane
8 Hindwell Farm
9 Clifford
10 Pontrilas
11 Abergavenny
12 Usk
13 Caerleon

DECEANGLI

ORDOVICES

DEMETAE

SILURES

Map 2. The Scapulan frontier.

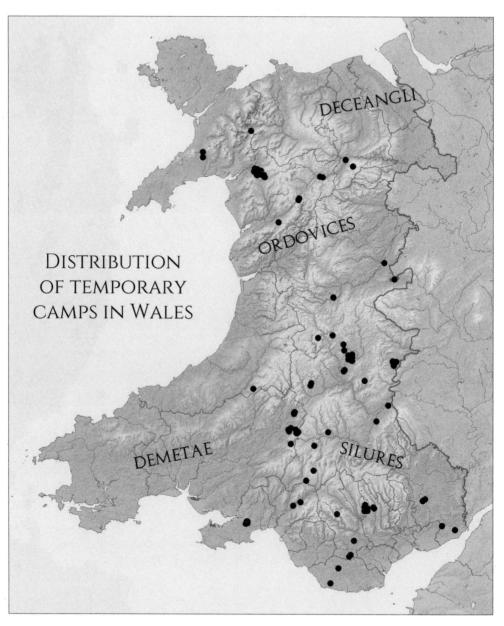

Map 3. Temporary camps in Wales.

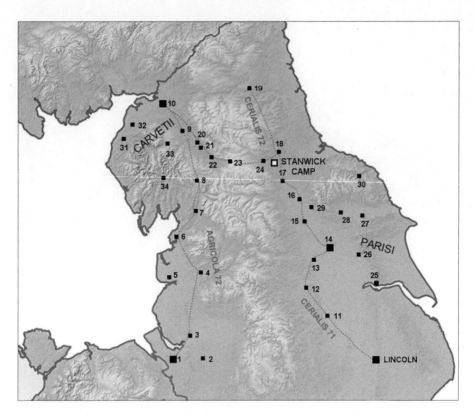

Map 4. Cerialis.

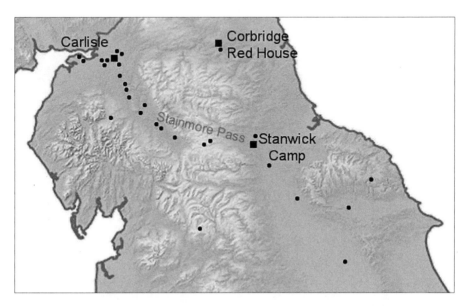

Map 5. Temporary camps.

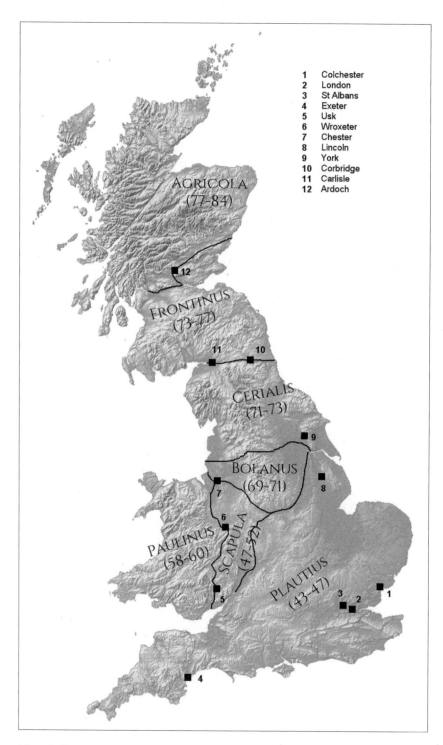

Map 6. Conquest.

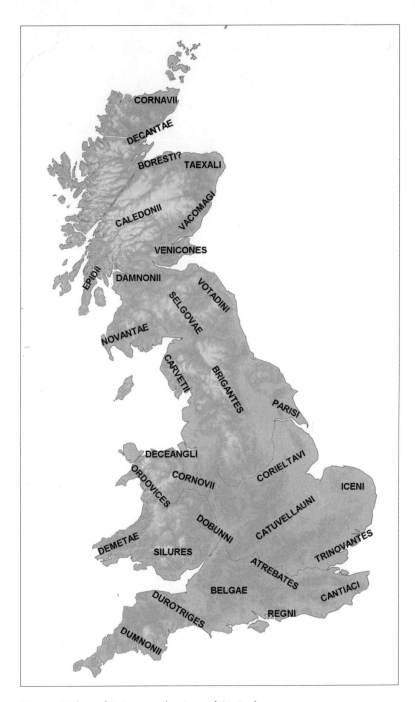

Map 7. Tribes of Britain in the time of Agricola.

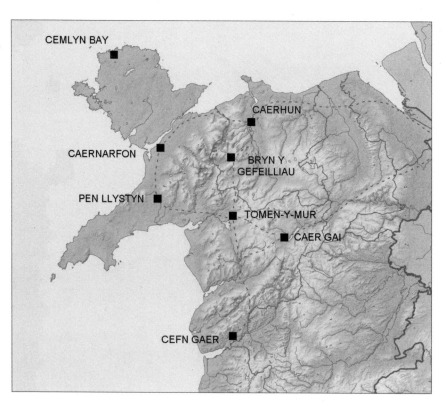

Map 8. Agricolan Wales.

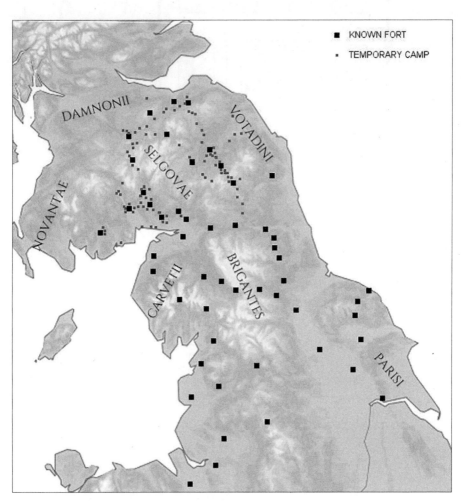

Map 9. Agricola's disposition in AD 78.

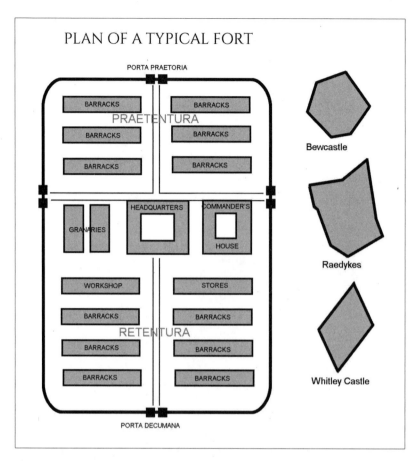

Map 10. A typical Roman fort of the time.

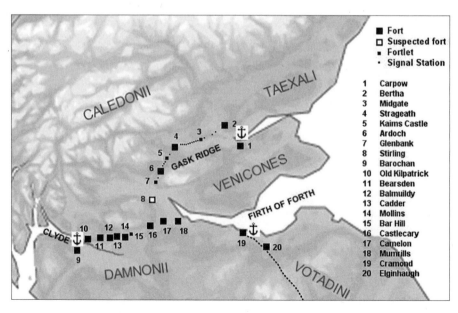

Map 11. Gask Ridge.

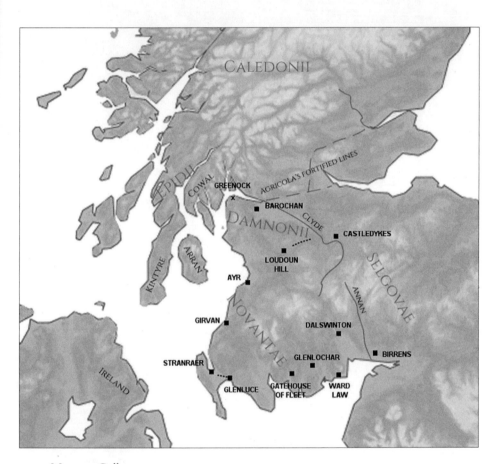

Map 12. Galloway.

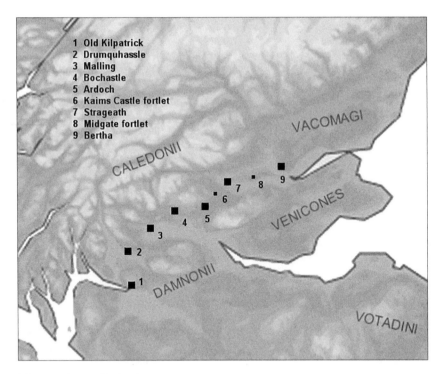

1 Old Kilpatrick
2 Drumquhassle
3 Malling
4 Bochastle
5 Ardoch
6 Kaims Castle fortlet
7 Strageath
8 Midgate fortlet
9 Bertha

VACOMAGI

CALEDONII

VENICONES

DAMNONII

VOTADINI

Map 13. Across Bodotria.

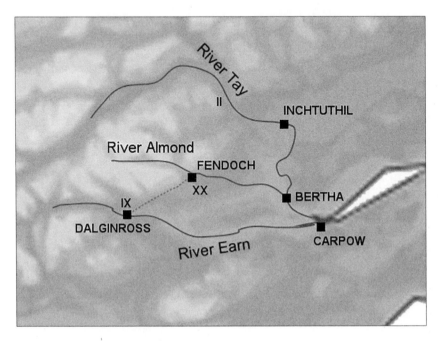

River Tay

II

INCHTUTHIL

River Almond

FENDOCH

XX

BERTHA

IX

DALGINROSS

River Earn

CARPOW

Map 14. Attack on the Ninth.

Appendix 6

SPEECHES OF THE COMMANDERS BEFORE MONS GRAUPIUS

Calgacus's Speech at Mons Graupius, from the Church & Brodribb translation

"Whenever I consider the origin of this war and the necessities of our position, I have a sure confidence that this day, and this union of yours, will be the beginning of freedom to the whole of Britain. To all of us slavery is a thing unknown; there are no lands beyond us, and even the sea is not safe, menaced as we are by a Roman fleet. And thus in war and battle, in which the brave find glory, even the coward will find safety. Former contests, in which, with varying fortune, the Romans were resisted, still left in us a last hope of succour, inasmuch as being the most renowned nation of Britain, dwelling in the very heart of the country, and out of sight of the shores of the conquered, we could keep even our eyes unpolluted by the contagion of slavery. To us who dwell on the uttermost confines of the earth and of freedom, this remote sanctuary of Britain's glory has up to this time been a defence. Now, however, the furthest limits of Britain are thrown open, and the unknown always passes for the marvellous. But there are no tribes beyond us, nothing indeed but waves and rocks, and the yet more terrible Romans, from whose oppression escape is vainly sought by obedience and submission. Robbers of the world, having by their universal plunder exhausted the land, they rifle the deep. If the enemy be rich, they are rapacious; if he be poor, they lust for dominion; neither the east nor the west has been able to satisfy them. Alone among men they covet with equal eagerness poverty and riches. To robbery, slaughter, plunder, they give the lying name of empire; they make a solitude and call it peace.

"Nature has willed that every man's children and kindred should be his dearest objects. Yet these are torn from us by conscriptions to be slaves elsewhere. Our wives and our sisters, even though they may escape violation from the enemy, are dishonoured under the names of friendship and hospitality. Our goods and fortunes they collect for their tribute, our harvests for their granaries. Our very hands and bodies, under the lash and in the midst of insult, are worn down by the toil of clearing forests and morasses. Creatures born to slavery are sold once and for all, and are, moreover, fed by their masters; but Britain is daily purchasing, is daily feeding, her own enslaved people. And as in a household the last comer among the slaves is always the butt of his companions, so we in a world long used to slavery, as the newest and most contemptible, are marked out for destruction. We have neither fruitful plains, nor mines, nor harbours, for the working of which we may be spared. Valour, too, and high spirit in subjects, are offensive to rulers; besides, remoteness and seclusion, while they give safety, provoke suspicion. Since then you cannot hope for quarter, take courage, I beseech you, whether it be safety or renown that you hold most precious. Under a woman's leadership the Brigantes were able to burn a colony, to storm a camp, and had not success ended in supineness, might have thrown off the yoke. Let us, then, a fresh and unconquered people, never likely to abuse our freedom, show forthwith at the very first onset what heroes Caledonia has in reserve.

"Do you suppose that the Romans will be as brave in war as they are licentious in peace? To our strifes and discords they owe their fame, and they turn the errors of an enemy to the renown of their own army, an army which, composed as it is of every variety of nations, is held together by success and will be broken up by disaster. These Gauls and Germans, and, I blush to say, these

Britons, who, though they lend their lives to support a stranger's rule, have been its enemies longer than its subjects, you cannot imagine to be bound by fidelity and affection. Fear and terror there certainly are, feeble bonds of attachment; remove them, and those who have ceased to fear will begin to hate. All the incentives to victory are on our side. The Romans have no wives to kindle their courage; no parents to taunt them with flight, man have either no country or one far away. Few in number, dismayed by their ignorance, looking around upon a sky, a sea, and forests which are all unfamiliar to them; hemmed in, as it were, and enmeshed, the Gods have delivered them into our hands. Be not frightened by the idle display, by the glitter of gold and of silver, which can neither protect nor wound. In the very ranks of the enemy we shall find our own forces. Britons will acknowledge their own cause; Gauls will remember past freedom; the other Germans will abandon them, as but lately did the Usipii. Behind them there is nothing to dread. The forts are ungarrisoned; the colonies in the hands of aged men; what with disloyal subjects and oppressive rulers, the towns are ill-affected and rife with discord. On the one side you have a general and an army; on the other, tribute, the mines, and all the other penalties of an enslaved people. Whether you endure these for ever, or instantly avenge them, this field is to decide. Think, therefore, as you advance to battle, at once of your ancestors and of your posterity."

Agricola's Speech at Mons Graupius, from the Church & Brodribb translation

"Comrades, this is the eighth year since, thanks to the greatness and good fortune of Rome and to your own loyalty and energy, you conquered Britain. In our many campaigns and battles, whether courage in meeting the foe, or toil and endurance in struggling, I may say, against nature herself, have been needed, I have ever been well satisfied with my soldiers, and you with your commander. And so you and I have passed beyond the limits reached by former armies or by former governors, and we now occupy the last confines of Britain, not merely in rumour and report, but with an actual encampment and armed force. Britain has been both discovered and subdued. Often on the march, when morasses, mountains, and rivers were wearing out your strength, did I hear our bravest men exclaim, 'When shall we have the enemy before us? – when shall we fight?' He is now here, driven from his lair, and your wishes and your valour have free scope, and everything favours the conqueror, everything is adverse to the vanquished. For as it is a great and glorious achievement, if we press on, to have accomplished so great a march, to have traversed forests and to have crossed estuaries, so, if we retire, our present most complete success will prove our greatest danger. We have not the same knowledge of the country or the same abundance of supplies, but we have arms in our hands, and in them we have everything. For myself I have long been convinced that neither for an army nor for a general is retreat safe. Better, too, is an honourable death than a life of shame, and safety and renown are for us to be found together. And it would be no inglorious end to perish on the extreme confines of earth and of nature.

"If unknown nations and an untried enemy confronted you, I should urge you on by the example of other armies. As it is, look back upon your former honours, question your own eyes. These are the men who last year under cover of darkness attacked a single legion, whom you routed by a shout. Of all the Britons these are the most confirmed runaways, and this is why they have survived so long. Just as when the huntsman penetrates the forest and the thicket, all the most courageous animals rush out upon him, while the timid and feeble are scared away by the very sound of his approach, so the bravest of the Britons have long since fallen; and the rest are a mere crowd of spiritless cowards. You have at last found them, not because they have stood their ground, but because they have been overtaken. Their desperate plight, and the extreme terror that paralyses them, have rivetted their line to this spot, that you might achieve in it a splendid and memorable victory. Put an end to campaigns; crown your fifty years' service with a glorious day; prove to your country that her armies could never have been fairly charged with protracting a war or with causing a rebellion."

Appendix 7

GAZETTEER OF BEST SITES
AND MUSEUMS

Archaeological Locations

Ardoch fort, Braco FK15 9LB – The best preserved fort ditches in the empire

Binchester fort, Bishop Auckland DL14 8DJ – With a stretch of Dere Street preserved

Brough fort, Stainmore CA17 4EJ – Excellent preserved fort platform

Caerhun fort, Conwy LL32 8TB – Well preserved fort platform

Caerleon legionary fortress NP18 1AE – Varied remains and museum

Castle Greg fortlet EH55 8RX – Excellent defences preserved in marshy ground

Cawthorn Camps, Pickering YO18 8HN – Incredible grouping of four camps

Gask Ridge (Kirkhill & Muir o'Fauld towers) PH3 1LG – Woodland walk with multiple remains

Gourdie Quarry PH1 4LF – The site for the stone used at Inchtuthil

Kaims Castle fortlet FK15 9LG – Impressive defences with an excellent view

Logie Durno camp, Bennachie AB51 5EH – The probable site of Mons Graupius

Maiden Castle fortlet, Stainmore CA17 4EU – Towering fortress on the heights of the pass

Raedykes camp AB39 3SX – Unusual and impressive temporary camp with well preserved ditches

Segontium fort, Caernarvon LL55 2LN – Excavated and preserved fort

Stanwick Camp DL11 7RU – Well preserved defences of a massive Brigantean capital

Tomen-Y-Mur LL41 4RE – An enigmatic site with fort, amphitheatre and more

Vindolanda NE47 7JN – The best excavated fort in Britain, with a museum and reconstructions

Museums

Chesters Museum, Chesters fort NE46 4EU

Dumfries Museum, Dumfries DG2 7SW

Grosvenor Museum, Chester CH1 2DD

Malton Museum, Malton YO17 7AB

National Museum of Scotland, Edinburgh EH1 1JF

Richmondshire Museum, Richmond DL10 4JA

Senhouse Museum, Maryport CA15 6JD

Trimontium Museum, Newstead TD6 9DQ

Tullie House Museum, Carlisle CA3 8TP

Verulamium Museum, St Albans AL3 4SW

Yorkshire Museum, York YO1 7FR

ENDNOTES

Introduction
1. Rome's First Frontier p. 201 (History Press, 2010)
2. Tacitus, Annals 2.69 (Loeb edition, 1931)
3. Tacitus, Annals 2.69 (Loeb edition, 1937)

1 *Ab Origine*
1. Tacitus: Agricola 4 (trans Church & Brodribb, Macmillan, 1877)
2. L'Annee Epigraphique, 1946 (CIL VI 41069)
3. Seneca: De Beneficiis' II.xxi (Loeb edition, 1935)
4. Columella: 'De Re Rustica' 1.1.14 (Loeb edition, 1941)
5. Pliny: 'Natural Histories' XIV.241 (Loeb edition, 1938)
6. Tacitus: Histories 4.48.1 (Church & Brodribb, 1873)
7. Tacitus, Annals 15.35 (Loeb edition, 1937)
8. Seneca Epistulae 29.6 (Loeb edition, 1917)
9. ILS 738
10. Columella: 'De Re Rustica' 4.3.6 (Loeb edition, 1941)
11. ILS 8451
12. Tacitus: A Dialogue on Oratory 28 (Modern Library, 1942)
13. Tacitus: Agricola 4 (trans Church & Brodribb, Macmillan, 1877)
14. Strabo: Geography IV 1:5 (Loeb edition, 1923)
15. Valerius Maximus: Memorable Deeds and sayings 2.6.7 (trans J H Walker, 2004)
16. Cicero: Flaccus 63 (trans. Yonge, 1856)
17. Plutarch: Life of Cato the Elder 23:1 (Loeb edition, 1914)
18. Quintillian Institutio Oratia XII:2 (Loeb edition, 1920)
19. Cicero: de Officiis 2.2 (Loeb edition, 1913)

2 *The British Situation*
1. Graham Webster, Rome Against Caratacus, p. 33 (Book club associates, 1981)
2. Frontinus, De Aquis 2.102 (Loeb edition, 1925)
3. Quintillian, Institutio Oratoria 6, 3.68 (Loeb, 1922)
4. Tacitus, Agricola 14

3 *Ad Signum*
1. Pliny, Epistulae 7.22 (Trans: Firth, Walter Scott, 1900)
2. Anthony Birley, The Fasti of Roman Britain (Oxford University Press, 1981)
3. Pliny, Epistulae 2.13 (Trans: Firth, Walter Scott, 1900)
4. Tacitus: Agricola 5 (trans Church & Brodribb, Macmillan, 1877)
5. Jaakko Suolahti: The Junior Officers of the Roman Army in the Republican Period (Annales Academiae Scientiarum Fennicae 1955, 46)
6. Adrian Goldsworthy, The Roman Army At War, p 124 (Oxford University Press, 1996)
7. Tacitus, Annals 14.29 (Loeb edition, 1937)
8. Tacitus, Annals 14.29 (Loeb edition, 1937)
9. Tacitus, Annals 14.29 (Loeb edition, 1937)
10. Julius Caesar, Alexandrian War 29 (Loeb edition, 1955)
11. Cassius Dio, Roman History 60.20 (Loeb edition, 1924)
12. Cassius Dio, Roman History 69.9 (Loeb edition, 1924)
13. Ammianus Marcellinus, History, 16.11 (Loeb edition, 1939)
14. V. E. Nash-Williams, The Roman Frontier in Wales p.7 (University of Wales, 1969)
15. Carmarthenshire Rivers Trust, 'Sustainability Committee's inquiry into access to inland water in Wales Response by Garth Roberts'
16. Tacitus, Annals 14.30 (Loeb edition, 1937)
17. Tacitus, Annals 14.30 (Loeb edition, 1937)
18. Lucan, Pharsalia 3.400, Trans: Ridley (Longmans, Green & Co., 1905)
19. Tacitus, Annals 14.30 (Loeb edition, 1937)
20. It is of note that although legend has the Ninth legion being massacred in Britain, the Boudiccan revolt is not their end, for they are mentioned later in the text, and indeed their last known attestation is on a tile stamp in Nijmegen dated to AD 121
21. Tacitus, Annals 14.38 (Loeb edition, 1937)
22. Suetonius, Life of Titus 4.1 (Loeb edition, 1914)

4 *Cursus Honorum*
1. Syme, Tacitus, p21 (Clarendon Press, 1963)
2. A. Birley, The Roman Government of Britain, p.89 (Oxford University Press, 2005)

3. Adam, Alexander, Roman Antiquities, p187 (Cadell, London, 1835)
4. James A. Field, Jr, The Purpose of the Lex Iulia et Papia Poppaea, p402 in The Classical Journal 40.7 (1945)
5. Cicero, Against Verres 2.1.9, trans C. D. Yonge (George Bell & Sons, London, 1903)
6. Cicero, Letters, Letter to Quintus 1.1.19, trans E. S. Shuckburgh (Collier & Son, New York, 1909)
7. Mitchell, Stephen, Anatolia. Volume 1. (New York: Oxford University Press, 1993)
8. Tacitus, Annals, 3.33 (Loeb edition, 1937)
9. Ulpian, Duties of a Proconsul, Book 1 (ed. A. Watson, University of Pennsylvania Press, 1985)
10. Tacitus: Agricola 6 (trans Church & Brodribb, Macmillan, 1877)
11. Tacitus, Annals, 14.51 (Loeb edition, 1937)
12. Tacitus, Annals, 14.47 (Loeb edition, 1937)
13. Suetonius, Life of Galba 15 (Loeb edition, 1914)
14. Tacitus: Agricola 6 (trans Church & Brodribb, Macmillan, 1877)
15. Suetonius, Life of Nero 32.4 (Loeb edition, 1914)
16. Livy, History of Rome 25.7 (trans Edmonds & Spillan, Harper & brothers, New York, 1871)
17. Tacitus: Agricola 7 (trans Church & Brodribb, Macmillan, 1877)
18. Tacitus: Agricola 7 (trans Church & Brodribb, Macmillan, 1877)
19. Tacitus, Histories 2.86 (Loeb edition, 1937)
20. Tacitus, Histories 3.59 (Loeb edition, 1937)

5 The British Situation Revisited

1. Tacitus: Agricola 16 (trans Church & Brodribb, Macmillan, 1877)
2. Tacitus, Annals, 14.39 (Loeb edition, 1937)
3. Frontinus, De Aquis 2.102 (Loeb edition, 1925)
4. Plutarch, Life of Galba 15 (Loeb, 1926)
5. Anthony Birley, The Roman Government of Britain p51 (Oxford University Press, 2005)
6. Tacitus: Agricola 16 (trans Church & Brodribb, Macmillan, 1877)
7. Tacitus, Agricola 16 (trans Church & Brodribb, Macmillan, 1877)
8. Tacitus, Histories 1.60 (Loeb edition, 1937)
9. Tacitus, Histories 2.57.1 (Loeb edition, 1937)
10. Tacitus, Histories 1.60 (Loeb edition, 1937)
11. Suetonius, Life of Nero 32.1 (Loeb edition, 1914)
12. Tacitus: Agricola 16 (trans Church & Brodribb, Macmillan, 1877)
13. Tacitus: Agricola 8 (trans Church & Brodribb, Macmillan, 1877)
14. Tacitus, Histories 2.97.1 (Loeb edition, 1937)

15. Statius, Silvae 5.2 79-80 (trans Slater, Clarendon Press, 1938)
16. Statius, Silvae 5.2 203-213 (trans Kline, Poetry in Translation)
17. Tacitus, Histories 2.66.1 (Loeb edition, 1937)
18. Tacitus, Histories, 2.86 (Loeb edition, 1937)
19. Tacitus, Histories, 3.44 (Loeb edition, 1937)
20. Tacitus, Histories, 3.44 (Loeb edition, 1937)
21. Tacitus: Agricola 7 (trans Church & Brodribb, Macmillan, 1877)
22. Tacitus, Histories, 3.45 (Loeb edition, 1937)

6 Para Bellum
1. Flavius Josephus, Jewish War, Book III, 1.2 (trans Whiston, Cambridge, 1737)
2. Silius Italicus, Punic III, lines 597-598 (Loeb edition, 1961)
3. Tacitus: Agricola 7 (trans Church & Brodribb, Macmillan, 1877)
4. Tacitus, Histories, 3.59 (Loeb edition, 1937)
5. Tacitus: Agricola 17 (trans Church & Brodribb, Macmillan, 1877)
6. D.C.A. Shotter, Petillius Cerialis In Northern Britain (Northern History, vol. XXXVI, 2000)

7 Governorship
1. Tacitus: Agricola 9 (trans Church & Brodribb, Macmillan, 1877)
2. Tacitus: Agricola 9 (trans Church & Brodribb, Macmillan, 1877)
3. Velleius Paterculus, History 1.13.4 (Loeb edition, 1924)
4. Livy Histories 2.56.9 (trans Roberts, Dutton & Co., New York, 1912)
5. Tacitus: Agricola 9 (trans Church & Brodribb, Macmillan, 1877)
6. Velleius Paterculus, History 1.13.3 (Loeb, edition 1924)
7. Tacitus: Agricola 9 (trans Birley, Oxford University Press, 1999)
8. Tacitus: Agricola 9 (trans Mattingly & Handford, Penguin, 1970)
9. Plutarch, Life of Cato the younger 21.6 (Loeb edition, 1919)
10. Tacitus: Agricola 9 (trans Church & Brodribb, Macmillan, 1877)

8 The British Situation, Reprise
1. Tacitus: Agricola 17 (trans Church & Brodribb, Macmillan, 1877)
2. http://www.theromangaskproject.org/?page_id=314
3. http://www.theromangaskproject.org/?page_id=323
4. Tacitus: Agricola 17 (trans Church & Brodribb, Macmillan, 1877)

9 Veni, Vidi, Vici
1. Hoffman, The Roman Invasion of Britain p.124 (Pen & Sword, 2013)
2. Hoffman, The Roman Invasion of Britain p.194 (Pen & Sword, 2013)
3. Grant, Roman Military Objectives in Britain under the Flavian Emperors, p. 83 (BAR British Series 440, 2007)

4. The inscription (CIL 7.22), now lost, was preserved in a drawing, and read:
NVMC
PROV
BRITA
(which could be expanded to NUMINI CAESARIS ET GENIO PROVINCIAE BRITANNIAE – 'To the divinity of the Emperor and the genius of the province of Britain')

5. Tacitus: Agricola 18 (trans Church & Brodribb, Macmillan, 1877)

6. Tacitus: Agricola 18 (trans Mattingly & Handford, Penguin, 1970)

7. An Inventory of the Ancient Monuments in Caernarvonshire: III West (RCAHMW 1964)

8. Tacitus: Agricola 18 (trans Church & Brodribb, Macmillan, 1877)

9. Tacitus: Agricola 18 (trans Church & Brodribb, Macmillan, 1877)

10. Tacitus: Agricola 18 (trans Mattingly & Handford, Penguin, 1970)

11. De Vita Agricola p.211 edited by Ogilvie & Richmond (Oxford University Press, 1967)

12. Tacitus: Agricola 19 (trans Church & Brodribb, Macmillan, 1877)

13. Tacitus: Agricola 19 (trans Church & Brodribb, Macmillan, 1877)

14. Tacitus: Agricola 20 (trans Church & Brodribb, Macmillan, 1877)

10 Hoc Est Bellum

1. Tacitus: Agricola 18 (trans Mattingly & Handford, Penguin, 1970)

2. Hugh Davies, Roads in Roman Britain p.123 (Tempus, 2002)

3. http://www.mcbishop.co.uk/oculus/derest.html

4. Tacitus: Agricola 21 (trans Church & Brodribb, Macmillan, 1877)

5. Rosalind Niblett, Verulamium p.77-78 (Tempus, 2001)

6. Carl Mazurek, Agricola 21 and the Flavian Romanization of Britain (accessed via https://www.mcgill.ca/classics/files/classics/2007-8-07.pdf)

7. Rosalind Niblett, Roman Hertfordshire, p.31-33 (Dovecote Press, 1995)

11 Ad Victoriam

1. Tacitus: Agricola 22 (trans Church & Brodribb, Macmillan, 1877)

2. Cassius Dio, Roman History 66.20.1 (Loeb edition, 1925)

3. Tacitus: Agricola 22 (trans Church & Brodribb, Macmillan, 1877)

4. Tacitus: Agricola 22 (trans Church & Brodribb, Macmillan, 1877)

5. Grant, Roman Military Objectives in Britain under the Flavian Emperors, p. 90 (BAR British Series 440, 2007)

6. Hyginus De munitionibus castrorum 56, trans Duncan B Campbell (Amazon, 2018)

7. Livy, History of Rome 35.14.8-9, trans Roberts (Dutton & Co., 1912)

8. Statius, Silvae 5.2 203-213 (trans Kline, Poetry in Translation)

9. Grant, Roman Military Objectives in Britain under the Flavian Emperors, p. 89 (BAR British Series 440, 2007)
10. Tacitus, Agricola 22 (trans Mattingley & Handford (Penguin, 1970)
11. Cassius Dio, Roman History 66.20.3 (Loeb edition, 1925)
12. Tacitus: Agricola 22 (trans Church & Brodribb, Macmillan, 1877)
13. Anthony Birley, The Roman Government of Britain p82 (Oxford University Press, 2005)
14. D. Fishwick, Templum Divo Claudio Constitutum, 179-180 (Britannia 3, 1972)
15. Grant, Roman Military Objectives in Britain under the Flavian Emperors, p. 92 (BAR British Series 440, 2007)
16. Martial, De Spectaculis vii 3, trans Shackleton Bailey (Loeb edition, 1993)

12 *Firmabatur*

1. Tacitus: Agricola 23 (trans Church & Brodribb, Macmillan, 1877)
2. Gordon Maxwell, A Gathering of Eagles p.27-28 (Birlinn, 1998)
3. Tacitus: Agricola 24 (trans Birley, Oxford University Press, 1999)
4. Tacitus: Agricola 24 (trans Church & Brodribb, Macmillan, 1877)
5. R B Warner, Tuathal Techtmar: a myth or ancient literary evidence for a Roman invasion, Emania (journal of the Navan research group) 13 (1995), 23-32

13 *The Eagle of the Ninth*

1. Tacitus: Agricola 25 (trans Church & Brodribb, Macmillan, 1877)
2. Tacitus: Agricola 25 (trans Mattingly & Handford, Penguin, 1970)
3. Tacitus: Agricola 25 (trans Birley, Oxford University Press, 1999)
4. Barry Cunliffe, Iron Age Communities in Britain: An Account of England, Scotland and Wales from the Seventh Century BC until the Roman Conquest (Routledge, 1971)
5. Grant, Roman Military Objectives in Britain under the Flavian Emperors, p. 100 (BAR British Series 440, 2007)
6. Grant, Roman Military Objectives in Britain under the Flavian Emperors, p. 101 (BAR British Series 440, 2007)
7. Tacitus: Agricola 26 (trans Church & Brodribb, Macmillan, 1877)
8. Simon Forder, the Romans in Scotland and the Battle of Mons Graupius, 79 (Amberley, 2019)
9. L'Annee Epigraphique, 1996
10. ILS 1077
11. Tacitus: Agricola 27 (trans Church & Brodribb, Macmillan, 1877)
12. Tacitus: Agricola 28 (trans Church & Brodribb, Macmillan, 1877)
13. Martial, To Faustinus in Epigrams, 6.60 (Bohn, 1897)

14 Mons Graupius
1. Tacitus: Agricola 29 (trans Church & Brodribb, Macmillan, 1877)
2. Tacitus: Agricola 29 (trans Church & Brodribb, Macmillan, 1877)
3. Julius Caesar, Gallic War 5.2 (Loeb edition, 1917)
4. Anthony Birley, The People of Roman Britain p.102 (University of California Press, 1980)
5. Tacitus: Agricola 29 (trans Church & Brodribb, Macmillan, 1877)
6. Virgil, Aeneid VI (trans Dryden, Collier & Son, 1909)
7. R. J. M. Pugh, The Killing Fields of Scotland: AD 83 to 1746 (Casemate, 2013)
8. Tacitus, Agricola 30 (Trans Birley, Oxford University Press, 1999)
9. Sallust, Histories 4.67.22 (trans J. C. Rolfe, Loeb, 1921)

15 Pugnare
1. Tacitus: Agricola 35 (trans Church & Brodribb, Macmillan, 1877)
2. Tacitus, Agricola 30 (Trans Birley, Oxford University Press, 1999)
3. Julius Caesar, Gallic War 4.33 (Loeb edition, 1917)
4. Silius Italicus, Punica 17.416-417 (Loeb edition, 1961)
5. Flavius Arrianus, Acies contra Alanos (accessed at http://members.tripod.com/~S_van_Dorst/Ancient_Warfare/Rome/Sources/ektaxis.html#translation)
6. Sallust, Jugurthine War 101.11 (Loeb edition, 1921)
7. L'Annee Epigraphique, 1951
8. Juvenal, Satire 4 (trans. Ramsay, Putman's, 1918)

16 Winter of Content
1. Tacitus: Agricola 38 (trans Church & Brodribb, Macmillan, 1877)
2. S. Wolfson, Tacitus, Thule and Caledonia: A Critical Re-interpretation of the Textual Problems (myweb.tiscali.co.uk/fartherlands)
3. Cassius Dio, Life of Titus 20 (Loeb edition, 1925)
4. Tacitus, Agricola 38 (Trans Birley, Oxford University Press, 1999)
5. S. Wolfson, Tacitus, Thule and Caledonia: A Critical Re-interpretation of the Textual Problems (myweb.tiscali.co.uk/fartherlands)
6. Plutarch, The Obsolescence of Oracles 2 (Loeb edition, 1936)
7. Plutarch, The Obsolescence of Oracles 18 (Loeb edition, 1936)
8. RIB 662 & RIB 663, both on display in the Yorkshire Museum
9. Tacitus: Agricola 39 (trans Church & Brodribb, Macmillan, 1877)
10. Tacitus, Agricola 39 (Trans Birley, Oxford University Press, 1999)
11. Suetonius, Life of Domitian 2.1 (Loeb edition, 1914)
12. Tacitus: Agricola 40 (trans Church & Brodribb, Macmillan, 1877)

17 A Private Citizen
1. Tacitus: Agricola 40 (trans Church & Brodribb, Macmillan, 1877)
2. Cicero, Against Piso 52 & 53 trans. Yonge, George Bell & Sons, 1891

3. Tacitus, Annals 3.9 (Loeb edition, 1931)
4. Trajan to Pliny (Pliny, Letters 43, Harvard Classics, 1909)
5. Tacitus: Agricola 41 (trans Church & Brodribb, Macmillan, 1877)
6. T.A. Dorey, Agricola and Domitian, Greece & Rome vol 7, 1960
7. Tacitus: Agricola 42 (trans Church & Brodribb, Macmillan, 1877)
8. T.A. Dorey, Agricola and Domitian, Greece & Rome vol 7, 1960
9. ILS 1011
10. Tacitus: Agricola 43 (trans Church & Brodribb, Macmillan, 1877)
11. Cassius Dio, Roman History 66.20 (Loeb edition, 1924)
12. Tacitus: Agricola 44 (Trans Birley, Oxford University Press, 1999)

Conclusion

1. Colin Wells, The Roman Empire pp.34-35 (Fontana, 1992)
2. Ulpian, Duties of a Proconsul, Book 1 (ed. A. Watson, University of Pennsylvania Press, 1985)

BIBLIOGRAPHY

Adam, Alexander, *Roman Antiquities* (Cadell, London, 1835)

"*Agricola's Campaigns*" (Special issue of Ancient Warfare, 1/1 2007)

Bastomsky, S. J., *The Not-so-perfect Man: Some Ambiguities in Tacitus' Picture of Agricola* (article, Monash University)

Birley, A., "*Iulius Agricola, Cn.*" in *Oxford Classical Dictionary* (Oxford University Press, 1996)

Birley, A., *Petilius Cerialis and the Conquest of Brigantia* (Britannia Vol 4, 1973)

Birley, A., *The People of Roman Britain* (Harper Collins, 1980)

Birley, A., *The Roman Government of Britain* (Oxford University Press, 2005)

Bishop, M. C., *A New Flavian Military Site at Roecliffe, North Yorkshire* (Britannia Vol 36, 2005)

Bishop, M. C., *The Pilum: The Roman Heavy Javelin* (Osprey, 2017)

Bishop, M. C., *The Secret History of the Roman Roads of Britain* (Pen & Sword, 2019)

Bonner, S. F., *Education in Ancient Rome* (Routledge, 2014)

Breeze, D., *Roman Scotland* (Batford, 2006)

Breeze, D., *The Antonine Wall* (Origin, 2020)

Breeze, D., *The Northern Frontiers of Roman Britain* (Batsford, 1993)

Campbell, D. B., *Mons Graupius AD 83* (Osprey, 2010)

Carcopino, J., *Daily Life in Ancient Rome* (Routledge, 1941)

Chrystal, P., *The Romans in the North of England* (Destinworld, 2019)

Cotterell, A., *Chariot* (Pimlico, 2004)

Cowan, R., *Roman Battle Tactics 109BC-AD313* (Osprey, 2007)

Davies, H., *Roads in Roman Britain* (History Press, 2008)

Dixon, S., *The Roman Family* (Johns Hopkins University Press 1992)

Fear, J., *Mons Graupius Identified* (accessed through http://www.lucasgnomite. co.uk/)

Fields, N., *Rome's Northern Frontier AD70-235* (Osprey, 2005)

Forder, S., *The Romans in Scotland and the Battle of Mons Graupius* (Amberley, 2019)

Gilliver, C. M., *The Roman Art of War: Theory and Practice* (Thesis, University College, London)

Goodman, M., *The Roman World 44BC-AD180* (Routledge, 1997)

Hanson, W. S., *A Roman Frontier Fort in Scotland: Elginhaugh* (Tempus, 2007)

Hanson, W. S., *Agricola and the Conquest of the North* (Batsford, 1987)

Hoffman, B., *The Roman Invasion of Britain, Archaeology versus History* (Pen & Sword, 2019)

Hopewell, D., Burman, J., Evans, J., Ward, M., and Williams, D., *Roman Fort Environs in North-West Wales* (Britannia Vol 36, 2005)

http://www.theromangaskproject.org/

Keppie, L., *The Legacy of Rome, Scotland's Roman Remains* (John Donald, 2015)

Leslie, A. F., Roman Temporary Camps in Britain (accessed through http://theses. gla.ac.uk/)

MacDonald, G., *The Roman Wall in Scotland* (Maclehose, 1911)

Mason, D. J. P., *Roman Britain and the Roman Navy* (History Press, 2009)

Mason, D. J. P., *Roman Chester, Fortress at the Edge of the World* (History Press, 2012)

Maxwell, G., *A Battle Lost, Romans and Caledonians at Mons Graupius* (Edinburgh University Press, 1990)

Maxwell, G., *A Gathering of Eagles* (Birlinn, 1998)

Moorhead, S. and Stuttard, D., *The Romans Who Shaped Britain* (Thames & Hudson, 2016)

Morris, B., *How important was Governorship of Agricola in the conquest and formation of Britannia?* (Accessed through Academia.edu)

Nagle, B., *The Silvae of Statius* (Indiana University Press, 2004)

Nash Williams, V. E., *The Roman Frontier in Wales* (University of Wales Press, 1969)

Niblett, R., *Roman Hertfordshire* (Dovecote Press, 1995)

Niblett, R., *Verulamium* (Tempus, 2001)

Ogilvie, R. M., and Richmond, I., *De Vita Agricolae* (Clarendon Press, 1967)

Pagan, V. E., *A Companion to Tacitus* (Blackwell, 2012)

Parker, A., *The Archaeology of Roman York* (Amberley, 2019)

Peddie, J., *Conquest: The Roman Invasion of Britain* (Sutton, 1997)

Rance, P., *Attacotti, Deisi and Magnus Maximus: The Case for Irish Federates in Late Roman Britain* (Britannia 32, 2001)

Bibliography

RCHM, *Roman Camps in England: The Field Archaeology* (Stationery Office Books, 1995)

Rogers, I., *The Conquest of Brigantia and the Development of the Roman Road System in the North-West* (Britannia vol 27, 1996)

Shotter, D., *Petillius Cerialis in Northern Britain* (Northern History XXXVI, 2000)

Shotter, D., *Roman Britain* (Routledge, 2004)

Southern, P., *Hadrian's Wall* (Amberley, 2019)

Strang, A., *Recreating a possible Flavian map of Roman Britain with a detailed map for Scotland* (Proceedings of the Society of Antiquaries of Scotland, 1998)

Syme, R., *Tacitus, Vols I & II* (Oxford University Press, 1958)

Tacitus, *The Agricola and the Germania*, trans. Birley (Oxford University Press, 2009)

Tacitus, *The Agricola and the Germania*, trans. Church & Brodribb (Macmillan, 1877))

Tacitus, *The Agricola and the Germania*, trans. Handford & Mattingly (Penguin classics, 1970)

Tibbs, A., *Beyond the Empire: A Guide to the Roman Remains in Scotland* (Robert Hale, 2019)

Wacher, J., *Excavations at Brough-on-Humber 1958-1961* (Society of Antiquaries, 1969)

Wacher, J., *The Towns of Roman Britain* (Batsford, 1978)

Warner, R. B., *Tuathal Techtmar: a myth or ancient literary evidence for a Roman invasion?* (Emania 3, 1995)

Webster, G., *Boudica: The British Revolt Against Rome AD 60* (Batsford, 1993)

Webster, G., Rome Against Caratacus (Routledge, 1993)

Webster, G., The Roman Invasion of Britain (Routledge, 1993)

Wells, C., The Roman Empire (Fontana, 1992)

Wilson, R., Roman Forts: An Illustrated Introduction to the Garrison Posts of Roman Britain (Bergstrom & Boyle, 1980)

Wolfson, S., T*acitus, Thule and Caledonia: the achievements of Agricola's navy in their true perspective.* Oxford, England: Archaeopress, 2008. 118pp. (BAR British series; 459).

Woodhead, A. G., *Tacitus and Agricola* (accessed through Jstor)

Wooliscroft, D. J. and Hoffman, B., *Rome's First Frontier* (History Press, 2006)

INDEX